LET HER KEEP IT

Jesus' Ordination of Mary of Bethany

A New Approach to
John's Gospel Through Its Use of Mosaic Oracles

By

Thomas W. Butler, Doctor of Ministry

Quantum Leap Publisher   Tracy, California

Library of Congress Catalog Card Number: 98-065357

ISBN: 09627161-1-1

Manufactured in the United States of America

Dedication

**This work is dedicated to women
who hear the voice of Jesus
calling them to become
shepherds of God's sheep**

**Thomas W. Butler, Doctor of Ministry
March 1998
Tracy, California**

Zora – De Colores!
May you find
the Word of God,
the Will of God,
the Wisdom of God
and the Love of God
in these pages!

Thomas W. Butler
August 1, 2005

ACKNOWLEDGMENTS

I am deeply grateful to my wife, Carolyn, and my children: Jason, Ben, and Sharolyn, who allowed me to sacrifice many hours of family time in order to do this research and to write. This endeavor has fed my soul, but it could not have done so had they not been tending to my heart. I'm grateful to my parents, Ted and Betty Butler, who have supported me in every endeavor that I have chosen to undertake.

I wish to thank the First United Methodist Church of Tracy, California, which granted a two-month study leave to me in 1995 during which the initial research for this book began. My many friends in this congregation have provided invaluable moral support as this volume began to come together.

Three persons have been especially helpful in the course of writing this book: my soul sister, Lori Woodruff; my friend and colleague Pastor Alice DeLaurier-O'Neil; and my friend and confidant, Art Cummings. Each of these people proofread the first draft and offered suggestions for making it easier to read and understand.

I am indebted to Chuck Powell of Quantum Leap Publishing Company, who has provided important guidance into the field of publishing, and to Dr. Virginia Mollenkott, whose professional opinion of my work gave me the courage to publish. Letha Dawson Scanzoni, editor and writing consultant, gave excellent counsel as to the final form of each chapter.

Most of all I am greatful to the hidden author and source of the Gospel that tradition has attributed to a man named John. I pray that with this volume some of the credit due to her will finally be paid.

Dr. Thomas W. Butler
Tracy, California
March, 1998

ABBREVIATIONS

The following abbreviations are used for books of the Bible.

Gn.	Genesis
Ex.	Exodus
Lv.	Leviticus
Nu.	Numbers
Dt.	Deuteronomy
Jos.	Joshua
1 Sm.	1 Smanuel
2 Sm.	2 Smanuel
1 Chr.	1 Chronicles
2 Chr.	2 Chronicles
Neh.	Nehemiah
Jb.	Job
Ps.	Psalms
Is.	Isaiah
Ez.	Ezekiel
Hos.	Hosea
Mi.	Micah
Mal.	Malachi

Mt.	Matthew
Mk.	Mark
Lk.	Luke
Jn.	John
1Jn.	1 John
2Jn.	2 John
3Jn.	3 John

Other Abbreviations:

Gk.	Greek
Heb.	Hebrew
LXX.	Septuagint
ed.	Edited by
NRSV.	New Revised Standard Version
lit. trans.	literal translation

TABLE OF CONTENTS

PART I
BACKGROUND

Chapter 1
Semeiotic Patterns in the Pentateuch

Chapter 2
Semeiotic Patterns in the Ordination and Consecration Rituals of the Pentateuch

Chapter 3
The Consecration of Nazirites

PART II
THE FOURTH GOSPEL IN A NEW LIGHT

Chapter 4
Semeiotic Patterns in the Gospel According to John

Chapter 5
Jesus Replaces the Temple Sacrifices

Chapter 6
The New Priesthood:
The Disciples of Jesus

PART III
INTRODUCTION TO A SEMEIOTIC TRILOGY

Chapter 7
The Setting of the Ordination Trilogy

Chapter 8
A Setting in Cosmic Time

Chapter 9
Understanding a Sign Called Bethany

Chapter 10
The Characters of the Trilogy

PART IV
THE ORDINATION TRILOGY

Chapter 11
The Ordination Trilogy: Act 1, Scene 1
The Examination of Martha and Mary

Chapter 12
The Ordination Trilogy: Act 1, Scene 2
The Raising of Lazarus

Chapter 13
The Ordination Trilogy: Act 2
The Ordination of Mary of Bethany

Chapter 14
The Ordination Trilogy: Act 3
Completing The Ordination of Jesus' Disciples

EPILOGUE

Chapter 15
Who Wrote the Gospel of John?

Chapter 16
The Rest of the Story

APPENDICES

Preface
Why This Book Was Written

That You May Know the Truth

Whenever I hear my brothers and sisters in Christ saying that nothing in Scripture can be found to support the idea that Jesus intended for women to be ordained as priests, I feel pain. For centuries women have been instructed to deny what they feel in their souls for that reason. The fact that an increasing number of women of all faith traditions are hearing and responding to the call to ordained ministry, in spite of an entrenched attitude in many churches against their taking on that role, suggests a tension between the action of the Holy Spirit and the ecclesiology of the institutional church.

Could it be that the Holy Spirit is working to break down the barriers that we Christians have erected between ourselves and God? We know from Scripture that the Spirit of God strives for wholeness, unity, shalom among God's people. Might not God's Spirit be prompting reconciliation between those who see themselves as gatekeepers of the sacred institution of the church, and those who are denied acknowledgement of God's call? From the perspective of the Gospel According to John, the incarnation of Jesus Christ fulfills this very purpose: to reconcile God's children by correcting flaws in the human understanding of what it means to serve as God's priests. In the Gospel, Jesus teaches his disciples to rely upon the authority of the Word, which he embodied, proclaimed and developed. He said, "If you continue in my word, you are truly my disciples; and you will know the truth, and the truth will make you free (Jn. 8: 31-32)."

Two Story Lines

It is in search of that liberating truth that this book
has been written. None of the insights in this study have
been devised by the author or others in recent history.
Rather, I believe they are revelations of a truth that, while
available for at least 1900 years, has remained hidden
because we, the church, have not had the eyes to see it. To
be set free from our blindness, we must first want to know
the truth, then be willing to follow the path that leads to it.
This work is intended to focus some light on the landmarks
in the Gospel of John that indicate where this truth has been
hidden all along. It requires the reader to become a kind of
detective, searching for clues to the ancient mystery of the
meaning behind this masterpiece of scripture. Let us begin
now to uncover those clues.

Carefully woven into the Fourth Gospel are *two*
story lines. The surface-level story bears a close
resemblance to the orthodox Jesus story of the Synoptic
Gospels. A second story is hidden by the Gospel's author
(or authors) through the ingenious use of metaphorical
language. It tells a Jesus story that is extraordinarily
unorthodox, though internally consistent, about how Jesus
and his disciples replaced every part of the ancient system
of worship in Israel. The centerpiece of this hidden story,
found in the eleventh, twelfth, and thirteenth chapters of
the Gospel, is that Jesus not only included women among
his disciples, he ordained at least two of them. He also
ordained an indeterminate number of men: many more than
the twelve that are acknowledged in the Synoptic Gospels.

The Pentateuch: An Ancient Cipher

To decipher the code language[1] within which this secret gospel is told, seekers of truth must refer to the Old Testament, especially the Pentateuch,[2] to learn how oracles were used in the Mosaic tradition. Understanding how symbols were incorporated into the ancient Hebrew traditions relating to the temple and the priesthood will help to open the eyes of the twenty-first-century disciple to the world view of the first-century community from which the Fourth Gospel came.

The holy scriptures of the Mosaic tradition, translated from Hebrew to Greek,[3] were the initial point of reference; the world view, from which the theology of the first-century disciples sprang. It is this theology, which presupposes an extensive knowledge and understanding of the Pentateuch, which is reflected in the Gospel According to John.

Applying the meaning of those Old Covenant symbols to the orthodox Jesus story, a method entirely consistent with the teaching methods used in both early Christian and first-century Jewish schools, brings to the forefront the theological perspective of a radically

---

[1]In discussing this code language, the Greek term for "s" (*semeia*) is intended to convey a meaning greater than first apparent, as do "metaphors," "oracles," and "symbols." *Semeia* bear further study.

[2]"The Pentateuch" refers collectively to the first five books of the Old Testament: Genesis, Exodus, Leviticus, Numbers, and Deuteronomy, also called the Torah or the Law of Moses, often called "The Law."

[3]The Greek version of the Old Testament is called the Septuagint, translated by approximately seventy scholars and therefore referenced as LXX.

unorthodox community of disciples.   This community
testifies through their hidden gospel that Jesus and his
disciples systematically replaced the Herodian temple, the
Mosaic festivals and sacrifices, and the Aaronic priesthood,
because all of these elements of the Hebrew tradition had
ceased to fulfill their symbolic functions as defined in the
Mosaic Law.

Jesus ordained his disciples as the new priests, and
carefully defined their roles in order to prevent them from
losing sight of their function, as the priests during the
Herodian period of the temple did. Jesus defined the new
priesthood so that it would not be a restricted tribe, as were
the Levites. The disciples were to include all of those who
were able to see Christ in Jesus and believe in him. That
group of disciples included women.

Mary's Anointing -- "Let Her Keep It"

In Jn. 11: 55 - 12: 8, Mary of Bethany anoints the
feet of Jesus with perfumed oil, then dries his feet with her
hair. Why did she do that? What does it mean? A
preliminary look at commentaries written on this passage
adds to the mystery. Most scholars agree that this is an
anointing story. Some scholars think that Jesus is being
anointed for his royal entry into Jerusalem as the Messiah.[4]
Others believe that the anointing of Jesus is in preparation
for his burial.[5] Neither interpretation is convincing.

---

[4]See C.K. Barrett, The Gospel According to St. John,
Westminster Press, Philadelphia, (first pub. 1955, 2nd ed. 1978), p. 409.

[5]See C.H. Dodd, The Interpretation of the Fourth Gospel,
Cambridge University Press, (1953), p. 370.

Some scholars acknowledge that translation of the anointing passage is difficult, and point out that it doesn't really qualify as an anointing story, because the anointing oil is applied to Jesus' feet, not his head. The head of a king or prophet would be anointed as a of office, while the entire body, including the head, but not restricted to the feet, would be anointed in preparing a body for burial. The problem is that the oil is *not applied to Jesus' head.* The oil *is applied to Mary's head*! Could it be that in serving Christ, Mary was anointed? If so, wouldn't that mean that Jesus anointed (ordained) Mary of Bethany?

The Beloved Disciple

Most comentators seem intent on asserting that the difficulties in translating this passage (Jn. 11: 55 - 12: 8) must be interpreted in some way that avoids consideration of Mary's role. Much more attention is given to discovering the identity of a character found only in the Fourth Gospel: a mysterious figure called "the disciple whom Jesus loved," or "the other disciple," or "the Beloved Disciple." Because of the assumption that Jesus called only male disciples, nearly every scholar, in spite of the anointing story, disregards the possibility that Mary of Bethany, or any woman, might be this mysterious, hidden figure.

One scholar lists Lazarus, Mary, and Martha as candidates for the role of Beloved Disciple. Then, after considering and discarding the candidacy of Lazarus, fails to apply his criteria to Martha or Mary, who fits the role as he defines it![6]   Another lists Mary and Martha as candidates, but quickly excludes them from consideration because at the end of the Gospel Jesus, while dying on the cross, appears to be referring to the Beloved Disciple when he says to his mother, "Woman, here is your son."[7]

Only one scholar, Maria Luisa Rigato, considers Mary to be a full-fledged disciple. In a brief article in an Italian periodical, Rigato presents her thesis that in John 12: 1-8 Mary of Bethany anoints the feet of Jesus as a prophetic gesture to acknowledge him as her King, the Anointed One of God, whose body, like the temple, is due to be destroyed.[8] In making this unusual gesture, says Rigato, Mary is anointed.[9] I have found nothing more than this one brief article, printed in Italian, by Rigato or anyone else, on this thesis.

---

[6]Raymond E. Brown, S.S., The Community of the Beloved Disciple, Paulist Press, New York, Ramsey, Toronto, (1979), pp. 191ff.

[7]See James H. Charlesworth, The Beloved Disciple: Whose Witness Validates the Gospel of John?, Trinity Press, Valley Forge, (1995), pp. xiv, xvii. Charlesworth identifies Thomas as the Beloved Disciple. We will deal with the passage (Jn. 19: 26) in which Jesus tells his mother to behold her son. It does not, as Charlesworth and others assume, disqualify Mary or women in general from being the Beloved Disciple.

[8]Maria Luisa Rigato, "Maria Di Betania Nella Redazione Giovannea (Mary of Bethany in John's Redaction," Antonianum: Periodicum Trimestre, editum cura Professorum Pontificii Athenaei, Antoniani de Urbe, Roma, (1991) p. 203f. (published in Italian).

[9]Ibid., p. 217.

Thesis: Mary of Bethany Is the Beloved Disciple

My studies have led me to this conclusion: **Mary of Bethany is the Beloved Disciple of the Fourth Gospel. In John 11: 55 through 12: 8, she officiates in a liturgical event (the consecration of the new Temple) by anointing the altar of that Temple (the feet of Jesus). This anointing results in her own anointing into a leadership role among the disciples, a role which Jesus affirms and defends with the words, "Let her keep it."**

My thesis is born out by a careful consideration of the Greek words, borrowed in most cases from the Septuagint (LXX) version of the Pentateuch, which were used in the writing of the Gospel According to John. These Greek terms support the interpretation that John's Gospel includes a hidden story line, one that includes the story of the ordination of Mary of Bethany as well as the ordination of other male and female disciples.

Biblical Evidence for Ordaining Women

Is this the Biblical evidence supporting the ordination of women that so many say does not exist? It certainly appears so, though to consider it the reader must be open to a different understanding of the Gospel than previously written. The key to seeing the pathway is a simple one: consider the possibility that Jesus had male *and female* disciples.

Recent studies in the emerging field of feminist theology have produced evidence that this idea has been historically and systematically repressed in the Christian church. The fact that some in the church recoil in anger and shock at such an idea is all the more reason for the

church of the twenty-first century to look at it carefully.
This liberating idea has persisted for two thousand years in
spite of intense repression. Could it be the truth? This
author is convinced that it is.

In the tension created by those with the courage to
offer a fresh "new" approach (though many of the ideas in
feminist theology are anything but new), the church is
feeling the birth pains of truth. Dr. Virginia Ramey
Mollenkott encourages a reconsideration of the ancient
metaphors in order to allow them to take new life as aids in
the formation of faith and the assertion of religious truth.
The hidden truth of the Gospel According to John is that
Jesus did, indeed, call women to be among his disciples,
and that he ordained all of his disciples, including the
women, and especially Mary of Bethany, to serve as priests
in God's House.

Field of Study

The present study considers the works of
contemporary historical critical scholars of the Gospel of
John, like Barrett and Brown, as well as the work of an
emerging group of neo-Aristotelian scholars who use a
method of literary analysis, variously called "poetics" (after
a work by Aristotle of that same name) or "post modern
literary criticism" or "reader-response criticism,"[10] which
promises to be a new paradigm for New Testament studies.

The former group might be identified as form-
critical historians who belong to what is being called "the
second quest." That is, they believe that it is possible, by

---

[10]See R. Alan Culpepper, Anatomy of the Fourth Gospel: A
Study in Literary Design, Fortress Press, Philadelphia, (1983), p. 81.

analyzing and dissecting scriptural text, primarily from the Synoptic Gospels, to identify the historical Jesus. Much valuable information has been generated in this quest, including careful studies of the words used in scripture. This study relies heavily on this important literary source.

The latter group begins with an entirely different set of assumptions when addressing themselves specifically to the study of scripture. They consider the Gospel as though it were a novel with a plot, characters, and settings; they consider not only who the author might be, but who the implied author might be and who the reader and the implied reader might be. All of this is considered to have been carefully structured to bring the reader to a different "world view" than the one the reader brings initially to encounter the Jesus story. To use this method, it is necessary to restrict our understanding of the "action" of the plot to the "narrative world of the Gospel of John,"[11] avoiding the assumptions that are easily made by inserting understandings derived from the Synoptic Gospels.

We will use tools suggested by Dr. R. Alan Culpepper in *An Anatomy of the Fourth Gospel*, applying the "Poetics" method to the Fourth Gospel. This method allows a new way of approaching scripture and at the same time offers a link to what some scholars are now acknowledging as the method that was probably used by first-century students of scripture.[12]

---

[11]This descriptive phrase and the advice to focus the study of John within it, come from Dr. Herman Weitjen, who was New Testament Professor at San Francisco Theological Seminary in 1995.

[12]The teacher poses a question regarding scripture. The student must support an answer with references to other parts of scripture. This didactic method (and a collection of commentaries developed using it) is

Methodology

Let us put ourselves into the mind-set of those first readers of this most extraordinary Gospel, expecting to learn more from the words within it than can at first be discerned. Let us use the method they may well have used to uncover the story that was hidden there in plain view for those who had eyes to see it. To do this we must first become familiar with the relevant parts of the Greek version of the Old Testament, looking especially at the specific Greek words used as oracles there. Then we will consider how the use of such words to describe places and times, to name people and describe what they do, tells the unorthodox story that I have just described.

The impatient reader will want to jump to the eleventh chapter, where an exegesis of the passages in the Gospel of John begins. This will allow such readers to see how the conclusions are drawn in this admittedly unorthodox study. Jumping ahead will deprive the reader, however, of the experience of discovery that awaits those who take the time to explore the more ancient texts and learn how to read the signs with which the gospel is written. This book can attempt to be nothing more than an introduction to a method of study and a "world view" that will certainly feed the spirits of those who attempt it. This is a serious and complex journey we are about to take, but I guarantee that you will not regret the time you spend taking any one of the steps outlined herein. Be patient. Start in the beginning, which is where the Teacher behind our Gospel begins.

---

called "midrash." See Michael A. Signer, "How the Bible Has Been Interpreted in Jewish Tradition," <u>The New Interpreter's Bible</u>, Abingdon Press, Nashville, (1994), vol. 1, p. 65f.

Chapter 1
Semeiotic Patterns in the Pentateuch

Mosaic *Semeia*

The first five books of the Bible, sacred writings attributed to Moses, are called the Pentateuch. These writings make extensive use of what English translators call "signs." In Greek, the language in which first-century Christians read the Pentateuch, they are called "*semeia.*" *Semeion* is the Greek term for a sign, characteristic, or mark which is designed to make a specific perception or insight possible.[13] The Mosaic writings are full of them.

In Genesis, for example, the lights in the sky are identified as signs to mark the passage of time (Gn. 1: 24). God puts a mark on Cain so that no one would kill him (Gn. 4: 15). God places a rainbow in the sky as a sign of the covenant between God and every living creature, never again to destroy the earth through flooding (Gn. 9: 12f). In Ex. 4: 6-9 Moses is encouraged by God to place his hand inside of his robe and then to withdraw it. It is leprous, "white as snow." Then God instructs Moses to replace his hand into his cloak and remove it again. It is restored to health, like the rest of his body. God instructs Moses to use both of these gestures as signs that will convince those to whom God is sending Moses that they should believe what Moses told them. Using the signs given to him by God, Moses is able to bring God's people to belief (Ex. 4: 28-31).

---

[13] See Karl Heinrich Rengstorf, "σημειον ," Theological Dictionary of the New Testament, (vols. 1-4 ed. Kittel, vols. 5-9 ed. Friedrich,) trans. and ed. Bromiley, Eerdmans, Grand Rapids, (vols. I, II: 1964; vol. III: 1965; vols. IV, V: 1967; vol. VI: 1968; vol. VII: 1971; vol. VIII: 1972; vol. IX: 1974), vol. VII, pp. 200-269.

The purpose of these signs was to sanctify believers, to enable them to comprehend and interact with that which is holy. The Sabbath day, for example, is a sign of what is shared by God and God's people (Ex. 31: 12-17). These signs were intended to be easy to read. The Mosaic lessons reflect the fact that an inability to read signs stems from an unwillingness to see and believe, not from the inadequacy of the signs themselves as means of communication (Nu. 14: 11, 22).

The descendants of Aaron were designated as the priests who were to maintain the covenant, to stand between God and God's people, to maintain the holiness of the sacred symbols. When 250 men who were not priests dared to approach the altar, carrying burning coals covered with incense, they were all consumed by the earth, and their censers were hammered into a plate to cover the altar of incense, as a sign that no one, except those designated by God, was to function as a priest (Nu. 16: 36-39).

Violating the boundaries established to define the sacred was viewed in the Pentateuch as a trespass against God, and the consequences were very serious, requiring God's intervention. When God's people spoke against God and were consequently dying of the venom of snakes, God instructed Moses to make an image of a serpent and place it on a pole. Those who looked upon it were healed from the venom's poison (Nu. 21: 4-9). A similar symbol, carried by Hermes or Mercury, appeared in Greek myths. It also appears in the Gospel of John as a sign understood by Jesus (Jn. 3:14). Today this same sign, "the caduceus," is used as a symbol for the medical profession, the universal symbol for healing. It achieves the purpose of all signs: crossing barriers of culture and language, it conveys an important level of meaning; it reveals a spiritual truth.

Semeiotic Pattern A:
The Meaning of Head, Body, Hand, and Foot

A close reading of the rituals of sacrifice in the Pentateuch brings to light two distinct patterns of *semeia*, used consistently to incarnate the covenant established between Yahweh and the people of Israel. The first of these *semeiotic* patterns of meaning makes use of four body parts: the head, the body (torso), the hand, and the feet, representing the relationship between the holiness of God and the profane reality of human existence.

The Head The consecrated head of the priest, the sacrificial animal or the horns of the altar represents holiness.[14]
　　　In Genesis 28: 10-22, Jacob lays his head on a stone and dreams of a ladder between heaven and earth on which angels are ascending and descending. He awakens from his dream and declares, "Surely the Lord is in this place -- and I did not know it! How awesome is this place! This is none other than the house of God, and this is the gate of heaven!" He sets up the stone on which he had rested his head, anoints it with oil and vows to return to that exact place to worship God.

---

[14]See **Gn**. 3: 15; **28: 11, 16-22**; 49: 26; **Ex. 29: 6, 7, 10, 12, 15, 17, 19; 34:** 8, **29-35; Lv**. 1: 4, 8, 15; 3: 8, 13; 4: 11, 15, 24, 29, 33; 5: 8; **8: 12,** 14, 20, **22-23;** 9: 13; 13: 29f, 40f; 14: 9, 18, 29; 16: 21; **21: 10f; Nu**. 5: 18; **6: 5, 7, 9, 11, 18; Dt**. 21: 12; **See also Ex. 28: 36-38;** Lv. 8: 9; (bold = best illustrations); See also H.F. Beck, "Consecrate, Consecration," The Interpreter's Dictionary of the Bible, vols 1-4: ed. Buttrick et. al., sup. vol: ed. Crim, Abingdon, Nashville - New York, (vols 1-4: 1962, sup. vol.: 1976), vol. 1, pp. 676-677; See also J. Muilenburg, "Holiness," The Interpreter's Dictionary of the Bible, op. cit., vol. 2, pp. 616-625, esp. 617: A.1.

Clearly Jacob realizes that there is a correlation between the holy house of God, his own head, and the stone. The stone is a sign. It signifies a holy place. His own head has been in contact with this stone, and in his dream he has become aware of the house of God. He is in awe of this extraordinary experience, which not only had deep meaning for him, but shaped forever the understanding of God's people regarding the nature of any "place" in which God could be encountered. We shall return again and again to this simple story to understand the rich metaphors within it and how they informed the understanding of "temple" in the Pentateuch and in the Gospel According to John.

In Ex. 28: 36; 29: 1-37 (Lv. 8: 1-36), Moses ordains Aaron and his sons. Included in the vestments for Aaron, the High Priest, is a turban on which is placed a diadem (a golden medallion) with the words "Holy to the Lord" printed in Hebrew. This is clearly a *semeion*, a sign, that identifies the head of the High Priest as holy.

The ordination process confirms this same *semeiotic* pattern. Anointing oil is poured on the head of the High Priest. The oil is a *semeion* for holiness. So, in fact, is the head of each sacrificial animal.

A bull and two rams, including one called "the ram of ordination," are prepared for sacrifice when the one to be ordained as a priest lays hands (presses hard) upon the head of the animal. It appears that a kind of exchange of holiness is being made. The animal is endowed with the identity of the ordinand, and the holiness of the animal, represented by the animal's head, is transferred to the ordinanand. When the animal is killed, it is the identity of the ordinand which ceases to exist. The innocence and holiness of the animal's head now abides in the ordinand.

After the animals are slaughtered, the ordaining priest touches the animal's blood with his finger, then touches the horns of the altar (the raised corners) and the right ear lobe of the ordinand. All of these ritualistic gestures treat the head (of the priest, altar, and animal) as the "place" of holiness.

The Body The washed body of the sacrificial animal correlates with the bathed and vested body of the priest, the washed hands and feet of the priest, and the anointed sides of the altar. It is the medium through which contact between God and humanity becomes possible.[15]

While the head of the sacrificial animal was placed on the altar as soon as it was severed from the body of the animal, the entrails and legs of the animal had to be washed with water before they could be placed on the altar. The head was holy, but the body and legs (or feet) were not holy until they were cleansed with water. Likewise, when a priest was ordained, he was first bathed (or bathed himself). Prior to wearing the vestments, the priest was required to bathe. The hands and feet of priests had to be washed before and after every sacrifice, "so that they (the priests) may not die (Ex. 30: 17-21)."

Clearly the *semeion* is that those portions of the sacrifice that lie between the sacred head and the profane

---

[15]See **Gn**. 2: 20-24; 6: 16; **17: 11**; **Ex**. 25: 10-22; 27: 1-8; 28: 6-35, 40-43; **29: 1-37**; **Lv**. **1: 9-17**; 3: 3-5, 9-11, 14-17; 4: 8-12; **5: 9**; 6: 10; **7: 3-6**; 8: 16, 21, 25; 9: 14, 19-21; 14: 9; 15: 13, 16f, 19f; **16: 11-28**; 22: 6; **Nu. 8: 5-26**; 16: 22; **19**: 7, 8, **12f**; 25: 8; **27: 16-17**; **Dt**. 7: 13; 28:4, 11, 18, 26; 30: 9. (bold = best illustrations); See also Eduard Schweizer, Friedrich Baumgartel, "σαρζ , σαρκικοσ, σαρκινοσ," Theological Dictionary of the New Testament, op. cit., vol. VII, pp. 98-151, esp. p. 109: 9f; 123: D.2; 138-140.

feet of the animal, and those portions of the priest that lie between the sacred head and the profane feet, must be cleansed for each sacrifice. Likewise, even the sides of the altar are consecrated, first with anointing oil and then with the blood of the sacrificial animal at each of the important seasonal festivals.

The Hand The hand is the *semeion* for the priestly function, literally the intermediary right hand of God.[16] It is with the priests' right hand that sacrifices are made, both in preparing the live animal for sacrifice through the laying on of hands and in the execution of the sacrifice itself. The hand is an important *semeion*, representing the power of God in one chosen to do the work of God. Moses, for example, is instructed to use his hand as a sign to convince God's people that he is God's representative (Ex. 4: 6f) or even to convince Pharaoh that he was God's representative (Ex. 7: 14-19; 8: 5-6, 17; 9: 8-10, 22).

When a priest was ordained, the blood of the ram of ordination was placed, not only on the right ear lobe, but also on the right thumb of the ordinand. Clearly there is a correlation between the *semeia* of the sacrificial animal and

---

[16]See **Gn. 22: 10f; 48: 14f; Ex. 4: 6f**, 20; 7: 4-5, **14f; 8: 5f,** 17; **9: 3, 22; 10: 12, 21, 22;** 13: **3, 9;** 14: **16f, 21, 26f; 15:6, 12, 20;** 17: **5f, 11, 12; 28: 41; 29: 9, 15, 19;** 34: 29; **Lv.** 1: 4; 3: 2-8, 13; 4: **4, 24, 29, 33-35; 8: 22-24; 9:** 17; **14: 14-20, 21-32; 16: 21; 21:** 19; **Nu.** 5: 18f; **20: 11; 27: 18-23; 31: 6; Dt.** 4: 34; **6: 4-9,** 21f; 7: 19; **15: 7-11; 26:** 4-8; **32: 40; 34: 9-12;** (bold = best illustrations); See also Eduard Lohse, "χειρ," Theological Dictionary of the New Testament, op. cit., vol. IX, pp. 424-434; also Walter Grundmann, "δεζιο σ," Theological Dictionary of the New Testament, op. cit., vol. II, pp. 37-40; also R.C. Dentan, "Hand," Interpreter's Dictionary of the Bible, op. cit., vol. 2, pp. 520-521.

the priest. Even the parts of the temple that are used by the priest (the brass utensils like censers used to carry coals to the altar and the knife used to kill the sacrificial animal) are consecrated with the same anointing oil that is used to anoint the priest (Lv. 8: 10-11).

The Feet The feet of the sacrificial animal correlate with the base of the altar and the feet of the priest, and represent the profane, that which must be cleansed before contact with God can be made.[17] The priest was required to perform priestly duties barefoot, and as has already been noted, the priest's feet and hands were to be bathed before and after each sacrifice was made. The feet of the sacrificial animal were separated from the body and offered as a separate "part" of the sacrifice. They too were bathed before they were offered. In the ordination process, the blood of the ram of ordination was placed on the right big toe of the priest being ordained.

This first *semeiotic* pattern appears whether one is considering the body parts of the priest, the body parts of the sacrificial animal, or the parts of the altar. There was a correlation of head, hand, body, and feet between all three components in the sacrificial liturgy. The fact that blood was applied to the head, hand, and feet of the High Priest as a sign of his office is especially significant for our study. The fact that the priest was required to reach into

---

[17]See Gn. 18: 1-4; 19: 1-2; 49: 33; Ex. 3: 5; 29: 20; 30: 19, 21; 40: 31; Lv. 8: 23, 24; 14: 14, 17, 25, 28; 21: 19; Dt. 32: 35; See also Konrad Weiss, "πουσ," Theological Dictionary of the New Testament, op. cit., vol. VI, pp. 624-631. The Hebrew words translated "foot" in the LXX also mean "feet," "sole," "heel," "hoof," "shin- bone," "step," "that which lies at the feet," "the walk, walk of life, or the way," or "a symbol of power."

the side of the sacrificial animal and remove the entrails with his hand is also important. The fact that priests were required to bathe before ordination and that their hands and feet were to be washed before and after each sacrifice will also be shown to be important, since all of these signs are used in the Gospel According to John.

That this pattern is so carefully preserved in the Gospel is one of the indications that the Gospel was written in such a way as to replicate it.   When the pattern's meaning is applied to the Gospel story, the understanding of that gospel's author(s) becomes more evident and radically different from what most Christians expect to see.

Semeiotic Pattern B: Separation and Remembrance

The second *semeiotic* pattern is more difficult to discern. It has to do with the importance of separating -- being set apart -- and remembering. Both separation and remembrance are used in the Pentatuech as a means of describing and celebrating the relationship between God and the people of God.

Separation   Separation represents the inherent circum- stance in the divine/human relationship. The people of God are separated from all other people. Among the people of God, one tribe is separated from all of the other tribes. This tribe is supported through the offerings made in the temple to God. No other provision is made for them. Those who became priests were separated from the community, set apart for their holy work.[18] Among the priests, the High Priest was set apart by a higher standard of holiness. He had first choice of the "priest's portion" of the temple sacrifices, meaning that the High Priest alone was assured of dining on the finest food available in all of Israel. In the Pentateuch, separation was used as a means of identifying what and who was holy.

Separation was also used to protect God's people, especially God's priests, from anything and anyone who became defiled. Defilement came through contact with anything having to do with death. When such defilement occurred, the one whose holiness had been spoiled had to be separated from the community. An elaborate set of procedures were used to assure that the defilement did not spread to others in the community. The same *semeia* could be used to identify one who had been chosen as a holy one as were used to identify one who was defiled.

Remembering The history of the people of God recorded in the Pentateuch is replete with circumstances through which the descendants of Abraham fail to remember their covenantal relationship with God. Disastrous consequences came from these failures: famine, exile from the homeland, and subjugation as slaves of the people of other cultures.

Remembering the covenant, on the other hand, maintaining the relationship with God by keeping God's laws and maintaining the pattern of festivals and sacrifices required by Mosaic law, were understood as the ways to financial prosperity, military prowess, and political success.

---

[18]See K.L. Schmidt, "αφοριζω ," Theological Dictionary of the New Testament, op. cit., vol. V, pp. 454-455; See also Lv. 20: 25-26; Nu. 12: 14f; 18: 24.

God remembers the covenant, and in so doing, rescues the people of God from the suffering that occurs when it is broken by human beings. There is an inherent unfairness in the relationship that relies so much on one party (God), and that creates a need for a system of worship through which guilt can be assuaged, where individuals and the heads of families, of tribes, and of the nation formed by the children of Israel, can express their remorse and implore God's forgiveness.

Remembering the covenant is an intrinsic part of every festival outlined in the Pentateuch. In the LXX the concept of remembrance is presented as central to the theology that binds the descendants of Abraham together and grants them their identity.

"Remember that you were a slave in the land of Egypt, and the LORD your God brought you out from there with a mighty hand and an outstretched arm; therefore the LORD your God commanded you to keep the sabbath day" (Dt. 5: 15 in the context of the ten commandments).

"Hear, O Israel: the LORD is our God, the LORD alone. You shall love the LORD your God with all your heart, and with all your soul, and with all your might. Keep these words that I am commanding you today in your heart. Recite them to your children and talk about them when you are at home and when you are away, when you lie down and when you rise. Bind them as a sign on your hand, fix them as an emblem (a frontlet) on your forehead, and write them on the doorposts of your house and on your gates" (Dt. 6: 4-9 the great commandment).

"Remember the long way that the LORD your God has led you these forty years in the wilderness, in order to humble you, testing you to know what was in your heart, whether or not you would keep his commandments. He humbled you by letting you hunger, then by feeding you with manna, with which neither you nor your ancestors were acquainted, in order to make you understand that one does not live by bread alone, but by every word that comes from the mouth of the LORD." (Dt. 8: 2-3)

"But remember the LORD your God, for it is he who gives you power to get wealth, so that he may confirm his covenant that he swore to your ancestors, as he is doing today. If you do forget the LORD your God and follow other gods to serve and worship them, I solemnly warn you today that you sall surely perish." (Dt. 8: 18-19)

"Remember and do not forget how you provoked the LORD your God to wrath in the wilderness; you have been rebellious against the LORD from the day you came out of the land of Egypt until you came to this place. Even at Horeb you provoked the LORD to wrath, and the LORD was so angry with you that he was ready to destroy you." (Dt. 9: 7-8)

"You shall offer the Passover sacrifice for the LORD your God, from the flock and the herd at the place that the LORD will choose as a dwelling for his name. You must not eat with it anything leavened. For seven days you shall eat unleavened bread with it--the bread of affliction-- because you came out of the land of Egypt in great haste, so that all the days of your life you may remember the day of your departure from the land of Egypt."(Dt. 16:2-3)

"When you reap your harvest in your field and forget a sheaf in the field, you shall not go back to get it; it shall be left for the alien, the orphan, and the widow, so that the LORD your God may bless you in all your undertakings. When you beat your olive trees, do not strip what is left; it shall be for the alien, the orphan, and the widow. When you gather the grapes of your vineyard, do not glean what is left; it shall be for the alien, the orphan, and the widow. Remember that you were a slave in the land of Egypt; therefore I am commanding you to do this." (Dt. 24: 19-22)[19]

Summary: The Importance of the Semeiotic Patterns

Each of these two *semeiotic* patterns of meaning is an important part of the symbolism used in the rites of the Hebrew temple, and is especially important in the rite of ordination of priests. Both patterns are replicated in the Gospel of John as signs pointing to the rite of ordination by Jesus of his disciples.

These same *semeia* are used as oracles in the Gospel of John to tell two truths that the authorities of that time could not accept, but that "those with eyes to see" would recognize: (1) that the disciples were ordained into a new priesthood by Jesus to replace the priesthood represented by temple authorities identified in the Gospel as "the Jews,"[20] and (2) this new priesthood included women.

---

[19]See O. Michel, "μιμνησκομαι," Theological Dictionary of the New Testament, op. cit, vol. IV, p. 675f.

[20]The term "the Jews" is borrowed from Neh. 2: 16 (NRSV) to identify the leaders of the religious establishment in Jerusalem. It is not intended, either in the Gospel or here, to reflect an antisemitic attitude.

Chapter 2
Semeiotic Patterns In the Ordination and Consecration Rituals of the Pentateuch

The Ordination of Aaron and His Sons

The ritual of ordination of the first High Priest, Aaron, and the first Chief Priests, Aaron's sons (Ex. 29; Lv. 8), begins with the separation of Aaron and his sons from the tribes of Israel (assembled at the entrance to the Tent of Meeting). They are ceremonially bathed by Moses, then invested with the robes and symbols of their priestly offices. As has already been noted, the ceremonial bathing is a necessary *semeion*, designating these particular people as holy before God and before the people of God.

The High Priest's vestments (Ex. 28) included a checkered tunic and an embroidered blue linen robe, fastened with an embroidered linen sash. Over this, the High Priest wore something called an *ephod*, an elaborate linen loin cloth or girdle.[21] Pockets were sewn into each of the shoulder pieces of the ephod to contain two onyx stones, engraved "as a gem-cutter engraves signets, . . . as stones of remembrance for the sons of Israel" (Ex. 28: 9-14).

---

[21]G. Henton Davies, "Ephod (Object)," The Interpreter's Dictionary of the Bible, Abingdon, Nashville-New York, (1962), vol. 2, pp. 118-119; See Gen. 3: 7; See also Albrecht Oepke, "ζωνη," Theological Dictionary of the New Testament, op. cit., vol. V, p. 302ff; See also John Gray, "The Book of Exodus," The Interpreter's One Volume Commentary on the Bible, Charles M. Laymon, ed., Abingdon, Nashville-New York, (1971), p. 61. Compare with Jn. 13: 4; 21: 7, 18.

Serving as a *semeion*, the ephod was used both as an item of clothing and as a religious symbol in its own right. Gray suggests that it was patterned after a tight-fitting apron or girdle worn by Egyptian priests.[22] According to Oepke, the term "ephod" is an Egyptian loan word meaning "an article of clothing of linen or leather . . . to gird up one's loins, to fasten one's clothes." He goes on to say that it functioned as "a pocket, . . . (figuratively) the close tie offers a term of comparison. Thus Yahweh bound Israel closely to himself like a girdle."[23]

Just as a pocket holds items, the ephod held *persons* who were esteemed as oracles, persons who aided in discerning and revealing the will of God. As a kind of pocket, the ephod contained the body of the High Priest, symbolizing his role as an intermediary between God and the people of God, aiding God's people in discerning God's will. The body of the High Priest was thus girded by the ephod, just as, in Oepke's words, "Yahweh bound Israel closely to himself like a girdle."

In the Hebrew tradition the High Priest's office served as a means by which the close relationship between God and God's people was maintained.

"The word "priest," here first mentioned in Exodus, is probably cognate with an Arabic word denoting a functionary who might officiate at sacrifices but was better known as the medium of oracles and divination. In view of the association of the primitive Tent of Meeting with oracles, Moses may have had such a function. The

---

[22] Gray, op. cit.

[23] Oepke, op. cit.

tradition of the consecration of Aaron as priest may reflect the divergence of the sacrificial office from that of the agent of oracles represented by Moses."[24]

In other words, the consecration of Aaron and his descendants provides for the transference of the oracle role as it was personified in Moses to another way in which God was represented to the people and the people to God. This way involved those who were separated from the community in order to function as priests, especially the High Priest. That such a transference occurred is supported by the carefully described nature of the clothing that the High Priest was to wear. The body of the High Priest was well covered with sacred clothing, held together by the tight-fitting ephod. The head was covered with a turban, on the front of which was a jewel-encrusted golden ornament on which were written the Hebrew words "Holy to the Lord" (Lv. 9: 9; Ex. 28: 36-38).

There is no mention in the Pentateuch of any footwear to be worn by priests. Apparently priests were expected to perform their duties barefoot, which is con-sistent with the instructions given to Moses when he stood before the burning bush and heard God say, "Come no closer! Remove the sandals from your feet, for the place on which you are standing is holy ground" (Ex. 3: 5).[25]

O'Sullivan suggests various meanings attached to going barefoot, which may shed light on why it is that priests were required to perform their duties barefoot.

---

[24]Gray, op. cit.

[25]See Oscar Cullman, Early Christian Worship, Wyndhall, (1953, 1987), p. 105.

"The special mention . . . of going barefoot is always done for some particular purpose, the meaning of which differs accordingly as the action is forced on one or is voluntary. To be forced to go barefoot was a sign of humiliation (Jb. 12: 19), especially if this shame was inflicted by one's enemies (Is. 20: 2-4); to go barefoot voluntarily was an expression of grief (2Sm. 15: 30; Mi. 1: 8) or of mourning for the dead (Ez. 24: 17-23) Sometimes the Lord demanded, when he appeared to men, that they should be barefoot as a sign of respect in approaching the place of the theophany (Ex. 3: 5; Jos. 5: 15) probably because sandals were considered unclean."[26]

Anything touched by God, that is all of creation including the ground, is holy. However, all ground touched by human beings is cursed; it has been defiled by human sin.

(God to Adam and "the woman") " . . . Cursed is the ground because of you; in toil you shall eat of it all the days of your life; thorns and thistles it shall bring forth for you; and you shall eat the plants of the field. By the sweat of your face you shall eat bread until you return to the ground, for out of it you were taken; you are dust, and to dust you shall return (Gn. 3: 17-19)."[27]

---

[26]Kevin O'Sullivan, O.F.M., "Barefoot," Encyclopedic Dictionary of the Bible, trans. and adapt of A. Van den Born, BijBels Woordenboek, 2nd Rev. Ed. (54-57), by Lois Hartman, McGraw-Hill, New York, (1963), p. 207.

[27]See Hermann Sasse, "γη," Theological Dictionary of the New Testament, op. cit., vol. I, pp. 677-680, esp. p. 679 "The Earth in Its Relation to God."

Thus, what the High Priest wore (the vestments) and did not wear (coverings of the feet) were *semeia* of the relationship between God and the people of God. The head of the priest was labeled by a signet as "Holy to God." The body of the High Priest was pocketed in an ephod as a sign of his holiness. The feet are bare so that they can be cleansed of the defiling dust, sin, with which they are in constant contact. The hands of the ordained and vested priest perform the functions of the intermediary between the holiness of God and the profane nature of humanity.

After vesting Aaron, Moses anoints the tabernacle and all that is in it (Lv. 8: 10-11). The holy altar is anointed seven times as are the altar's utensils and the basin at its base. Seven was a sacred number.[28]

The parts of the altar are sprinkled with holy oil to consecrate them.   Once again, the *semeia* appear. Corresponding to the symbolic parts of the priest's body, the horns of the altar represent the holy head. The utensils used on the altar represent its "hands," and the sides of the altar represent its "body." At the "foot" of the altar is the basin.   All are consecrated in order to facilitate the maintenance of a covenantal relationship between the Holy God and a people who continually need to be cleansed of their sinfulness.

The next step in the ordination process is when Moses pours some of the anointing oil on Aaron's head

---

[28]See M.H. Pope, "Seven, Seventh, Seventy," The Interpreter's Dictionary of the Bible, op. cit, vol. 4, pp. 294-295. "Passover and Tabernacles are seven-day festivals.   The New Year, the Day of Atonement, and Tabernacles all occur in the seventh month.   The Feast of Weeks and Jubilee were based on the square of seven . . . Seven days is the period for ordination of priests and consecration of altars. . . . The sacrificial blood is sprinkled seven times, and so too the anointing oil."

(Lv. 8: 12). The anointing with oil applied to the head of the High Priest is, according to Franz Hesse, linked with holiness and "separation for the sphere of Yahweh."[29] C. Houtman says that perfumed anointing oil marked the High Priest with a fragrance associated only with the temple, thereby protecting the High Priest from death as a consequence of encroaching upon the holiness of God.

"By anointing "his" (God's) fragrance is transmitted to his dwelling and its inventory (Ex. 30: 26-9) and to the priests, devoted to his service (Ex. 30: 30). So YHWH's fragrance becomes attached to his house and his attendants. So they are marked by his personality. . . . Persons who do not possess YHWH's fragrance cannot be his servants (See Nu. 17: 5). When they fulfil priestly duties, they encroach on YHWH's holiness. It will be fatal for them (Nu. 16; 2 Chron. 26: 16ff)."[30]

Semeiotic Pattern in Ritual Sacrifices

This *semeiotic* pattern appears in the blood sacrifices. In the ordination sacrifice, the pattern appears when Moses presents the bull for a sin offering[31] along with two rams, one for a burnt offering and one called "the ram of

---

[29] Franz Hesse, "χριω , χριστοσ, αντιχριστοσ, χρισμα, χριστιανοσ," Theological Dictionary of the New Testament, op. cit., vol. IX, p. 500f.

[30] C. Houtman, "On the Function of the Holy Incense (Exodus XXX 34-8) and the Sacred Anointing Oil (Exodus XXX 22-33)," Vetus Testamentum, XLII, vol. 4, (1992), pp. 458-465.

[31] See Lv. 8: 14. The LXX says the animal is a calf.

ordination," for sacrifice. All three of these animals are sacrificed in the same way as any animal is sacrificed: separating the head, the body, and the feet (the lower legs and hooves) of the animal. Just as the head, hand, body, and feet of the priests are anointed with oil, and the horns of the altar, the altar utensils, the side of the altar and the basin at the foot of the altar are consecrated with oil, so it is with the *semeiotic* parts of the sacrificial animal. The head, (entrails from the) body, and feet are anointed with oil before they are burned (Lv. 8: 14-29).

This is the *semeiotic* pattern for all animal sacrifices in the Pentateuch. First the worshipper leans hands upon the head of the animal to be sacrificed. This is an intentional transfer of the identity of the worshipper to the animal,[32] just as anointing is an intentional transfer of holiness from God to the one being anointed, and the laying on of hands is an intentional transfer of authority from one prophet to another or from a teacher to a student.

After this "leaning on of hands" has been done, the animal is slaughtered and separated from its life's blood, which is poured out into the basin at the foot of the altar. Then the animal is separated into its parts: the head and feet are severed from the body, and the entrails and fat of the animal are removed from its belly by the priest's hand.

The head is placed on the altar without any further treatment, but the entrails and the feet are first washed in water before being placed upon the altar (Lv. 8:21). The

---

[32]See David Daube, The New Testament and Rabbinic Judaism, University of London, The Athlone Press, (1956), pp. 224-245 n. 38. Daube pointedly calls this the leaning on of hands (*samakh*) as opposed to the "laying" or "placing" (*shith*) of hands. *Samakh* is preferred in any temple ritual, be it sacrifice or ordination.

important thing about each sacrifice is that the animal is separated. Over and over again in the Levitical instructions for sacrifices the words, "this is a sacrifice, an odor pleasing to the Lord" are repeated. The sacrifice symbolizes the broken, torn, divided, separation between God and those who seek reconciliation with God. It represents the idea that human beings cannot live without the covenant that reconciles this natural separation.[33]

The sacrifice must have been difficult to watch. The worshipper leans hands on the head of the sacrificial animal before it is killed, then watches as the priest proceeds to butcher the animal right there in front of God. The worshipper is prompted by this gory scene to *remember* the covenant, to resist temptations to break it again.

Just as the High Priest "remembers" the tribes of Israel by wearing the symbolic jewels near his heart, and those who see the High Priest "remember" that he is "Holy to God" by reading the inscription on the emblem on his turban, the worshipers are to "remember" the relationship between themselves and YHWH at the times of sacrifice.

Thus, separating and remembering are two central *semeiotic* themes of the temple sacrificial rites. All of the sacrifices reflect this symbolism, regardless of the festival or the nature of the sacrifice itself. Even the bread, cake, or unleavened bread are broken before the oil is added to them when the the offering of well-being is made.[34]

---

[33] See Gn. 1: 4, 6, 7f. The pattern is established that creation occurs as a process. First, that which is created is separated from that which is not created, then created things are separated from other created things (i.e.: water is separated from land, day lights are separated from night lights, etc.), then they are named.

[34] Also called the cereal, grain, or peace offering.

The leaning on of hands and the shedding of the blood of life are inducements to "*remember*" the covenant. The separation of the head, the body, and the feet and the breaking of bread signify the breaking (separation) of the covenant, which is re-established by the sacrifice. The head, body, and feet of priest, altar, and sacrificial animal are *semeia* which the faithful use to "remember" that the separation between holy God and worldly worshipper is mended through the mediating ritual of sacrifice performed by the priest.

In the Mosaic ordination service, the blood of the sacrificial animals, symbolically their life, is sprinkled by the priest on the horns (the head) of the altar, on the sides (the body) of the altar, and poured out at the base (the feet) of the altar. Symbolically, there are three dimensions to the covenant represented here: God is at the head, the priest is at God's side, and the people of God, who receive their life from God, are at God's feet. The sacrifice "gives life" to this whole relationship; it "incarnates" it.

In the rite of ordination of the High Priest (Lv. 8: 22f), the blood of the ram of ordination is applied to the priest's right earlobe (head), his right thumb (hand), and right big toe (foot).

As the sacrificial rite comes to a close, the right hand of the priest is used for the elevation of the offering (Lv. 8: 27).[35] Essentially what this involves is placing all of the "parts" of the offering into the upturned palms of the worshiper, then (by placing his right hand under the worshipper's hands) lifting up their hands and the offering before the altar, and thus, symbolically, before God. In

---

[35]This is called the elevation offering or the wave offering in some translations.

this way the priest functions as God's right hand, enabling the worshiper before God.[36]

To complete the sacrifice of the ram of ordination, the entrails removed from the side of the animal, one cake of unleavened bread, one cake of bread soaked with oil, one wafer, and the right thigh of the ram are lifted up as elevation offerings, then they are placed on hot coals on the altar with the burnt offering and "turned into smoke." "This was an ordination offering for a pleasing odor, an offering by fire to the Lord," (Lv. 8: 25-29).

When the sacrifice is completed, Moses (or later the ordaining High Priest) makes another elevation offering of the (right) breast of the ram, then keeps that portion for himself. The priest's portion includes those parts of the sacrifice which lie between the head and the right side (the shoulder or breast), or the right side and the feet (the thigh) of the sacrificed animal's carcass. The priest stands between God and the people of God, and his portion is that which lies between the two extremes of the animal's body, which represents the covenant. Eating portions of the sacrifice results in the incarnation of the covenant in the body of the worshipper and the priest.

----

[36]See Konrad Weiss, "αναφερω ," Theological Dictionary of the New Testament, op. cit, vol. IX, p. 60f. This word, (*anafero*) meaning "lift up" (a sacrifice), bears a similarity to "αιρω " (*airo*) which means "to lift up a hand to make an oath," or "to lift one's own life before God (See Jn. 10: 18; 17: 15). Similarly, "επαιρω " (*epairo*) means the raised hand as a gesture of prayer or blessing at departure. (See Jn. 17: 1); See Joachim Jeremias, "αιρω ," and "επαιρω ," Theological Dictionary of the New Testament, op. cit., vol. I, p. 185, 186.

The Mosaic Theology of Creation, Ordination, Sacrifice

The ordering of creation, the ordering of the priesthood and the ordering of every sacrificial ritual in the Pentateuch all follow the same pattern and reflect the same theology.

The head of the sacrificial animal is placed upon the altar without any treatment. It represents God and is holy to God. For the burnt offering, the entrails and feet of the animal are first washed in water, before they are placed on the altar for burning.

It is significant that the head is holy but the side and feet of the animal, which has come into the temple as an animal without blemish, are not. The cleansing of the sacrifice signifies that the body and feet of the sacrifice are not holy and must be cleansed before they can be given to God, apparently because they are unclean. Since the animal, like all things in creation, is a good creature of God, this might seem to be a theological error.

In fact, it is not an error, when viewed as a symbol of the created order. According to Gn. 1: 1-5, God created light and then separated the light from the darkness. One way of reading that is to recognize that God slips between the light and the darkness; God divides the light and the darkness by being the contact point between them. This serves as a metaphor for all of creation. On one side of God is light, and the created order. On the other side of God is darkness, which theologians in both the Old Testament and the New Testament use as a sign to represent the mistaken belief that existence is possible without God. In the Gospel of John, darkness represents the world outside of the covenant community. As the reconciling agent, God is the intermediary between reality and oblivion, life and death, light and darkness, living by virtue of the covenant and stumbling about, spiritually lost in the darkness. God is the Maker and Sustainer of the covenant. Human beings are incapable of establishing or maintaining the covenant on their own, so God provides all that is required to establish, maintain, and renew it. In fact, the theology goes much further than that, because the worshippers, the "other party" to the covenant, are also emanations from God. They are created by the Word of God (Jn. 1: 3-4; Gn. 1: 26f).

It follows that if human beings and everything else in creation are emanations from God, then there can be no relationship *between* them; they are all parts of one being. Yet the ancient theologians recognized that human beings feel separate from God, separated by sinfulness. If a return to wholeness is to be possible, then a relationship must be represented both theologically and symbolically in the rites.

There must be some dividing line, some separation between God and God's creation. This dividing line is intrinsic in the very nature of existence. God separates in order to create. In Gn. 1, God's first act of creation is to separate the light from the darkness. Next God separates "the waters (above) from the waters (below)." Then the dry land is separated from the waters below, and so on. Separation is what makes it possible for anything to exist in a form other than God. It becomes an objective reality because it is separate from other parts of reality. Not only is God the "agent" of the separation, God is also the "interface" between all elements of creation. God not only causes the separation, God is the medium by which one part of the creation can have a relationship to any other part of the creation. How can this correlation between God and the created order be represented by a *semeion* in the temple rituals?

The ancient theologians considered the neck to be the dividing line between what represents God and what does not represent God in a sacrificial animal and in one dedicated to God. The head is sacred. The body and the feet are profane, separated from the sacred. When the High Priest is anointed, the sacred anointing oil is applied to his head. Before and after the priest performs the sacrifices, he must, under penalty of death, wash his hands and his feet (Ex. 29: 17-21), because his hands and feet represent that which is not holy, and they must be cleansed in order to perform the holy rituals.

The vestments of the High Priest reflect this same theology. As has been noted, the High Priest wears a turban upon which a jeweled emblem is sewn, inscribed with the words "Holy to The Lord" (Ex. 28: 36-38). It is no accident that this emblem and these words are placed on the priest's head when he is wearing his priestly clothing.

The bare feet require frequent bathing as well, especially before ascending the altar and again upon descending from the altar. The hands, covered with blood from "handling" the elements of the sacrifice, must also be cleansed both before and after they are used to present the sacrificial elements on the altar.

When the sacrifice is made, incense is used in addition to perfumed oil and wine (Ex. 30: 22-38). The aroma of the incense is the same as that of the oil. The scent of the oil on the priest's head is the same scent as the oil used to consecrate the temple or tabernacle, and it is the same as the scent of the incense which fills the Holy of Holies (Ex. 30: 1-10). The aroma of that incense is holy and pleasing to God. When the sacrifice is made, "it is a

holy sacrifice and a pleasing odor before God."[37]   The
incense is designed to protect the holiness of God from the
stench of death.   That stench must have been powerful
indeed when one considers the vast numbers of animals that
were sacrificed on the temple altar and all of the blood that
must have been coagulating at the base of the altar --
especially during festivals like the Passover, when the head
of virtually every family in Jerusalem sought to have a
lamb that had been sacrificed in the temple on their dinner
table!   Virtually every family in Israel and the diaspora
longed to be in Jerusalem for Passover. At those times,
without the incense, the temple would have wreaked of
dead flesh as in a slaughter house.   The burning incense on
the altar of incense and the perfumed oil on each sacrifice
served to separate the stench of death from the sacred
precincts of the temple.

It is not that God really needs to be protected from
the stench of death, of course, but for the sake of the
worshipers, there needs to be one place in the world where
death cannot enter, where life is always present, where the
holiness of God is constant. The Pentateuch is very clear
that the aroma to be used in the temple is to consecrate the
objects in the temple, the sacrifices, and the High Priest.
It is to be used for no other purpose (Ex. 30: 37-38).

The sacrifice provides a tactile, visual and auditory
worship experience (the laying on of hands, seeing the
animal butchered, the sounds of animals, and the roar of
the altar fire). It also provides an olfactory experience,
since the smell of the incense and the ointment, along with
the smoking flesh, pervade the scene.

---

[37] These words appear at the conclusion of the Levitical instructions
for every sacrifice.

Lv. 17 makes it clear that any animal that is slaughtered must be brought to the temple for sacrifice. In practice, this meant that the temple was a virtual slaughterhouse and butcher shop. The parts of the animal that were sacrificed (except for the priest's portion) were not edible. The remainder, with a few exceptions (ordination and atonement), was eaten by the people as part of the feast. This completed the sensory experience of the sacrificial feasts by providing taste. Indeed, the covenant was "eaten" and became part of the worshipper's flesh. No doubt the worshipper comes away from the worship event with some of that perfume lingering on her or his clothing, reminding the faithful one of the experience long after the benefits of the feast have passed.

Chapter 3
The Consecration of Nazirites

A Costly Separation Ritual

While the Pentateuch clearly identifies priests as men and even restricts access to the holiest precincts of the temple to men, there was one significant ritual in which the worshipper could be a man or a woman. A Nazirite, clearly considered equivalent in holiness to the High Priest, could be *male or female*.[38]

A Nazirite was a person from any tribe, not like the priests who came exclusively from the tribe of Levi. They were persons whose lives were dedicated to God, often for a particular purpose, sometimes from birth. They were accorded a status essentially equal to that of the High Priest, though they did not perform the duties of a temple priest. Their work, whatever it might be, was considered to be the work of a holy person. Their particular gifts or capacity to accomplish their work were considered *semeia* of their holiness. Samson was a Nazirite and a warrior (1 Sam. 9-11). Samuel was a prophet, a priest and a Nazirite from birth as a consequence of his mother's vow (1 Sam. 1: 11). The prophet Amos proclaimed that just as God "raised up" prophets, God "raised up" Nazirites (Amos 2: 11). Nazirites were understood as people who had been set apart, as a consequence of their own vow or the vow of

---

[38] See J.C. Rylaarsdam, "Nazirite," Interpreter's Dictionary of the Bible, op. cit., vol. 3, pp. 526-527.

their mother,[39] as holy to God. They were called into ministry, ordained by the power of the Holy Spirit, and consecrated by their own costly choice to accept the way of life that identified them as Nazirites.

According to Nu. 6, it was possible for women as well as men to take Nazirite vows, the completion of which involves the Nazirite virtually co-celebrating the sacrifice with the priest, including the leaning on of hands upon the sacrifice and the elevation offering. While the Nazirite does not ascend the altar, he or she does ascend the steps to the Holy of Holies, a privilege not only denied to other "laity," but normally restricted to the High Priest and the Chief Priests. It would appear that a significant exception was made for women, who were normally excluded from the holiest area of the temple; they were permitted to enter the Court of the Priests when they consecrated their vows.

A Nazirite would have had to separate herself or himself from all others, remaining apart from the community for the sake of maintaining a sacred vow to God and demonstrating consecration by

> (1) abstaining from wine and strong drink, vinegar or wine vinegar, grape juice, grapes (fresh or dried) or any grape product;
>
> (2) allowing the hair to grow long, never taking a razor to cut it;
>
> (3) never going near a corpse;[40]
>
> (4) consecrating the head (anointed in the manner prescribed below), and

---

[39]Theoretically either parent could make this vow, but only mothers are recorded as having done so.

[40]Compare this with Lv. 21: 11, the restrictions imposed upon the High Priest. They are identical.

(5) living as one "Holy to the Lord (Ex. 28: 36-38)."

The obligation to observe the holiness codes was higher for Nazirites than it was for Levites. It was equivalent to the requirements of the High Priest.[41] While the Pentateuch does not prescribe that the ritual pertaining to a Nazirite must be performed by the High Priest, it seems likely that the High Priest would be the officiant at such an event, since only the High Priest would seem to qualify by an equivalent definition of holiness.

To complete a Nazirite vow (Nu. 6: 13f), any person, man or woman, would have to bring an enormously costly gift to the temple. That gift would include

(1) a male lamb without blemish a year old
to be used as a burnt offering;

(2) an ewe lamb without blemish a year old
to be used as a sin offering;[42]

(3) a ram (a mature sheep or goat) without
blemish for a peace offering;

(4) a basket filled with unleavened bread,
cakes of choice flour mixed with oil, or
unleavened wafers spread with oil;

(5) a grain offering (Nu. 15: 1-4) of:
- 1/10th ephah (about 1 litre) of choice flour
- mixed with 1/4 hin (about 1.5 liters) of oil,
- (with the ram), 2/10 ephah (about 2 liters)
  of fine flour
- mixed with 1/3 hin (just over a litre) of oil;

---

[41]Compare Nu. 6: 1-12 with Lv. 21: 1-24.

[42]A *female* animal (an ewe) is used only for this sacrifice, the atonement sacrifice, and the rite for the purification of one who has been healed of leprosy.

(6) drink offerings (Nu. 15: 5-10) including:
- 1/4 hin of wine (about 3 liters) for each sacrificial lamb and
- 1/3 hin of wine (about 2 liters) for the sacrificial ram.

The wine was poured over the parts of the sacrifice that were burned on the altar to provide a pleasing odor to the Lord and probably to aid in its burning.

The monetary value of the above gifts was calculated according to the age and sex of the person making the vow as follows:[43]

Male:	20-60 yrs.	50 shekels (about 250 denarii)
Female:	20-60 yrs.	30 shekels (about 150 denarii)
Male:	5-20 yrs.	20 shekels (about 100 denarii)
Female:	5-20 yrs.:	10 shekels (about 50 denarii)
Male:	1 mo. -5 yrs.	5 shekels (about 25 denarii)
Female:	1 mo. -5 yrs.	3 shekels (about 15 denarii)
Male:	over 60 yrs.	15 shekels (about 75 denarii)
Female:	over 60 yrs.	10 shekels (about 50 denarii)

The priest could assess an alternative (and presumably lower) value for persons making the Nazirite vow who could not afford these amounts.[44]

Assuming the Nazirite is a woman between the ages of twenty and sixty years of age, and using these values, the ritual that she would be required to complete is as follows (Nu. 6: 13-20):

---

[43]See Lev. 27.

[44]I have translated these values from shekels to denarii to facilitate comparison with the value of the pure oil of spikenard used by Mary of Bethany in the anointing story in Jn. 11: 55-12: 8.

(1) The priest brings the Nazirite before the Lord. (i.e.: the Nazirite is met at the Nicanor gate by the priest, who escorts her into the court of the Israelites and stands next to her, facing the altar.)

(2) The priest offers a sin offering to atone for the worshiper's sins according to the guidelines of Lv. 4: 32-35:

> (a) The Nazirite leans her hands on the ewe lamb's head. This signifies that the identity of the Nazirite, including the state of holiness (or sinfulness) of that person is transferred to the lamb.
>
> (b) The priest slaughters the lamb near the altar (by cutting its throat).
>
> (c) The priest sprinkles some of the lamb's blood on the horns of the altar.
>
> (d) The priest pours the blood of the lamb into a basin at the base (foot) of the altar.
>
> (e) The priest places his hand inside the body of the lamb and removes the entrails and fat, then burns them on the altar. The Nazirite's sins are forgiven.

(3) The priest offers a burnt offering according to the guidelines found in Lv.1:

> (a) The Nazirite leans her hands on the male lamb's head.
>
> (b) The priest slaughters the lamb on the north side of the altar.
>
> (c) The priest dashes the blood of the lamb on all sides of the altar.
>
> (d) The priest cuts the lamb into "parts:"
> - the head is severed from the body,
> - the legs are severed from the body,

- the side of the body is cut open and the priest removes the entrails and fat with his hand.

(e) The priest arranges the head and fat of the lamb on the wood piled on the coals on the altar.

(f) The priest washes the entrails and feet of the lamb with water.

(g) The priest places the entrails and the feet of the lamb along with the head and the fat on the smoldering fire.

(4) The priest offers the sacrifice of well being (the peace offering) according to the guidelines found in Lv. 3:12.

(a) The Nazirite lays her hands on the ram's head.

(b) The priest kills the ram by the doors of the Tabernacle.

(c) The priest dashes the ram's blood on the altar.

(d) The priest removes from the body of the lamb:
-the fat that covers the ram's belly,
-both kidneys and all of the fat on them,
-the appendage of the liver,
-the fat on the thighs.

(e) The priest places these removed parts of the ram on the altar fire, turning them into smoke.

(5) This is followed by the grain or cereal offering as explained in Lv. 2: 1-2.

(a) The Nazirite pours oil on a portion (handful) of the grain offering (including the unleavened bread).

(b) The Nazirite puts frankincense on a portion (handful) of the grain offering (including the unleavened bread).

(c) The priest takes the memorial (the prepared portion) of the grain offering and "turns it into smoke" (i.e.: burns it on the altar.)

(6) As a final step in making these three blood offerings, the priest offers the drink offering,[45] pouring the wine over the "parts" on the altar.

(7) The Nazirite shaves her head entirely, while standing at the entrance to the Tent of the Meeting.

The Nazirite is now face to face with God. No veil may separate the Nazirite's head from the countenance of God, so she shaves off completely the hair that has been the sign of her personal covenant. Note that other priests "shall not make bald spots upon their heads, or shave off the edges of their beards (Lv. 21: 5)." The High Priest may not even dishevel his hair, let alone remove it (Lv. 12: 10), because disheveled hair was a sign for someone who was unclean (Lv. 13: 45). On the other hand, one who had been cured of leprosy was required to shave off all hair from his or her body (Lv. 14: 8-9) and a priest unbinding a woman's hair before the Lord was part of a test for adultery (Nu. 5: 18).

Consider how extraordinary it would be for a woman to complete a Nazirite vow. Unless she was supported by a wealthy father or husband, the likelihood of a woman ever accumulating enough wealth to provide all of the sacrifices was slim, especially given the fact that the male head of her family could prevent the ritual simply by objecting to it (Nu. 30: 1-16). Then consider the cultural barriers in place to prevent women from going further into

---

[45]See Otto Michel, "σπενδομαι," Theological Dictionary of the New Testament, op. cit., vol. VII, pp. 528-536, esp. 531-533. "The act consisted of pouring out the wine on the altar, God's table, or on the burnt offering, Ex. 30: 9, Nu. 28: 24." Presumably, this produced a flaring up of fire as the alcohol ignited.

the temple than the Court of the Women. Once admitted to the Court of the Israelites (men's court), the Nazirite woman would have to be admitted to the sacred precincts of the priests. It must have been a very rare event when a woman was admitted to this part of the temple. It seems likely that it would have occurred (especially during a busy time like the Festival of the Passover) only in the middle of the night. Nothing in the scriptures suggests that such a ritual had to be conducted late at night, but the practical demands of scheduling time on the altar as well as the normal barriers to admitting women may have required it.

The ritual sacrifices for a Nazirite took at least three times as long as others, since they included every kind and purpose for sacrifice, so an extended period of time would have been required. Finally, consider the end result for a woman completing a Nazirite vow: she would be bald! This would at once be a sign of her devotion to God and a social oddity that could not have been ignored. It seems likely that women rarely completed this vow.

The conclusion of this ritual includes a unique and extraordinary step:

(8) *The Nazirite places her consecrated, but now severed, hair under the sacrifice of well being. This involves a personal sacrifice unequaled in any other ritual except circumcision.*[46]

(9) The priest now places the elements of the sacrifice (all of the elements that have been prepared in steps 1-8: the (boiled) shoulder of the ram, one unleavened, oil-soaked

---

[46]See Gn. 22: 7-14. After Isaac was saved by the substitution of a sacrificial ram, no form of human sacrifice, except circumcision and this offering of severed hair, was allowed in Israel.

cake, and one unleavened, oil-soaked wafer, in the
Nazirite's upraised hands, then

(10) The priest raises the Nazirite's hands, now filled with
the elements of this specific sacrifice, presumably including
the locks of hair.

(11) The priest keeps these offering elements along with
the lamb's breast and thigh as his portion (Nu. 6: 20).

(12) The Nazirite may now drink wine, the vow having
been consecrated and fulfilled.

Nazirite Consecration and Ordination of Priests

The ritual for the consecration of a Nazirite (Nu. 6) can be
compared to the ritual for the ordination of Aaron and his
sons (Lv. 8).

Particularly important is the fact that the Nazirite
vows are taken voluntarily, while the ordination ritual falls
upon those who inherit their function in the Hebrew
community. Only Levites may be priests, and only a direct
descendant of Aaron may become High Priest (Ex. 29: 9).
However, any holy man or holy woman may choose to take
the Nazirite vow. While the level of holiness of a Nazirite
was comparable to that of the High Priest, the Nazirite was
not permitted to perform the sacrificial rites of a priest in
the temple, *except during the completion of his or her own
vow, when privileges restricted to the High Priest (i.e.:
permission to ascend the steps to the sanctuary) were given.*

Both rites serve to separate a person from the
community for the sake of serving God within the
community, and both require that the separated person be
holy. The standards for holiness are higher for the High
Priest than for other priests (Lv. 21).

"The priest who is exalted above his fellows, on whose head the anointing oil has been poured and who has been consecrated to wear the vestments, shall not dishevel his hair, nor tear his vestments. He shall not go where there is a dead body; he shall not defile himself even for his father or mother [as a Levite could (Lv. 21: 1-3)]. He shall not go outside the sanctuary and thus profane the sanctuary of his God; for the consecration of the anointing oil of his God is upon him: I am the Lord" (Lv. 21: 10-12).

Compare this to the standards required of a Nazirite.

"When either men or women make a special vow, the vow of a Nazirite, to separate themselves to the Lord, they shall separate themselves from wine and strong drink; they shall drink no wine vinegar or other vinegar, and shall not drink any grape juice or eat grapes, fresh or dried. All their days as Nazirites they shall eat nothing that is produced by the grapevine, not even the seeds or the skins. All the days of their Nazirite vow no razor shall come upon the head; until the time is completed for which they separate themselves to the Lord, they shall be holy; they shall let the locks of the head grow long. All the days that they separate themselves to the Lord they shall not go near a corpse. Even if their father or mother, brother or sister, should die, they may not defile themselves; because their consecration to God is upon the head. All their days as Nazirites they are holy to the Lord. (Nu. 6: 1-6)"

Both the High Priest and the Nazirite are "Holy to the Lord." Their consecration is upon the head (whether it is by the *semeion* of uncut hair or an anointed head, the hair of which is not disheveled).

When the High Priest is ordained, the second lamb is called the Ram of Ordination. It is sacrificed along with a Grain Offering after its parts are elevated. For the Nazirite, the second lamb is a ewe lamb called the Peace Offering. It is sacrificed first, and then a Grain offering is made after parts of the Peace Offering and the Grain Offering are elevated. The composition of the two elevation offerings is the same except for one important difference: at the place in the rite when blood from the Ram of Ordination is touched to the right earlobe, the right thumb, and the right big toe of the priest being ordained, the Nazirite shaves his or her own head and places the hair under the elevation offering. There appears to be a *semeiotic* equivalence between the threefold touch of blood and the severance of hair. In fact, they appear to be correlated. The touch of the sacrificial blood brings holiness to each one of the *semeiotic* parts of the newly ordained priest. The shaving of the hair that serves as a sign of holiness for the Nazirite ends the Nazirite's time of holiness. Afterwards, the one who has completed the Nazirite vow can drink wine.

While ordination begins a lifetime of holiness for the priest, consecration of the Nazirite vow ends a period of holiness for the holy man or woman. In the early days of this vow, the Nazirite might live a lifetime as a holy person (as a warrior, a king, a prophet or even as a priest). In the latter years, emphasis appears to have been made upon the sacrifice used to consecrate the vow, and the period of time between the making and the consecration of the vow could be as short as thirty days.[47]

---

[47]See Rylaarsdam, op. cit.

If a High Priest is defiled, either by being in proximity to a corpse or by injury to the head, hand, body, or foot, he is disqualified to serve (Lv. 21: 16-24). If a Nazirite is inadvertently in the presence of one who dies, then the period of holiness must be started all over again (Nu. 6: 9-12).

Unlike the Levite priests who served in lesser roles, the High Priest was not permitted to draw near to a dead person, not even to the corpse of a near relative. The language of the restriction applied to Nazirites is almost identical to that for the High Priest.

Summary

While it is true that the Pentateuch does not indicate that women were not permitted to be priests who practiced the rites of sacrifice, the passage regarding Nazirites does indicate that women as well as men could be consecrated and considered as holy in Israel as the High Priest. It is significant that Nazirites were allowed to participate in the elevation offering during their own service of consecration and that they were permitted to climb the steps to the sanctuary. Of great importance for our study is the ritual a Nazirite follows with her or his hair during the completion of the Nazirite vow.

Later we will see that these ritual acts bring light to bear on the female identity of the mysterious figure in the Fourth Gospel called the Beloved Disciple. The fact that Mary of Bethany performs rituals that use all of these *semeia* suggests that she was a Nazirite.

Chapter 4
Semeiotic Patterns in the Gospel of John

The Transfer of Semeiotic Patterns[48]

Our study thus far has focused on the role that signs and patterns of signs play in the Pentateuch. As indicated in the preface of this work, we are starting from the assumption that the original students of the Gospel of John were very familiar with the Pentateuch, or more accurately, they were familiar with the Greek version of the Pentateuch called the Septuagint. Our thesis relies on an extension of that assumption, namely that this familiarity with the Greek version of the ancient Hebrew scriptures included an appreciation for the precise choice of words used in that version. These words conveyed what first-century readers would have seen as holy writ. These words would have been considered holy in two ways. (1)Having been used in a document that conveyed the words of God, great care would have been given to preserving and using those exact words (even though these words had been originally written in Hebrew). (2)Many of these words were actually oracles, metaphors that contained the mysterious power to convey meaning beyond their common use. As such, the exact language of the Septuagint would have been a matter of careful study.

What remains to be shown is that these Greek words from the Septuagint were in fact chosen as key words in the Gospel According to John. We shall begin by considering

---

[48] See the Appendix C: <u>Concordance of Mosaic and Johannine Oracles</u> for a listing of transferred *semeia*.

a term that has long been associated with the New Testament, and especially with the Gospel According to John.

The Word

The Greek term used in both the LXX and the New Testament for the mediating aspect of God is "λογοσ"(*logos*) -- word. It is through the Word that all things are created. Nothing exists without having been brought into being by the Word. It is through the Word that God is known or "seen" and the covenant is remembered. Those who see or know the Word remember the covenant and live in the light of the Word. Those who do not see or know the Word live in the darkness of the world.

When the covenant is remembered, it is restored or reconciled. The faithfulness of God is revealed in the constancy of God's remembrance of the covenant. The faithfulness of the people of God is reflected in their remembrance of the covenant. When the people forget the covenant or take it for granted, they lose faith, and their relationship with God is broken. The separation between God and God's people grows wider. It becomes necessary for God to slip between God and God's creation to reconcile the separation. That is when the Word of God is spoken, when the Word of God can be seen, when faith or belief in God becomes the all-important response to the divine initiative.

The Gospel of John begins with a prologue that is patterned after the first five verses of the first story of

creation in Genesis.[49] "In the beginning was the Word, and
the Word was with God, and the Word was God . . ." "In
the beginning when God created the heavens and the earth
. . . God said, 'Let there be light,' and there was light."
Word is a *semeion* and light is a *semeion*. Each points to
the divine role in creation.

The author of the Fourth Gospel understands the
significance of the ancient symbolism of temple sacrifice:
separating and remembering. The theologian behind the
Gospel of John uses different words to affirm the same
dynamic: seeing and believing. "To see" is to separate
truth from untruth, light from darkness, to differentiate and
discern.[50] "To believe" is to remember the covenant, and
thus to live in faith.[51]

In the New Testament, especially in the Gospel of
John, believing is a present reality. The theologian behind
the Gospel presents the Jesus story of the Synoptic Gospels
with a significant difference: Jesus is not the long-awaited
Jewish Messiah, but the pre-existent *logos*, the Word
incarnate in the world, the Holy One walking upon the
earth, abiding within the creation (Gn. 3: 8). Jesus
personifies the suffering of God that comes as a
consequence of the separation between God and those God

---

[49]Compare Gn. 1: 1-5 with Jn. 1: 1-5.

[50]See Wilhelm Michaelis, "οραω , ειδον , Βλεπω , (etc)," Theological Dictionary of the New Testament, op. cit., vol. V, pp. 315-382, esp. pp. 324-334; 361-366; See also Heinrich Seesemann, "οιδα," Ibid., pp. 116-119; Friedrich Buchsel, "ιστορεω (ιστορια)," Ibid., vol. III, pp. 391-393.

[51]See Rudolf Bultmann, Artur Weiser, "πιστευω ," Theological Dictionary of the New Testament, op. cit., vol. VI, pp. 174-228, esp. 222-228; also Kittel and von Rad, "δοζα," Ibid., vol. II, pp. 232-255, esp. p. 249.

has created, especially those who are entrusted with the task
of "striving with both God and human beings," the people
of God, the children of Israel, the descendants of Jacob
(Gn. 32: 28).[52]

In the prologue, the theologian behind the Gospel of
John is presenting the assertion that the Word is the
primordial emanation of God through whom all things are
created and have life. The Word is the Light of God,
which shines into the darkness of a world that chooses not
to see that Light. The gospel story presented in John is the
eternal drama of God reconciling the separation between
God and God's people through the Word.

The disciples of Jesus, for whom the Gospel
According of John is written, are facing the prospect of
living in a world in which the temple in Jerusalem, the
priests, and the sacrifices associated with the temple have
all ceased to mediate between God and God's people. The
Gospel explains, using the *semeia* of the Pentateuch, how
God slips into human history, and how and why the Word
has become flesh in Jesus of Nazareth.

The Temple

The setting for much of the Fourth Gospel is the Temple in
Jerusalem. Actually the Temple in Jerusalem in the time of

---

[52]See Gn. 32: 28; also Walter Gutbrod, "Ισραηλ, ισραηλιτησ,
Ιουδαιοσ, Ιουδαια, Ιουδαικοσ, etc.," Theological Dictionary of the
New Testament, op. cit., vol. II, pp. 356-390. "(In the Old Testament)
'Israel' is originally a sacral term. It denotes the totality of the elect of
Yahweh and of those united in the Yahweh cult." (p. 357) "In John
Ισραηλ . . . is the people of God. To be related to it is to be related to
God's people, and consequently to God . . . (Israel) is thus almost a supra-
temporal entity." (p. 385).

Jesus was the second Temple. Originally the people of God worshipped in a tent called the Tabernacle. The instructions in Ex. 25-27; 35-40 are for the Tabernacle. It was portable, and God decided when it moved (Ex. 40: 35). The people literally "followed" God. It was a holy place built by the great prophet of the Exodus, Moses, and by his brother, Aaron, the first High Priest, father of all priests.

Before Moses and Aaron, Jacob's ladder dream gave rise to the idea that a place on earth could be the location of God's house. The top (head) of the ladder was in heaven, the bottom (feet) of the ladder was in a place he called Bethel, which means "House of God." Angels climbed between. Later, Jacob wrestled with one of these angels, though he thought that his struggle was directly with God. That struggle ended with an injury to Jacob's hip. He called this place Penuel meaning "face of God" because he believed that there he was able to *see God* (Gn. 32: 24-32).   Later, Moses, whose face glowed after each time he was permitted to speak with God (Ex. 34: 29f), defined the sacred dimensions and components first included in the Tabernacle. It was David, the Great Shepherd King, who determined that a permanent and glorious structure should be built (1 Chron. 17: 1-12). His son, Solomon, the wisest and wealthiest of all of Israel's kings, fulfilled the vision and built the first Temple on a site chosen by David: a threshing floor that could be the same location as Abraham had prepared to sacrifice Isaac and the same site that Jacob had called "the House of God."[53]

---

[53]2 Chron. 2-5, esp. 3: 1; See G.A. Barrois, "Moriah," The Interpreter's Dictionary of the Bible, George Buttrick, ed., Abingdon, Nashville-New York, (1962), vol. 3, p. 438f.

Jacob's vision is the source of the *semeia* of the Tabernacle and the Temple. The Temple is the house of God, where God touches the earth. It is the intersecting point between the Holy God (head) and the profane earth (feet) and in between is the priest who interacts (physically, bodily) with God and humanity.

All of this, including Jacob's injured hip, is represented in the rituals of animal sacrifice performed in the Temple. "Therefore to this day the Israelites do not eat the thigh muscle that is on the hip socket, because he struck Jacob on the hip socket at the thigh muscle (Gn. 32: 32)." While the people of Israel do not eat the meat from the sacrificed animal's thigh, the priests do (Lv. 8: 25). It is their portion. It represents their *semeiotic* role. They are literally sustained by the covenant, being dependent upon the food that has been sacrificed to God.

The house of God, therefore, was a vision of Jacob[54] who struggled with both God and humans (Gn. 32: 28). That is, he "saw" the connection between God and humans. Later, Moses would build the tabernacle to fulfill this same function. Still later a stationary Temple was built in Jerusalem. This Temple was designed to enable the priests to enact the *semeiotic* symbols of the ancient covenant with God.

The second Temple, however, though it was built in the same location as the first (the previous one had been

---

[54]Jacob's name (a name is a *semeion* or sign) was changed from Jacob (which means "takes by the heel (foot)" as a blessing by the angel or God with whom he had been struggling. His new name was Israel, which means "One who struggles with God." See Gen. 27: 36 note b.; 32: 28 note k., New Revised Standard Version.

destroyed)[55] was lacking in two important ways. First, it was constructed by Herod, who had a reputation as a great builder; and he had a political motive (to ingratiate himself with the people of Israel, whom he ruled on behalf of Rome). Comay[56] quotes Josephus[57] that "Herod esteemed this work (building of the second Temple) to be 'the most glorious of all his actions . . . and that this would be sufficient for an everlasting memorial for him." It was, in other words, built as a memorial to Herod, not a place to remember the covenant with God. Second, it was built by a ruler who saw it as a way to maintain power by uniting the Roman authority with the authority of the priests of Israel. Herod's purpose was not to separate God's people as a holy nation, but to unite God's priests with a nation that did not worship God. In these two respects, the Herodian Temple, in spite of its grandeur, could not provide a sanctified place for the sacred rites of Israel.

Herod began building the new Temple about 20 years before Jesus came on the scene. Herod chose to build an enormous earthen platform which was called the Temple Mount. It was literally a mountain. Upon this artificial mountain were built the new Temple and adjacent buildings, including Herod's own palace (which was elevated above the altar and sanctuary). The whole project was still under construction during the time of Jesus, a full

---

[55]See Comay, op. cit., p. 132-191 for a history of the Herodian temple; see also Alfred Edersheim, The Temple, Kregel Publications, Grand Rapids, (1997). This book makes extensive use of photographs of a useful model of the temple made by Mr. Alec Garrard of Norfolk, England. Edersheim's work is dated 1874.

[56]Ibid., p. 141 f.

[57]Antiquities of the Jews, Book XV, Chapter 11.

generation after Herod's death in 4 B.C. It was destroyed again in 70 A.D., only 20 years after completion, and it has never been rebuilt. The destruction of the Temple was an event of enormous importance for the first-century Christians, who understood that Jesus had replaced the Temple as the center of faith.

There was another important discrepancy in the Temple during the Herodian period. The role of the High Priest, a position inherited from one generation to another among the descendants of Aaron, had become a position gained through political influence. The Jews had been subjected to the power of Rome by the Roman triumvir, Pompey, who installed Hyrcanus II as High Priest, over his brother, Aristobulus II. In 42 BC (when Julius Caesar was assassinated) an internal Roman struggle resulted in the mutilation of Hyrcanus. His ears were chopped off, disqualifying him to serve as High Priest (Lv. 21: 16-23). King Herod, for political reasons, "discarded the principle that the office was hereditary; it became not even a life appointment, but one held at the king's pleasure."[58] He appointed several persons to this position, then removed them from office or had them killed. The High Priest's vestments were kept by Herod in the Antonia fortress adjacent to the Temple and only released when required for special feast days.[59] The Anointed One was supposed to be Holy to God. Priests were supposed to be removed from their roles only by God's action or by God's law, not by any political authority. To desecrate that high office was to destroy the High Priest's ability to provide the service for which he had been anointed.

---

[58]Ibid., pp. 137.
[59]Comway, Ibid., p. 134f.

It can be implied from the Gospel of John that there were people in Israel who were very much against the building of the Herodian Temple in Jerusalem in spite of its beauty and grandeur. They opposed the authority of the High Priest, as unthinkable as that would have been to previous generations of faithful Jews.[60] The priests of this generation, led by their High Priest, functioned to widen the separation between God and God's people. They had forgotten the covenant, forgotten their *semeiotic* priestly role. Some of them had forgotten that their purpose was to be the right hand of God in helping the people to lift up their sacrifices before God whenever the people broke their covenant. They had, instead, become intermediaries between Caesar's agent, Herod, and God's people. They functioned as political operatives rather than as priests. The metaphor of the priestly role had become frozen. In fact, it had died. The right hand had become "white as snow." The priesthood was dead. It was time to return that right hand to the bosom of God, to resurrect it as a sign of a living relationship between God and God's people.

---

[60]Raymond E. Brown, Community of the Beloved Disciple, Paulist Press, New York/ Ramsey/Toronto, (1979), p. 40f.; M.H. Shepherd's refutation of Brown's thesis, citing support from Mark 1: 44 and Luke 17: 14, is not convincing. "Neither Jesus nor his orthodox Jewish disciples were so radical as to repudiate either the priesthood or the sacrificial system of the temple, for they accepted these institutions as God-given in the law." "Priests in the (New Testament)," The Interpreter's Dictionary of the Bible, Abingdon, New York, Nashville, (1962), p. 890.

Chapter 5
Jesus Replaces the Temple Sacrifices

Introduction

The theologian behind the Gospel of John sees in the ministry of Jesus a sign that the Word has come to replace the Temple. In Jn. 2: 18f. Jesus responds to the challenge of his authority for driving money changers out of the Temple. The Jews ask, "What sign can you show us for doing this?" He says, "Destroy this Temple, and in three days I will raise it up." The Jews respond, "This Temple has been under construction for forty-six years,[61] and will you raise it up in three days?" John explains clearly that Jesus is talking about the Temple of his own body. This is a clue to a much wider understanding of Jesus' intent, which the Fourth Gospel explains in the symbolic language of Mosaic *semeia*.

In addition to replacing the enormous building complex of the Temple with his own body, the Gospel According to John provides clues for those with eyes to see that Jesus also meant to replace all of the sacrificial rites that occurred within the Temple. By identifying the *semeia* of each festival in the Old Testament terms of separating and remembering,[62] then locating these same *semeia* in the

---

[61]Comay, op. cit., using Josephus as her source, says that the temple was under construction for 46 years totally. By the time that the Gospel of John was written (ca. 120 AD) that 46 years would have been complete and the temple's destruction in 70 AD an historical event.

[62]See Lev. 23. Sabbath: vs. 3f; Passover: vs. 5f; First Fruits: vs. 9f; Weeks: vs. 15f; Trumpets: vs. 23f; Atonement: vs. 26f; Booths: vs. 33f.

Gospel, now defined in terms of seeing and believing, this part of what might be called the "sub plot" of the Gospel emerges into view.

The Sabbath

The Sabbath, God's holy day of rest, occurred every seventh day, beginning at sundown of what we would call Friday evening. Its function was to separate work from worship and to remember God the Creator.

The fourth commandment (Ex. 20: 8 LXX) reads, "Remember the Sabbath to keep it holy."[63] By keeping the Sabbath each believer could participate in making a sign for God that the covenant was being remembered, and thus maintained.[64] Ex. 19: 5-6 makes it clear that in keeping the covenant, God's people preserved their identity as a holy nation of priests. Nu. 1: 53 makes it clear that the Levites understood their role to be that of guardians, keeping the Temple (protecting its holiness) and keeping God's laws (observing every ritual statute), keeping the traditions that recall God's offer of salvation.

The observance of the Sabbath began at sundown in remembrance of the watch kept by God and by God's people on the Passover night when God brought the people of Israel out of Egypt (Ex. 12:42).

In Jn. 5: 1-18 and again in Jn. 9: 1-41 Jesus breaks the Sabbath. In fact, he abolishes it with the words, "My

---

[63]Trans. by Sir Lancelot C.L. Brenton, The Septuagint with Apocrypha: Greek and English, Orig. Pub. Samuel Bagster & Sons, Ltd, London, 1851, Fifth Printing Feb. 1995 in the U.S.A., p. 96.

[64]Georg Bertram, "Φυλασσω , Φυλακη ," Theological Dictionary of the New Testament, op. cit., vol. IX, p. 236-244.

father is still working, and I am also working (Jn. 5:
17)."[65] Why? Why would the Word, with God in creation,
break the Sabbath? The prologue to the Gospel provides a
hint. "In the beginning . . ." guides a reader with even the
most basic knowledge of the Pentateuch to the first chapter
of Genesis. The subject of the first five verses of the
creation story is *light*. The prologue says that in the Word
was light and that the light shines in the darkness (Jn. 1: 4-
9). In the Pentateuch, the first day of creation is the day of
light. It is because light exists that it is even possible to
consider that time passes. For the author or authors of this
gospel, the Day of the Lord is not "a watch in the night,"
but "the dawn of creation," the first day, not the last day.

A complete consideration of Jn. 5: 1-18 and Jn. 9:
1-41 will reveal a rich set of metaphors for the spiritual
life. At this point what is important is that the case is made
to support the assertion that Jesus replaced the Sabbath.

"With what did Jesus replace the Sabbath?" Again
the creation story provides the model. In Genesis, the
pattern for creation is that God calls (or brings forth) each
new part of creation (as in birth), then names it and then
blesses it as good. When Nicodemus, one of the great
teachers of the law, comes to Jesus in the dark of night (Jn.
3: 1-21), Jesus tells him that in order to see the kingdom of
God he will need to be born anew. Jesus teaches
Nicodemus to see the kingdom of God by being reborn of
water and spirit. The imagery of baptism and the promise
of new life, rebirth, re-creation, and resurrection is offered
in place of the Sabbath. The Sabbath recalls the *first*
creation. Jesus brings the *new* creation.

---

[65] Eduard Lohse, "σαββατον ," Theological Dictionary of the
New Testament, op. cit, vol. VII, pp. 1-35, esp. pp. 26-28.

The Festival of First Fruits

First Fruits (Lv. 23: 9f) is the name of the festival that was celebrated at the beginning of the harvest. Ostensibly, this is the gift presented to God from the first (and best) of the crops and livestock that are produced in each season. These first fruits are separated from the rest of the crop and brought to the Temple, where God's providence over the course of Israel's history is remembered. First fruits also serve as a practical means of support for the priests in the Temple. The priests are entitled to this portion (a tithe) of every farmer's crop or herd, in addition to the "priest's portion" of every other sacrifice.[66]

The priests and their families, in other words, were provided with the best of every product that their agrarian culture could provide. Their needs were met abundantly. In fact, the Chief Priests and certainly the High Priest, lived in relative luxury.

Jesus in this gospel has a different understanding of the role of the priest and what it is that sustains or nourishes a priest. In Jn. 4: 1-42, Jesus teaches his disciples to "see how the fields are ripe for harvesting (vs. 35)" and reveals to them that such a harvest is "food to eat that you do not know about (vs. 31)." What he is talking about is not the harvest of grain or the firstborn of any herd. He means those who are coming into a relationship with him, prepared to become disciples. He is replacing the nourishment of the body through food with the nourishment of the spirit through a new kind of sustenance.

---

[66]See Dt. 18: 4; 26: 1-15; Nu. 18: 8-12. Also See Gerhard Delling, "απαρχη ," Theological Dictionary of the New Testament, op. cit, vol. I, pp. 484-486.

The role of the disciple/priest is defined in terms of planting and harvesting these spiritual first fruits, recognizing that they will harvest even "that for which you did not labor. (vs. 38)" Separating the first fruits from the rest of the harvest and remembering God's history of providence is replaced in the Fourth Gospel with seeing the harvest of those who would share a relationship with God and believing that each disciple is spiritually fed by bringing other believers into discipleship.

The Festival of Weeks

Fifty days after the Festival of First Fruits, the Festival of Weeks is held. This is the occasion of the completion of the harvest, a time when food is available in greatest abundance. Numerous animals, first fruits, and bread baked with leaven are offered as elevation offerings before the Lord (Dt. 16: 9-12). Most importantly, however, at this festival the landless Levites, the widows, orphans, and strangers are to receive shares of the freewill offerings that the faithful bring to their Temple. These faithful are to separate a generous portion of their harvest to share with those less fortunate and remember that they were once slaves in Egypt. The Festival of Weeks required the faithful to be generous to widows, orphans, priests, and gentiles every year. Every seventh (sabbatical) year, that generosity was to last all year long.

"If there is among you anyone in need, a member of your community in any of your towns within the land that the LORD your God is giving you, do not be hard-hearted or tight-fisted toward your neighbor. You should rather open your hand, willingly lending enough to meet the need,

whatever it may be. . . Since there will never cease to be
some in need on the earth, I therefore command yuou,
'Open your hand to the poor and needy neighbor in your
land'" (Dt. 15: 7-8, 11)

In John 12: 8, Jesus paraphrases the first part of Dt.
15: 11, ("You always have the poor with you . . .")
leaving the remainder of the verse unsaid and adding, "but
you do not always have me." Later we shall consider the
important implications of the words left unsaid in this
passage. For now let us simply note that Jesus substitutes
himself as the reason for being generous as in the sabbatical
year or the Festival of Weeks. He emphasizes that the
opportunity to be generous to the poor is always at hand,
but the opportunity to consecrate this moment is brief.

Later (Jn. 12: 20-26), Jesus interprets the fact that
some Greeks have come seeking to see him to be a sign that
"the hour has come for the Son of Man to be glorified."
He explains this interpretation by borrowing from the
semeion of an abundant harvest, a harvest that cannot be
made without first planting seed. "Very truly, I tell you,
unless a grain of wheat falls into the earth and dies, it
remains just a single grain; but if it dies, it bears much fruit
(Jn. 12: 24)." Clearly, the first fruit as Jesus sees it in the
Gospel According to John is the fruitful seed, planted in the
ground, the seed that "dies" and is buried and then bears
much "fruit." Obviously the theology here is that Jesus
knows that he is the grain (the bread that is offered as a
sacrifice) and that he must die in order for people from the
wider world (represented by the Greeks) to become his
disciples.

The Festival of Trumpets

The Festival of Trumpets is based upon the account in
Exodus 19 of a most extraordinary event in Israel's history:
the day that the seventy leaders of Israel met God face to
face! The account is rich in metaphors.

"And it came to pass on the third day, as the morning drew
nigh, there were voices and lightnings and a dark cloud on
mount Sina (sic): the voice of the trumpet sounded loud,
and all the people in the camp trembled. And Moses led
the people forth out of the camp to meet God, and they
stood by under the camp. The mount of Sina was
altogether on a smoke, because God had descended upon it
in fire; and the smoke went up as the smoke of a furnace,
and the people were exceedingly amazed. And the sounds
of the trumpet were waxing very much louder. Moses
spoke, and God answered him with a voice. And the Lord
came down upon the mount Sina on the top of the
mountain; and the Lord called Moses to the top of the
mountain, and Moses went up. And God spoke to Moses,
saying, Go down, and solemnly charge the people, lest at
any time they draw nigh to God to gaze, and a multitude of
them fall. And let the priests that draw nigh to the Lord
God sanctify themselves, lest he destroy some of them (Ex.
19: 16-22 LXX)."[67]

Two trumpets were made for use in the Temple
(Nu. 10: 1-10). They were long, slender metal instruments
capable of making only two (or with great effort, three)
loud notes. They were to be blown by the priests whenever

---

[67]Brenton, trans., Septuagint, op. cit.

the encampment moved and whenever burnt (flesh) offerings or peace (bread) offerings were made. They were "reminders." "At cockcrow trumpet signals ended the nightly feast of lights in the Court of Women. At Passover blasts were blown on the trumpets before the slaying of the lambs."[68]

The loud sound of the trumpet is the obvious *semeion* that connects this passage with the Gospel of John. The sound (phoneo) is also translated "loud speaking, calling, or crying (of people)" and can be used to mean "to summon, to send for, to cause to come" as it is in Jn. 1: 48 ; 2: 9; 4: 16; 9: 18, 24; 10: 3; 11: 28; 12: 17, and 13: 13.

In Jn. 10: 3, Jesus describes himself as the good shepherd who "calls his own sheep by name and leads them out." It is the sound of his voice that causes the people of God to move, not the sound of the trumpet.

A most interesting parallel, though, is in its secondary meaning: "crowing."[69] In Jn. 13: 38 and 18: 27 the crowing of the cock is used by Jesus as a sign by which Peter will recognize that he has failed to fulfill his promise to "lay down my life for you." It was a reminder that the sacrifice was being made, and being made by Jesus alone.

The Day of Atonement

That Jesus replaces the Festival of Atonement is a gross understatement. The *semeia* in this festival bear exceptional value in the Gospel According to John.

---

[68]Gerhard Friedrich, "σαλπιγξ ," Theological Dictionary of the New Testament, op. cit, vol. VII, p. 83.

[69]Otto Betz, "Φωνεω ," Theological Dictionary of the New Testament, op. cit., vol. IX, p. 303.

Lv. 16 dictates that between the offering of a bull for a sin offering and the offering of a ram for a burnt offering, two goats are to be sacrificed. One is sacrificed as a sin offering to atone for the sins of the nation of Israel. The other, the scapegoat, is set free to wander in the desert. On its head, too, the High Priest lays his hands to transfer the sins of the nation. This is the only animal brought to the Temple for sacrifice that is ever permitted to leave the Temple alive. The scapegoat is paired with another goat, which is sacrificed to "cover up" or "wash away" or "expiate" the sins of the nation.[70]

Whenever blood is drawn in any sacrifice and sprinkled upon the altar, atonement is made for the sins of the worshipper. On the Day of Atonement, the High Priest must first make an offering of a bull to atone for his own sins and the sins of his family. He enters the sanctuary alone and sprinkles the blood of the bull seven times on the mercy seat. Then he comes out of the sanctuary, places the two goats before the entrance to the sanctuary and draws lots. One of the two goats is sacrificed, and its blood is brought into the sanctuary and sprinkled directly on the mercy seat seven times to atone for the sins of the nation. Then the High Priest comes out of the sanctuary to sprinkle the blood of the bull and of the goat on the horns of the altar to cleanse it and hallow it from the uncleanness of the people of Israel. Next, the High Priest presents the live goat before the altar and releases it to another priest, who leads it out into the wilderness and sets it free. When all of this has been done, the High Priest re-enters the sanctuary,

---

[70]See Johannes Herrmann, "ιλασκομαι, ιλασμοσ," Theological Dictionary of the New Testament, op. cit. vol. III, pp. 301-310.

disrobes and washes his body, then puts on the vestments again. When he comes out, he offers parts of the bull and parts of the goat as burnt offerings for himself and his family and for the nation. The remaining parts of both animals are then taken outside of the camp and burned. Both the priest who leads the scapegoat into the wilderness and the priest who carries the sacrificed bull and goat outside of the camp for burning must bathe before they can return to the camp. While all of this is going on, everyone in the nation is to deny themselves (i.e.: fast) and refrain from working (i.e.: treat the Day of Atonement as a Sabbath day.) The High Priest corrupts his role in the atonement saying,

"You do not understand that it is better for you to have one man die for the people than to have the whole nation destroyed. He did not say this on his own, but being High Priest that year he prophesied that Jesus was about to die for the nation, and not for the nation only, but to gather into one the dispersed children of God. So from that day on, they planned to put him to death" (Jn. 11: 50-51).

Clearly the writer of the Gospel sees the irony of the High Priest declaring that Jesus is to be the atonement sacrifice. We will consider the fact that there is another, one who is paired with the one that is sacrificed, one that is allowed to leave the Temple and is set free in the wilderness. For now, Jesus is clearly the atonement sacrifice in the Gospel.

Our thesis, however, is that Jesus set out to replace the sacrifice of atonement. For support for that thesis, we must find how the *semeia* from the Pentateuch, used to "separate" and "remember" are used in John to "see" and "believe." What happens to the goats in the Temple and what is done with the blood of one of them is what is important.

Jesus, in Jn 10: 1-18, makes reference to anyone who does not enter the sheepfold by the gate, but climbs in by another way. That person is a thief. Jesus uses the analogy of the sheepfold to describe the Temple. The Chief Priests, considered in this Gospel to be "hired hands" of the Roman empire, do not enter the Temple by the main gate, but by the "back door" gates through which the sacrificial animals, wood, water, and oil are received. The shepherd, however, is permitted to enter by the gatekeeper and, once inside, proceeds to call the sheep, which represent those who are worshipping there. These sheep know his voice and follow him out. Jesus is replacing the practice of slaughtering livestock in the Temple. He not only drives the moneychangers out (Jn. 2: 13-16), but he figuratively enters the most sacred precincts of the Temple and calls out the sheep waiting there for sacrifice out. "The thief (Chief Priests and the High Priest) comes to steal and kill and destroy. I came that they may have life, and have it abundantly (Jn. 10: 10)."

The Festival of Atonement is the one time each year when the High Priest, and only the High Priest, can enter the Holy of Holies in the Temple and offer a sacrifice on the Altar of Incense (which is never used otherwise to burn sin offerings) to atone for the sins of the nation. This is the occasion where a second sacrifice, the scapegoat, is released into the wilderness to carry away the nation's sins. Jn. 1: 29 records the words of John the Baptist, who says, seeing Jesus, "Here is the Lamb of God who takes away the sin of the world!"

The atonement sacrifice is a goat. A lamb is more highly valued[71] and the sacrifice that John the Baptist foresees will not only atone for the sins (plural) of the nation of Israel, but for the sin (singular) of the whole world.

If Jesus abolishes the practice of sacrificing animals in the Temple, how does he intend for atonement to be accomplished?

"For this reason the Father loves me, because I lay down my life in order to take it up again. No one takes it from me, but I lay it down of my own accord. I have power to lay it down, and I have power to take it up again. I have received this command from my Father" (Jn. 10: 17-18).

Jesus expects to be the atonement sacrifice. Indeed, the blood of the sacrifice will be sprinkled on the altar (his own feet!). Atonement is the theme that is woven throughout the monologue provided by Jesus in chapters 14 through 17 of the Gospel. Jesus achieves the goals of the sacrifice of atonement through instruction and prayer prior to allowing his own body to be sacrificed.

The Festival of Booths

The Festival of Booths (Lv. 23: 33-36; Nu. 29: 12-40) involved eight days in which the people of Israel constructed temporary booths, small huts made of matted

---

[71]See Lev. 27: 9f. The value to God was the same (both were holy as long as they were without blemish) but the priests could assess the value of any animal or offering. This was necessary in the case of freewill (votive) offerings, which could not be given a standard value.

straw in which they (at least symbolically) lived. A term similar to the one translated here as "booths" was used for the Tabernacle, the mobile Temple, the dwelling place of God. During the time of this festival, a successively larger number of animals was sacrificed each day in the Temple in remembrance of the time when God's people dwelled in huts and worshipped God in one. For the festival, the people separated themselves from their homes in the promised land and lived again as their ancestors had lived, in order to remember them and remember what God had given them when they were brought to the promised land.

The *semeion* here is obviously the hut, the little house or dwelling place. At the beginning of the Gospel (Jn. 1: 35-39), two of the disciples of John the Baptist, following John's witness as to the identity of Jesus, choose to follow Jesus. He turns and asks them, "What are you looking for? (NRSV)" A better translation would be "Whom do you seek?" They answer him, "Rabbi." Then they ask him a question. "Where are you staying?" A better translation is "Where do you abide (dwell)?" He answers them, "Come and see." They come to see where it is that Jesus dwells and abide with him that day.

There is only one day in the Gospel according to John. This is the first day of creation, the day of light, the day when "the Word became flesh and dwelt among us," the day of resurrection. Any disciple of Jesus ought to be able to answer the question posed by those first two disciples. "Where does Christ abide?" "Christ abides in me." Clearly the dwelling place of God and of the people of God, the sheep of the Good Shepherd, is not a hut built of matted straw. Nor is it the Herodian Temple. Christ dwells with those who seek him, and, upon finding him (seeing where he abides), they abide with him.

In Jn. 14: 1-4 Jesus says to his disciples, "You know where I am going. Believe in God, believe also in me. In my Father's house are many dwelling places." Your booth is in my Father's house, not in a straw hut. I am going to prepare your place there. You do not need to build a booth for yourself. Jesus replaces the Festival of Booths.

The Passover Observance

The Passover Festival (Lv. 23: 5-8; Nu. 28: 16-25) was the most important of all of the festivals in Israel. It consisted of one day for an offering and seven days for a festival, during the first day of which no work was to be done. Unleavened bread was to be eaten on each of the seven days. Whole burnt offerings were made throughout the week. They consisted of a total of two calves, one ram, seven lambs that were a year old without blemish (and flour mixed with oil for each), along with the whole burnt offerings and drink offerings that were offered on a daily basis on "normal" days.

Chaim Raphael has provided a modern Passover Haggadah[72] with a useful English translation of the traditional liturgy (called the *Seder*) for those who cannot read Hebrew.

"'Haggadah' means, literally, a recital. The Bible enjoins us to tell (hagged) our children the story of the Exodus from Egypt. The Haggadah is, then, the tale that is told at the annual feast -- Passover -- which celebrates this

---

[72]See <u>Passover Haggadah</u>, with a new trans. by Chaim Raphael, Behrman House, Inc., New York, 1972, p. 15.

deliverance. The word 'Seder' we apply to this gathering around the table on the eve of Passover, means, literally, 'program,' indicating that the ritual is carefully prescribed."

This carefully prescribed ritual consists of a meal of symbolic elements of food: signs designed to remind the participants of the salvific events from the past. The meal is divided into four parts, each part beginning with a toast over a glass of wine. (1) The First Cup introduces "the sanctification," which on Friday night is the reading of Gn. 1: 31-2: 3, where God finishes creation, blesses it, and rests on the seventh (the Sabbath) day. The prayer over this first cup is: "Blessed is our Lord, God, King of the universe, who creates the fruit of the vine." On Saturday night, the following blessing over the first cup is added.

"Blessed is God who creates the light of fire. Blessed is God who has let us see the line between sacred and profane -- between light and darkness. He set the holiness of Sabbath apart from the six days of work. He set the people of Israel apart for holiness. Blessings to God who showed us the nature of holiness."[73]

Those gathered around the table say, "Thanks be to God who kept us alive and sustained us and brought us to this moment." Then all drink the first cup, "To life!"

Next, the host washes his hands in preparation for eating the Karpas (a plant such as celery or parsley), but without a blessing. Then everyone receives the Karpas, dips it into salt water and eats it in the spirit of an hors

[73]Ibid.

d'oeuvres after reciting a blessing: "Blessed is our Lord, God, King of the Universe, who creates the fruit of the soil."[74]

Next, the host separates the middle of three flat crackers of unleavened bread called *matzah*. This middle *matzah* is broken in two and half is put away for the "afikoman" (dessert). The prayer over the "Seder plate" which contains the remaining matzah bread was originally written in Aramaic, so that everyone could understand it.

"This is the bread of affliction which our ancestors ate in the land of Egypt. Let all who are hungry come and eat. Let all who are in need come and celebrate Passover. This year we are here: next year, in the land of Israel! This year we are slaves: next year, free men!"

The youngest child present then poses four questions about the Seder which provide opportunity for the host to tell the story of the Exodus and explain the meaning of each symbol in the feast. The host says a blessing over the second cup of wine and those present recite the same toast as they did for the first cup.

Then, all drink the second cup of wine, toasting "to freedom!" Everyone washes their hands after saying a blessing. "Blessed be God who made each *mitzvah* (commandment) bring us holiness and laid on us the washing of hands before food." Then two more blessings are said, one on "bread" and the other over the matzah. "Blessed be God, who brings food out of the earth. Blessed be God, who made each *mitzvah* bring us holiness, and laid on us the eating of *matzah*." A similar blessing is

---

[74]Ibid., p. 23.

said over the bitter herb (symbol of slavery) and the haroset (symbolizing the mortar used by the slaves).

Then, a fine meal provided by the host is served to all of the guests. It concludes with a game of "hide and seek" during which the youngest person present produces the afikoman from its hiding place. The afikomen is broken and shared with all present as a reminder of the Paschal (lamb) sacrifice. This concludes the official part of the meal, which is followed by the singing of Psalm 126, then a grace after the meal. The consumption of a third glass of wine, toasting "to peace!" follows the same toast as given for the first two.

Now, an extra glass is placed on the table and all of the glasses are filled a fourth time. This is the Elijah cup over which a series of Psalms[75] are read, interspersed with prayers glorifying God. Then, the blessing is given, toasting: "To Jerusalem!"

The Seder is rich with metaphors. It is difficult for most Christians, upon first encountering a full Seder (much abbreviated here), not to recognize contact points with the Lord's Supper.

While no liturgical account of the Passover meal occurs in the Gospel According to John, the festival is named nine times[71] and the metaphors are easily recognizable. In fact, the entire Gospel could be considered a Haggadah for the Lord's Supper, which replaces the Passover meal.

---

[75]Ps. 79: 6-7; 69: 25; Lam. 3: 66; Ps. 115; 116; 117; 118: 1-4; 118: 5-20, 21-24 (predicts the coming of the Messiah), 25-29; 136 (antiphonally); 103: 1.

[71]Jn. 2: 13, 23; 6: 4; 11: 55; 12: 1; 13: 1; 18: 28, 39; 19:14.

The first sign of this is in Jn. 2: 1-25. It is concerned with wine to be used at a marriage feast. Verse 6 refers to "six stone water jars for the Jewish rites of purification, each holding twenty or thirty gallons." Where would one expect to find 120 to 180 gallons of purification water in stone jars? What does it mean that this purification water was converted by Jesus into wine? What *semeion* does wine represent? Could it be that the reader is expected to "see" that the water used in the Temple for sanctification was transformed by Jesus into the first cup of Passover wine? Does it not seem likely that the first sign that Jesus provides is one that sanctifies a covenant?

The Passover is identified as "The Passover of the Jews" in Jn. 2: 13; 6:4; 11:55. Why? Is there another Passover other than "The Passover of the Jews?" For the first- century Christian community from which the Fourth Gospel came, the answer is "Yes, there was a Christian Passover: the Lord's Supper." For Christians who were familiar with the Jewish Passover, what would be the meaning of a toast: "To life!" over a cup of wine after this prayer: "Blessed be the Lord, God, King of the Universe?" Jn. 1: 1-5, as has already been shown, correlates well with the story of creation in Gn. 1.[72]

How would a first-century Christian, familiar with the Jewish Seder, understand the significance of the breaking of the middle matzah? This is the bread of affliction. "This is my body, broken for you."

---

[72]Consider the uncanny similarity between the prayer of blessing over the first cup provided for a Saturday night Seder with our observations regarding the Pentateuch's use of "separate" and "remember."

The second reference to the Passover in the Fourth Gospel is at Jn. 6: 4, in the context of the story in Jn. 6: 1-15 of the feeding of the 5,000. The reference appears to be an interjection, an interruption in the story, yet it comes between a reminder that people were following Jesus because he provided them with signs and the question that Jesus poses to Philip about where they were going to get enough bread to feed all of those people. What is the prayer said over the broken matzah? "Let all who are hungry come and eat." Can there be any question by those who know the words, "I am the bread of life; whoever comes to me will never be hungry (Jn. 6: 35)," that in this gospel Jesus is presented knowing the Passover liturgy and intentionally replacing it?

The centerpiece of this study and of the Gospel is the trilogy of stories that appear in chapters 11, 12, and 13. Each chapter includes at least one reference to the Passover. It is mentioned again in chapters 18 and 19 when accounts are given of the betrayal and trial of Jesus and again in chapter 21 at a resurrection appearance. It seems clear that the author(s) of this gospel expected that those with eyes to see would recognize the signs revealing the assertion that Jesus replaced the Passover.

Chapter 6
The New Priesthood: The Disciples of Jesus

Replacements

We have seen how the Temple and each of the festivals for which sacrifices were made in that Temple, were replaced by Jesus, according to the perspective of the writer(s) of the Fourth Gospel. Instead of a Temple building being located at the feet of Jacob's dream ladder (Bethel or "House of God," where God touches the earth), Jesus becomes the new Temple, and his feet become the feet of Jacob's ladder. In place of angels ascending and descending the ladder, or priests struggling with God and humanity, Jesus installs his disciples to mediate between God and God's people.

Indictment of the Old Priesthood

The function of the Aaronic priests was to speak for God, to serve as intermediaries between God and God's people, to translate, to mediate, to slip between the two. The priests of Israel had lost the ability to do that, so the author(s) of the Gospel of John represents them as a man who never speaks, who dies, and whose life is only restored because Jesus calls him forth (creation language) from the grave. The man in the story is Lazarus, and his story may be interpreted as semeiotic. Lazarus is "born again."[72] Symbolically, Jesus is calling the priesthood back into life. The Gospel presents Jesus and his disciples seeking, not to

---

[72]Jn. 11: 1-44. The story of the raising of Lazarus.

destroy the Temple and the priesthood and the system of sacrificial worship, but to replace all of them.

R. Abba puts the Johannine indictment against the priesthood into perspective:

"The chief functions of the postexilic priesthood are the care of the vessels of the sanctuary and the sacrificial duties of the altar: only the priest may sacrifice (Nu. 18: 5, 7). But the priesthood also retains its ancient prerogative of giving - i.e.: instruction in the ways and requirements of God (Mal. 2: 6-7, See Jer. 18: 18) As the custodian of sacred tradition, the priest had always been the authority par excellence in all matters relating to the law. He, no less than the prophet, was a medium of revelation. But, whereas the revelatory experience of the prophet was personal and direct, that of the priest was collective and mediated, either through divination or through his training in the accumulated knowledge of the past."[73]

"The priesthood was thus the custodian of past revelation and legal precedent before any written word was available for the guidance of the people of God. Hence, the priest was both the teacher and the administrator of justice (See Dt. 17:8-9; 21:5). He was the spokesman of God before the people, as well as the representative of the people before God."[74]

For the priesthood to have ceased to function in these ways meant that the covenant between God and God's

---

[73]R. Abba, "Priests and Levites," Interpreter's Dictionary of the Bible, op. cit., vol. 3, p. 889.
[74]Ibid., p. 891.

people was broken. The priesthood of the Herodian period
had ceased to maintain the *semeiotic* functions of the
Temple and of the sacrificial festivals. In some cases they
had utterly violated them, as was the case with the High
Priest's substitution of a man for a ram on the day of
atonement. Worst of all, the priesthood had failed to keep
the *semeia*, metaphors for the relationship between God and
God's people alive. They had allowed them to atrophy, to
freeze, to die.

Word, Sacrament, and Disciple

According to the theological perspective of the
Fourth Gospel, when faced with this situation, God chose
to slip in between God and God's creation to re-define the
covenant in more universal terms, to bring new life to the
original *semeia* in terms that correspond to "head, body,
hand, and feet": word, sacrament, and disciple.

For the theologian behind the Gospel of John, the
realm of the sacred was defined by the Word. Since Christ
was understood to abide in every true disciple, the Word
was incarnate in each one of them. They were the true
priests, intermediaries between God and the chosen people
of God (the children of Israel) who chose to follow God in
Christ (Jn. 1: 11-13). Their witness brought God into
view, so God's people could "see" God and "believe," that
is, live as sanctified witnesses themselves, that the Word
was abiding within them, an ever-expanding community of
priests. This idea was not new. Ex. 19: 3-6, 9b-11 reads:

"Then, Moses went up to God; the Lord called to him from
the mountain, saying, 'Thus you shall say to the house of
Jacob, and tell the Israelites: You have seen what I did to

the Egyptians, and how I bore you on eagles' wings and
brought you to myself. Now, therefore, if you obey my
voice and keep my covenant, you shall be my treasured
possession out of all the peoples. Indeed the whole earth is
mine, but you shall be for me a priestly kingdom and a
holy nation. These are the words that you shall speak to
the Israelites . . . the Lord said to Moses: 'Go to the
people and consecrate them today and tomorrow. Have
them wash their clothes and prepare for the third day,
because on the third day the Lord will come down upon
Mount Sinai in the sight of all the people.'"

The model for an entire community, indeed an
entire nation of priests, consecrated to receive the Lord on
the third day, was already established in the Pentateuch. In
John those "priests" were called "disciples." They were to
be the new right hand of God.

"Sacrament" was the emerging word for the new
liturgical rites, including Baptism and the Eucharist, which
provided "outward and visible signs of an inward and
spiritual grace." "Originally the Latin *sacramentum* meant
a soldier's oath of allegiance, but in Christian usage it
became the equivalent of the Greek *musterion*, a mystery.
. . Sacraments involve or imply a promise or a
commitment, and they are mysteries in the sense that they
do not disclose their meaning to unbelieving eyes."[75]
Sacraments were, and are, signs.

The new priesthood would move about in the world.
It represented the feet of God. By separating some of the

---

[75]See Alan Richardson, "Sacrament, Sacramental Theology," A
Dictionary of Christian Theology, ed. Richardson, Westminster,
Philadelphia, (1969), p. 300.

followers of Jesus from the community for the sake of providing the priestly functions, the people were assured that they would remember the covenant that had been established by the Word for them, that some would be empowered to teach others how to read the signs, how to "see" so that all could believe. Their models were the prophets and teachers of the Old Testament, as witnessed in the Didache, a first-century ecclesiastical guidebook:

"Now appoint for yourselves bishops and deacons worthy of the Lord, men meek and not avaricious, and upright and proved; for they, too, render you the service of the prophets and teachers. Therefore neglect them not; for they are the ones who are honored of you, together with the prophets and teachers."[76]

The Greek term for bishop, *episkopos,* was first used mean "visit," usually by God (Gn. 50: 24, 25). Then it referred to the overseer on behalf of God (Neh. 11: 22).[77] Eleazar, the third son of Aaron, whose name is used generically in the Old Testament to refer to the priesthood, is called by this term, having "oversight of all the Tabernacle and all that is in it, in the sanctuary and in its utensils" (Nu. 4: 16). In John, the role corresponding to bishop is one of the roles that Jesus uses to identify himself: the shepherd, who watches over the sheep (Jn. 10).

---

[76]Teaching of the Twelve Apostles, Ed. with a trans., intro and notes by Roswell D. Hitchcock and Francis Brown, Charles Scribner's Sons, (New York), 1885, XV, p. 27.

[77]See Hermann W. Beyer, "επισκεπτομαι, επισκοπεω, επισκοπα, επισκοποσ, αλλοτριεπισκοποσ," Theological Dictionary of the New Testament, pp. cit., vol. II, pp. 599-622.

Diakonos is a Greek word (διακονοσ) which identified the role of a servant, serving at table. It is derived from two root words, *dia*, meaning "through," and *koniortos*, meaning "dust." Dust is the "stuff" of creation (Gn. 2: 7), the ground, the earth, the part of the world which represents the defilement of human sin. The *Diakonos* walks through this defiling dust on behalf of God. Influenced by the example of Jesus, who took upon himself the role of a slave in teaching the disciples (Jn. 13: 1-20), the deacons were those who delivered the food to the faithful when they gathered for their daily sacramental meal together. The title *Diakonos* represented a fundamental truth about the new priesthood: it would move with the people. It would walk upon the earth, maintaining contact with those who did not feel holy to the Lord, getting its feet (and hands) dirty in service to God.

A third term, πρεσβυτεροσ *(presbuteros)*, meaning "elder" was used in Genesis to identify an older person (Gn. 18: 11; 35: 29), but later was used in reference to the fabled College of Seventy who wrote the Septuagint and in reference to the Council of the Sanhedrin, Israel's supreme court. In Neh. 2: 16, the elders are closely identified with priests, identifying "the Jews" as they are in John. "The officials (elders) did not know where I had gone or what I was doing; I had not yet told the Jews, the priests, the nobles, the officials (elders), and the rest that were to do the work."[78]

---

[78]Gunther Bornkamm, "πρεσβυσ, πρεσβυτεροσ, πρεσβυτησ, συμπρεσβυτεροσ, πρεσβυτεριον, πρεσβευω ," Theological Dictionary of the New Testament, op. cit, vol. VI, pp. 651-683. In 2 Jn. 1 and 3 Jn. 1, the elder is a specially valued teacher, bearer of the Johannine traditions (attributed by Bornkamm to Conzelmann, note 126, p. 672).

Seeing and Believing

These three roles can be defined in terms of
"seeing" and "believing." A bishop or overseer is one who
"sees" the Word made flesh when the Eucharist is served
or a baptism is given. A deacon is one who brings the
sacrifice, the sacrament, to those who worship. An elder
literally "lifts up" the "outward and visible signs of an
inward and spiritual grace" before God. In Jn. 4: 23, Jesus
asserts that true worship is spiritual. The deacon, the elder,
and the bishop, are considered to be holy before God.
They are the New Testament equivalents to servant, priest,
and Chief Priest in the Old Testament.

Semeia Transferred

The transfer of *semeia* from the Old Testament
system of sacrificial worship to the New Testament can be
seen in the Gospel of John in much more obvious ways than
those already mentioned. For example, though his head,
hands, and feet are not severed from Jesus' body, they are
injured severely enough to cause them to bleed and his side
is cut open, fulfilling each step in the liturgy of sacrifice.

Jesus also receives the signs required for the
ordination of a High Priest. The blood of the sacrificial
lamb (his body) is applied to his head, his hands, and his
feet. Ironically, the ritual is performed not by the High
Priest of the Temple, directly, but by Roman soldiers,
"hired hands," who not only substitute a crown of thorns
for the anointing oil on his head, but who vest him, as a
mockery, with a robe which represents their own (Greek)
idea of authority, rather than the proper (Hebrew)
vestments of the High Priest.

The consecration of the Temple's altar by Moses (following the example of Jacob, who anoints a stone with oil to mark the sacred place he called the House of God), has a direct parallel in John's Gospel when Mary of Bethany anoints the feet of Jesus as will be shown in the following chapters. The preparation of Aaron and his sons for ordination that Moses provided, bathing them and later instructing them to wash their hands and feet before and after officiating at each sacrifice, is reflected in the washing of the feet of the disciples by Jesus.

Even more obvious is a part of the tradition of the Eucharist which is not quoted directly in the Gospel According to John, but which is woven throughout it: The words of institution of the Lord's Supper. These words are clearly instructions to Jesus' disciples and succeeding generations of disciples to understand and remember his crucifixion as a sacrifice. "This is my body, broken for you . . . This cup is the new covenant in my blood, which is shed for you . . . " The worshipper need only receive these elements to receive his or her personal identification with the sacrifice, a tranference of identities which occurred in the Old Testament through the leaning of hands on the head of the sacrificial animal.

To See the Signs

The parallels are both obvious and subtle. The *semeiotic* role of the incense required to protect the holy atmosphere of the Temple is found in the Gospel According to John in the perfumed ointment which Mary of Bethany applies to the feet of Jesus, the aroma of which "fills the house." "The house," being "the house of God," the new Temple, the church.

To see the signs is nearly impossible for the uninitiated reader. Even for those who are alerted to the importance of signs, there are subtle ones that can easily be missed. We shall search for such signs as well as attempt to understand how they were used.

Signs were used intentionally in the writing of the Gospel According to John. They represent the language of the initiated, those who knew and understood the ancient oracles of the Old Testament. By using signs, the initiated would be able to see the truth, while those who were not people of faith or who were not spiritually ready to hear the extraordinary news contained beneath its code, would be protected. In a hostile environment, the signs used in the Gospel of John may well have been a protective shield against those who would have destroyed its unique and precious message.

Chapter 7
The Signs and Historical Setting
of the Ordination Trilogy

A Preview

Three stories in John: the raising of Lazarus by
Jesus in chapter 11, the anointing of the feet of Jesus by
Mary of Bethany in chapter 12, and the washing of the feet
of the disciples by Jesus in chapter 13, constitute a trilogy,
a three-act play, whose subject is the ordination of the
disciples of Jesus as priests. It tells how, liturgically, Jesus
transferred authority to his disciples to preside over the new
sacrifice in the Temple of Jesus.

The purpose of the Lazarus story is two-fold: It
establishes the qualifications of Martha and Mary of
Bethany for ordination by hearing their confessions of faith
in Jesus even as he faced his own death. It also establishes
the authority of Jesus to bring a dead priesthood,
represented symbolically by Lazarus, back to life.

The purpose of the foot-washing story is to complete
the ordination of the disciples, following the *semeiotic*
pattern established in the Pentateuch when first Jacob, then
Moses, anoints the altar that is to become "the place"
where God can be found and worshipped.

The centerpiece of the trilogy is the anointing story
in Jn. 11: 55 - 12: 8. By paying close attention to the
semeiotic patterns found in the rituals for the ordination of
the High Priest and the consecration of the Nazirite, we
will be able to discern that in this story Jesus ordains Mary
as a bishop, and charges her with responsibility for keeping
the tradition of his death. Martha is portrayed as a deacon
and all of the disciples are installed as elders.

Support for this exegesis is found in the abundant oracular signs, borrowed from the Pentateuch and scattered throughout the entire gospel. These signs are reinforced by the *semeiotic* parallels between the Old Testament's legal codes for the Temple, priests, and sacrifices and the patterns carefully provided in the Gospel for those with the eyes to see them. These stories' settings of time and place, the representative identities of their characters, the words of institution (of ordination) woven into the dialogue between Jesus and Judas and the provocative and unforgettable nature of the ordination liturgy as a whole, constitute a strong case for the assertion that the trilogy of stories is written to convey an unorthodox perspective of the nature of the ministry of Jesus and the roles to be played by a diverse group of disciples. It clearly suggests, to those who are alert to the meaning of the signs woven into it, that Jesus ordained his disciples, and that on Mary of Bethany he bestowed the most important role of keeper of the tradition, a role associated even today in most Christian denominations, with the authority of the bishop.

This story contrasts with the more orthodox perspectives of the ministry of Jesus found in the synoptic gospels. Hints are provided as to why it may have been necessary to hide the story itself and the identity of the key source of the tradition that the hidden story conveyed. Namely, that the orthodox, male authorities in the first-century church, lead by Peter, were not ready to place such authority in the hands of women, even though one female disciple was what this gospel calls "the beloved disciple."

The picture that emerges from the trilogy is of a structured priesthood of disciples, inclusive of women and men, with a special emphasis on the important role of women in the first-century "Johannine" house church.

The Trilogy

The writer of the Fourth Gospel carefully links the three stories in the center of the Gospel by naming characters and repeating a total of twelve times references to *feet*. The characters identified in Jn. 11: 1-2 as Mary of Bethany, her sister, Martha, and their brother, Lazarus, are acknowledged again in Jn. 12: 1-11. The action described in detail in Jn. 12: 1-11 is summarized in Jn. 11: 1-2, though the summary seems unnecessary to the story except as a means of emphasizing the linkage between the common set of characters. In addition to Jesus, Lazarus appears to be the key figure in Jn. 11: 1-44 with Mary and Martha in supporting roles. Mary appears to be the key figure in Jn. 12: 1-11 with Lazarus and Martha in supporting roles. Though these three are the only characters identified by name as people whom Jesus loved, none of them is mentioned anywhere else in the Gospel except in Jn. 13: 23 where "One of the disciples -- the one whom Jesus loved -- was reclining in the bosom of Jesus" in the context of a supper before the Passover (Jn. 13: 1-2). Clearly, the evangelist intends a connection between the characters listed in Jn. 11: 5 and Jn. 13: 23.

In Jn. 11: 1-44, Mary is identified as the one who wiped the feet of Jesus with her hair. In Jn. 11:32, Mary falls at the feet of Jesus and begins her confession of faith. In Jn. 11: 44, Lazarus is resurrected, but comes out of the tomb with his head, hands, and feet bound in burial cloths. In Jn. 12: 3, Mary anoints the feet of Jesus with perfumed oil and dries them with her hair. In Jn. 13: 1-14, Jesus washes the feet of the disciples in a pericope where feet are mentioned eight times. The term for feet, *podas,* is mentioned in only one other place in the Gospel, when

Mary Magdalene "saw two angels in white, sitting where the body of Jesus had been lying, one at the head and the other at the feet" (Jn. 20:12).

The repetitive use of feet in the context of death and resurrection narratives (Jn. 11: 44; 20: 12) as well as the liturgical (Jn. 12: 3; 13: 1-14) and devotional (Jn. 11: 32) use of feet in these passages alone unites the three stories as a literary unit, a trilogy, a drama in three acts. This trilogy is the centerpiece of the Fourth Gospel.

Signs

By studying these three passages as oracle,[79] not as historical,[80] the presence of numerous signs becomes apparent, pointing to a deeper meaning than is at first visible. The identity of an undefined group of disciples (as opposed to the synoptic gospels which limit the disciples to

---

[79] "From   orare to speak, utter, pray, *Greek and Roman Antiquity:* The medium by which a god reveals hidden knowledge or makes known the divine purpose; also the place where the revelation is given; the response of an oracle to a question or petition; a place of communication from God, as the Holy of Holies of the Jewish temple; also, an inspired prophet; the revelation received from such a place or medium; *plural:* the Scriptures." A. Merriam-Webster, Webster's New Collegiate Dictionary, G.&C. Merriam Co., Springfield, Mass, (1953), p. 590.

[80] "From Greek *"historikos,"* see HISTORY, "Of, pertaining to, or of the nature of history, narrating, dealing with, or based upon history; true to history; as *historical* evidence, fidelity or novels; HISTORY: from *"historia"* history, from *"histor"* knowing. A narrative of events, a tale; a story; a record of facts about a person, as a case history, which lists details relating to ancestry, environment, experiences, and the like, . . . a systematic written account of events, particularly of those affecting a nation, institution, science, or art, usually connected with a philosophical explanation of their causes." A. Merriam-Webster, Ibid, p. 392.

the twelve) including women, and led not by Peter but by Mary of Bethany, emerges for those who have eyes to see. In addition, once these signs are understood, the structure and identities of the people of the "Johannine church" emerge. The *semeiotic* structure of the Gospel itself reveals its original purpose: as a textbook for the training of disciples in the Johannine school.[81]

The use of the oracle as a literary form is consistent with the prophetic tradition of the Old Testament,[82] but distinct from its use in other parts, especially the synoptic gospels, of the New Testament.

By defining *logos* as "oracle," the entire Old Testament tradition becomes a source for spiritual signs with which to convey the meaning of the incarnation. This

---

[81] "The Johannine concepts of discipleship and Jesus' role as teacher (both of which are related to the role of the Beloved Disciple) suggest that the community engaged in study and interpretation of the teachings of Jesus and the scriptures (Jn. 2: 22). The Gospel's reflection of these activities strongly suggests that the Gospel was written within a school." R. Alan Culpepper, The Johannine School, Scholars Press for the Society of Biblical Literature, Missoula Montana, (1975), p. 274 (The author's Ph.D. thesis to Duke Univ. in 1974).

[82] Jeremiah, for example. See Andrew W. Blackwood, Jr., Commentary on Jeremiah, Word Books, Waco, (1977), p. 14f. "The most cursory analysis will show that Jeremiah was not a systematic theologian or philosopher; he was a prophet with rare poetic skill . . . He expressed ("the Word of the Lord") usually, in a poetic oracle which he delivered -- often in peril -- to a hostile audience." See also Nu. 24: 4, 16; Dt. 33: 8-11; Ps. 18: 7-24, esp. 13-15, 118 (where *logos* occurs 24 times and *logion* occurs 22 times, suggesting that the two terms were used interchangeably); Is. 5: 24; 28: 13; Also Kittel, "λογιον," Theological Dictionary of the New Testament, op. cit., vol. IV., p. 137.

is particularly important with regard to the "plot"[83] of the Gospel: the replacement by Jesus of every covenant symbol extant in the cultic life of Israel. His authority to replace the Temple, the festivals, the sacrifices, the priesthood and even to reinterpret and supervene the Torah itself is grounded in the assertion that Jesus is the pre-existent *logos*, the fulfillment of the law and the prophets, the One by whose example and direction holiness is defined. Indeed, the presence of the *logos* is what is sacred about the Torah.[84]

The Gospel establishes itself as scripture by following Old Testament scriptural patterns, found in oracles dealing with holiness.   This literary device,

---

[83]R. Alan Culpepper, Anatomy of the Fourth Gospel, Fortress, Philadelphia, 1983, pp. 84f. explains the function of "plot" in the Gospel: to give meaning to events in a story which has an ending.

[84]See Gerhard Kittel, "*lego, logos, rama, laleo, logios, logion, alogos, logikos, logomaxeo, logomaxia,*" Theological Dictionary of the New Testament, op. cit., vol. IV, pp. 69-143, esp. pp. 128ff. "The situation in the Fourth Gospel is thus quite different. At the time of the Synoptists, as Ac. and Pl. show, the *logos* is the message about Jesus. There is an unmistakable material tendency to regard Jesus Himself as the One who gives and is this Word, not only in His addresses, but in His whole earthly manifestation. This created in the Synoptists, and most strongly on Jewish Christian soil, a hesitation to apply the term *logos* in its developing specific sense to Jesus Himself, since at this stage of development, i.e., before the development was complete, it might give rise to misunderstanding.   Now, however, the restraining factor is the definitiveness of the specific use, which may be seen in the prologue to Jn. as nowhere else in the NT. Once the *logos* saying of the prologue was possible, there could hardly be any further place for the kind of use still found in Mk. 2: 2; 4: 33 "He (= the *logos*) spoke the *logos* to them." Kittel points out (pp. 128 - 131) that in Jn. the *logos* refers not only to the Word of God, but to the pre-existent Word of creation (Gn. 1: 1) and the Word of Law (p. 134f.) so that the Torah's pre-existence and rabbinical sayings about the Torah as *logos* become, in Jn., references to Christ.

patterning new teachings after old ones, known as "midrash," is well known among rabbinical scholars.[85]

The midrash method is deceptively simple. When expounding upon the meaning of a scriptural text, a scholar makes reference to other, similar, texts. By showing how the language, symbols, metaphors or signs in one part of the scripture are used to convey a particular meaning, the teacher or student supports the interpretation of the text at hand.

The use of the oracle as a literary form, however, carries with it some inherent problems, especially for modern scholars expecting a coherent, chronological order in the text.[86] The order, when using this form, is dictated by the meaning being conveyed, not the historical or chronological or even the logical sequence of events. In the Fourth Gospel the systematic replacement of the Herodian Temple in Jerusalem, along with the Mosaic festivals, sacrifices, and priesthood, implies a logical order, but when

---

[85]For a more complete consideration of *midrash*, see Michael A. Signer, "How the Bible Has Been Interpreted in Jewish Tradition," The New Interpreter's Bible, Abingdon Press, Nashville, (1994), vol. 1, p. 65f. "The word *midrash* encompasses both a method of expounding the biblical text and a name for a collection of discourses . . . The collections of *midrash* . . . constitute a separate literary genre.

[86]Blackwood, op. cit., p. 14, for example, commenting on the structure of Jeremiah, "When the reader understands the historical situation in which a particular oracle was delivered, the essential message is, usually, quite clear. The arrangement of the oracles and other materials, by a long series of editors, is, alas, not always so lucid as the oracles themselves. Sometimes we find a clear progression from one oracle to another; sometimes oracles are grouped by subject matter; sometimes the arrangement demonstrates rare editorial skill. In other places there is no discernible link between a passage and what precedes and what follows."

the orthodox (as in the synoptic gospels) Jesus stories are retold using symbolic elements from these Mosaic oracles, the result is what most scholars see as a confused pattern. Once the meaning of these oracles is discerned, the importance of each story is lifted out of history into a more "divine" and coherent perspective.

The purpose of the oracle is the same in the Fourth Gospel as it is in the Old Testament: it allows the scholar who has eyes to see, a means by which to expound or theologize about divine or holy things, to step from the historical world into a narrative world in which reality is "seen" from God's point of view (i.e.: a cosmic perspective.)

Interestingly, the oracle, as a literary device for communicating divine truth, is found not only in the ancient Hebrew literature of the Torah, but in the ancient literature of the Hellenistic world.[87] The Gospel of John is a masterpiece of oracular literature, written to link seekers of Truth from cultures in both worlds. It relies upon Hebrew texts translated into Greek (called The Septuagint, abbreviated LXX), which was used extensively by both early Christian and Hebrew communities during the first two centuries of what modern scholars now call "the Common Era (CE)."[88]

Discerning a scriptural sign involves first "seeing" the sign, then "understanding" it. To "see" a sign, the seeker of Truth (scholar) must watch for terms that seem odd or out of place, unusual in their context, unnecessary

---

[87]For example, the references to the cryptic messages from the Oracle at Delphi in the Illyad and The Odyssey by Homer. A priest delivered oracular replies to the queries of seekers of Truth.

[88]See Signer, op. cit.

except that they suggest a reference beyond the context in which they are found. To "understand" a sign, especially in the Gospel of John, the seeker must locate the Greek term in the LXX, usually in the Torah. Once this antecedent use of the Greek word in the Old Testament context has been identified, its significance in the New Testament context becomes more readily apparent.

What is remarkable about this method of instruction is how well it correlates with post modern approaches to Biblical studies, sometimes called "Reader-Response Criticism." This method assumes that both the author and the reader contribute to the meaning in any narrative text.[89] When oracles are used in scripture, the reader must contribute to the process of communicating spiritual truth by discerning the meaning of each sign in order to "see" and "understand" the meaning of the text. This would be especially important when using the midrash method to study and expound upon a particular passage of scripture.

The Use of Historical Time in the Setting

The use of historical time in the setting in John is different from that in the parallel passages in the synoptic gospels,[90] which causes no small amount of confusion

---

[89]See the "Eye" of Reader - Response (Diagram) in the Appendix.

[90]Elisabeth Schussler Fiorenza, In Memory of Her: A Feminist Theological Reconstruction of Christian Origins, Crossroad, New York, (1983), pp. 152-153, 330-331. Fiorenza reads Jn. 12: 1-8 through a lense created by the Gospel of Luke, which prevents her from a deeper consideration of its importance in John.

among Johannine scholars.[91]   Only Brown, following a
caution voiced by de Jonge[92] seems clear that the Fourth
Gospel is not primarily a source for historical
information.[93] The purpose of Brown's The Community of
the Beloved Disciple is to uncover the identity of the
Beloved Disciple, a figure who only appears in the Fourth
Gospel. In the process of analyzing what Brown sees as
historical influences on the community from which the

---

[91]D. Daube, The New Testament and Rabbinic Judaism, op. cit.,
pp. 301-324, compares the four anointing stories, suggesting that they are
all included as a means of refuting the suggestion that Jesus was buried in
disgrace ("Niwwul"). Barrett, op. cit, p. 409, argues that this motivation
does not apply to the Gospel of John, since John provides for the proper
disposal of Jesus' body at a later time in the Gospel (19: 39). He says
that, "the peculiarly Johannine features seem secondary." Culpepper, op.
cit., pp. 51ff., discusses narrative time, but refers to 11: 2 as "one of the
well-known anomalies of the gospel" and calls it "an internal analepsis
which has the appearance of being a repeating analepsis inserted to
reintroduce Mary, but the anointing is not narrated until the following
chapter. In other words, it is a misplaced analepsis which functions as a
prolepsis since it refers to the anointing, which is yet to come."

[92]M. de Jonge, "Jesus: Stranger from Heaven and Son of God,"
SBLSBS, 11, Scholars Press, Missoula, (1977), p. 199. "A Gospel may
be used only with great circumspection as a historical source."

[93]Raymond E. Brown, The Community of the Beloved Disciple,
Paulist Press, New York-Ramsey-Toronto, (1979), p. 17. "Primarily, the
Gospels tell us how an evangelist conceived of and presented Jesus to a
Christian community in the last third of the first century, a presentation
that indirectly gives us an insight into that community's life at the time
when the Gospel was written. Secondarily, through source analysis, the
Gospels reveal something about the pre-Gospel history of the evangelist's
Christological views; indirectly, they also reveal something about the
community's history earlier in the century, especially if the sources the
evangelist used had already been part of the community's heritage.
Thirdly, the Gospels offer limited means for reconstructing the ministry
and message of the historical Jesus."

Fourth Gospel came, a methodology is suggested that
produces useful results. Brown establishes a set of criteria
for his study, which this study will follow. In order to
minimize the element of self deception (Brown's words), he
resolves to: (1) base his conclusions on the existing Gospel,
not on any reconstructed sources, (2) stress those passages
in John which are significantly different from the
Synoptics, and (3) when arguing from silence, confine
himself to silence about matters which John could scarcely
have passed over accidentally.[94]

In addition to Brown's criteria, this study will be
disciplined by two more boundaries:
(4) with very few exceptions, only canonical scriptures will
be used as sources to discern the meaning of signs,[95] and
(5) definitions of signs, though they may be derived from
Old Testament sources, will be restricted to meanings that
are used consistently within the narrative world of the
Fourth Gospel.

The approach of reader-response criticism,[96] as
applied by Culpepper,[97] has made it possible to look upon
the Gospel of John as the literary creation of a faithful
community and, as such, to reach a deeper and more
spiritually satisfying understanding of the Gospel using the

---

[94]Ibid. p. 21f.

[95]This canonical boundary, except for the importance of
Nehemiah, could be limited to the Pentateuch.

[96] See Wolfgang Iser, The Act of Reading: A Theory of
Aesthetic Response, Johns Hopkins University Press, Baltimore and
London, (1978, fourth printing 1987); Umberto Eco, The Limits of
Interpretation, Indiana University Press, Bloomington and Indianapolis,
1990; George Aichele et. al, The Postmodern Bible, Yale University
Press, New Haven and London, (1995).

[97]R. Alan Culpepper, Anatomy of the Fourth Gospel: op. cit.

same tools one would use to analyze a work of fiction: considerations of character and plot, narrative time and story time, the implied perspectives of the author, the narrator, the intended reader, and the actual reader. With such tools, the undue pressure applied by historical analysis, which requires the elimination of some parts of the text and rearrangement of its order to fit an anticipated chronological pattern, can be avoided.

As Schweitzer pointed out nearly a hundred years ago,[98] the Gospels, including the Fourth Gospel, were not written as histories, but as instruments designed to communicate and facilitate the growth of faith. The Gospel According to John uses symbols or signs to convey meaning. Identifying those symbols and drawing the meaning that can be seen from them is an enjoyable and renewing experience, but to gain such renewing insights, some historical expectations and preconceptions must be suspended.

---

[98] Albert Scwheitzer, The Quest for the Historical Jesus:, Macmillan Company, New York, (1906 in German, 1st English Edition 1910, ninth printing 1964), p. 398f. prophesied accurately: "Whatever the ultimate solution may be, the historical Jesus of whom the criticism of the future, taking as its starting-point the problems which have been recognized and admitted, will draw the portrait, can never render modern theology the services which it claimed from its own half-historical, half-modern, Jesus. He will be a Jesus, who was Messiah, and lived as such, either on the ground of a literary fiction of the earliest Evangelist, or on the ground of a purely eschatological Messianic conception . . . Jesus means something to our world because a mighty spiritual force streams forth from Him and flows through our time also. This fact can neither be shaken
nor confirmed by any historical discovery. It is the solid foundation of Christianity."

Having said that, there are some observations made by historical critical scholars (like Brown, Daube and Barrett) that are useful. This study will begin with a consideration of those observations, then move into an analysis of the oracular signs in the Gospel, using the tools of poetics, in order to arrive at a full exegesis of the three pericopes of the trilogy.

The settings in John, especially of the sequence of the three stories in Jn. 11, 12, and 13, are different from the most of the synoptic settings. Luke 7: 36-50 sets the anointing story toward the beginning of Jesus' ministry, following inquiries from John the Baptist in the house of an unnamed Pharisee, who watches the action to determine who Jesus is.

In Luke's version, a sinful woman of the city bathes Jesus' feet with her tears, then while kissing his feet, anoints them with expensive ointment from an alabaster jar. Luke seems to see the story as both an entrapment story and as a presage of Jesus' burial.

Mk. 14: 1-9 and Mt. 26: 6-13 set the anointing story in Bethany two days before the Passover meal, in the house of Simon the Leper before Judas goes to the High Priest to arrange the betrayal. Both Gospels seem to use the story as a motivation for the betrayal. Mark's version, copied by Matthew, has an unnamed woman break open an alabaster jar and pour anointing oil over Jesus' head.

In John, the setting is a full six days (not two) before the Passover observance. This pericope is positioned between the event generally recognized as the greatest sign in the Gospel, the raising of Lazarus (Jn. 11: 1-48) and the sign that signals to Jesus that "The hour has come for the Son of Man to be glorified," the arrival of Greeks seeking to see Jesus (Jn. 12: 20-25).

By placing the pericope between such obviously important signs, the writer of the Gospel indicates its importance in the overall structure of the Gospel. It functions as the denouement[99] of the plot,[100] leading to the Gospel's dramatic climax: the Passion of Jesus. It is placed so that those who have eyes to see will not fail to notice it, though those who are not alert to the signs usually fail to see its value, glossing over significant parts of the story, assuming they are "transition passages."

The period of six days before the Passover was used by the Jews as a time of purification (Jn. 11: 55).[101] Six days before the Passover began would place the event on Sunday. The Greek term used to describe the meal ($\delta\epsilon\iota\pi\nu o\nu$ -- deipnon) indicates that it was a supper meal. The time, therefore, is what we would call Saturday evening. Barrett notes[102] that this meal was connected with the Habdalah or service denoting the separation of the Sabbath from the rest of the week.[103] That it was, indeed, to be understood as a Habdalah meal is consistent with the intent of the trilogy (i.e.: ordination involves "setting

---

[99] "[F. denouement, fr. denouer untie] The final revelation or occurrence which clarifies the nature and outcome of a plot; also, the passage in which it occurs." A. Merriam-Webster, op. cit., p. 221.

[100] See Culpepper, Anatomy, op. cit, pp. 77ff. for a consideration of the plot in the Fourth Gospel.

[101] See Nu. 9: 6-12. After purification, Israelites who have been defiled by coming near a corpse are allowed to celebrate Passover. See also Lev. 8: 33-35 re: time required for ordination of Aaron and his sons.

[102] Barrett, op. cit., p. 411.

[103] Barrett ends his comment on the Habdalah with, "It must be added that John himself shows not the smallest knowledge of or interest in the Habdalah ceremony, and may well have been unaware of its existence."

apart" or separation) and because the note in Jn. 11: 55 indicates that this is a time for purification (during which one must be separated from others), I suggest that John intends for the reader to set the event about to be described in a temporal context consistent with the one motivating others to be in or near Jerusalem almost a week before Passover: They were required to separate from everyone else, to purify themselves before Passover began.

Later we will see that Mary and her sister, Martha, send a message to Jesus out of concern for "Lazarus" who is "ill." The Gospel tells us, in fact, that Lazarus is dying when that message is sent. If, as we will show, Lazarus is really the priesthood, and the tomb in which the priesthood dies is the Herodian temple, and if Mary of Bethany is a Nazirite, then she clearly had a need to go through the rite of purification that many were seeking to complete before the Passover observance.

If the six-day period of purification required of a Nazirite began after sundown on *Sabbath*, then that period would have ended on the Day of Preparation, i.e.: the day before the Passover: Friday, which begins after sundown on what we would call Thursday night. That timing fits the timing of the account of the arrest and midnight trial of Jesus at the house of the High Priest (Jn. 18: 12-18).

We are also told in Jn. 11: 55 that "many went up from the country to Jerusalem before Passover." The Greek term ανεβασαν -- *anebasan* means literally "they climbed." The Herodian Temple was located on an enormous and recently constructed "Temple Mount."[104]

---

[104]See Comay, op. cit., p. 155f. The Temple Mount, which elevated the temple up to 154 feet above the ground, was held in place by a retaining wall built of huge stones, some estimated to weigh over 100

Barrett indicates[105] that this term is "a word of pilgrimage." For John it may have been more than that. The theological importance of the Temple as a holy place, as we have seen, is grounded in Gn. 28: 10-17: Jacob's ladder dream.

The Temple, in other words, represents the connecting point between heaven and earth, where angels ascend and descend. Pilgrims who seek a closer relationship with God must ascend the Temple mount to do so. In John, Jesus replaces the Temple (Jn. 2: 13-22). "Destroy this Temple, and in three days I will raise it up." This is understood to be a sign to those who ask by what authority he drove the money changers out of the Temple.

Barrett quotes Brown when he suggests that another sign is merely a literary conjunction.[106] Jn. 7: 11, 13, to which Barrett refers, are part of John's account of the secret attendance by Jesus at the Festival of Booths. As was pointed out in chapter five, during the Festival of Booths (or Tabernacles) the faithful children of Israel were to "live in booths for seven days . . . so that your generations may know that I (Yahweh) made the people of Israel live in booths when I brought them out of the land of Egypt" (Lv. 23: 33-36, 42-43). The theological import of this festival is to cause the faithful to remember that God abides with them, and they abide with God.

The Tabernacle ("Tent of the Meeting") was the first house of God in Israel. It was distinguished from

---

tons.

[105]Barrett, op. cit., p. 409.

[106]Ibid., p. 410. "See Jn. 7: 11, 13. The parallel suggests to Brown that, "Jn. may have been reusing traditional material in order to effect the transition to the new paragraph. 55ff. are in any case an editorial link."

Solomon's Temple and Herod's Temple because it moved
with the people, who literally "followed" God.   God
appeared as a pillar of fire at night and a pillar of cloud by
day.[107]   The faithful were required to "climb up" to
Solomon's Temple and to climb even higher to Herod's
Temple, rather than to "follow" it.   In each case, seekers
had to find the place where God abides.

The Beginning of the Plot

         The plot of the Gospel begins with the first
exchange between Jesus and two seekers.

**"When Jesus turned and saw (two of John the Baptist's
disciples) following, he said to them, 'What are you
looking for?'   They said to him, Rabbi, (which
translated means 'Teacher') 'Where are you staying?'
He said to them, 'Come and see.'"** (Jn. 1: 38)

στραφεισ δε ο Ιησουσ, και θεασαμενοσ αυτουσ
ακολουθουντασ, λεγει αυτοισ, Τι ζητειτε; Οι δε
ειπον αυτω, Ραββι, ο λεγεται ερμηνευομενον
διδασκαλε, που μενεισ; Λεγει αυτοισ, Ερχεσθε
και ιδετε.

("Having turned but Jesus, and beheld them following, says
to them, What (Whom) seek ye?   And they said to him,

---

[107]Ex. 13: 21, 22. In this same chapter, take note of 13: 9 where
the remembrance of salvation from Egypt is to be "as a sign on your hand
and as a reminder on your forehead, so that the teaching of the Lord may
be on your lips; for with a strong hand the Lord brought you out of
Egypt."

Rabbi, which is to say, being interpreted, Teacher, where abidest thou? He says to them, Come and see.")[108]

Before they become disciples of Jesus, these two seekers must acknowledge that they are seekers. "Whom do you seek?" is the initial question posed to a seeker. The answer one would expect to hear is "I seek God," or within a Christian community, "I seek Jesus Christ." Discipleship begins with an awareness that one is seeking God. The response of Jesus is to call the seeker to him and to invite the seeker to "see" him.

The second question in the text is similar to the first, and also reveals the purpose of the Gospel. To a Christian seeking to know Christ more deeply, "Teacher, where do you abide?" might be read as "Where does God abide?" or "Where does Christ abide?" The Gospel of John implies that there is an obvious answer to one seeking to become a disciple: "Christ abides in me."[109] In responding to these two questions, seekers learn how to see Christ and witness to Christ's presence in their lives.

In Jn. 7:11, the Jews (leaders among the Temple priests) were asking "Where is he?"

---

[108]Our exegetical studies will include a three-fold presentation of each passage: (1) as translated in the New Revised Standard Version of the Holy Bible, then (2)the Greek and (3)a literal English translation by George Ricker Berry, The Interlinear Literal Translation of the Greek New Testament, Zondervan, Grand Rapids, (1st printing 1958, 19th printing 1977), p. 243. Those with an extensive understanding of Greek will want to skip the literal translation. Those with no understanding of Greek will want to skip both the Greek and the literal translations. Those with a limited understanding of Greek may choose to consider all three.

[109]See Jn. 8: 31; 14: 23; 15: 4-10; Culpepper, op. cit., p. 115, suggests that the Gospel may have been written by a school. Indeed, it may have been written as that school's textbook for making disciples.

"They were looking for Jesus and were asking one another
as they stood in the Temple, 'What do you think? Surely
he will not come to the festival, will he?' Now the Chief
Priests and the Pharisees had given orders that anyone who
knew where Jesus was should let them know, so that they
might arrest him." (Jn. 11: 56-57)

In Jn. 7: 14f., Jesus is teaching. Where? In the
Temple. The Temple (Jesus himself) is teaching in the
Temple (that is, in the Herodian Temple). Those who say
they don't know where Jesus is do not know where God
abides. If they did, they would find God there. It all
comes to a head in Jn. 7: 25-31:

"Some of the people of Jerusalem were saying, 'Is not this
the man whom they are trying to kill? And here he is,
speaking openly, but they say nothing to him! Can it be
that the authorities really know that this man is the
Messiah?" Jesus cries out, "You know me, and you know
where I am from . . .Then they tried to arrest him, but no
one laid hands on him, because his hour had not yet come.
Yet many in the crowd believed in him and were saying,
"When the Messiah comes, will he do more signs than this
man has done?"

At both the Festival of Booths and the Festival of
the Passover, the faithful were to recall the salvation history
of the people called by Jacob's new name: Israel.[110]
Jn. 11: 57 implies that the Pharisees really do know
where Jesus is, that is, where Jesus abides. The fact that

---

[110]See Gen. 32. Jacob again encounters the angels at "God's
camp" and spends another night.

they "give orders" implies that they are using a military approach to what is really a theological problem: the priests in the Temple don't know where God is. They are not acting as priests, but as mercenary soldiers, paid by the Roman government.

This theme is repeated with roles reversed when the Roman soldiers do the work of the priests: first they "ordain" Jesus (and prepare him for sacrifice) by laying hands on his head (Jn. 19: 2), pressing down hard a crown of thorns,[111] and vesting him with a robe that corresponds both to the High Priest's robe (Ex. 28: 31f) and the curtain in the Temple (Ex. 26: 31f). Then they anoint him by lifting a branch of hyssop to his mouth containing a sponge filled with sour wine. This also served to mark him in the way the lintels of the door posts of the faithful had been marked at the time of the Passover.[112] In crucifying him (Jn. 19: 18), the soldiers separated his extremities from his body, though they did not break the legs as was customary (Jn. 19: 32-33).[113] Then they pierced his side (Jn. 19: 34)

---

[111]As pointed out earlier (footnote #32), Daube, Ibid., p. 224ff. distinguishes between "placing one's hands" on someone or something (*sim or shith* -- for a blessing) and "leaning one's hands" on someone or something (*samakh* -- for ordination or sacrifice). The later involved hard pressure, was used to transfer one's identity to another, either in preparing an animal for sacrifice or creating a substitute for one's self as when Moses laid hands on (*samakh*) Joshua to authorize him as leader of Israel or when Moses ordained Aaron and his sons as high priests. The former was used for a blessing; the latter for ordination and sacrifice.

[112]I am grateful to Dr. Herman Weitjen for this insight.

[113]Daube, op. cit. p. 301ff. says this was to avoid "Niwwul" (disgrace). Disfiguring any person's body, alive or dead, was believed to impair the body's ability to be resurrected. If bones were broken, the body might not rise at all. John deals with these concerns by reporting Jesus' teaching (12: 24) that though a grain of wheat dies (and "rots" in

so that blood and water came gushing out (pouring out his life's blood at his feet: the base of the altar). John presents the ironic picture of foreign soldiers performing the sacrificial rites entrusted to the Temple priests, though neither the soldiers nor the priests realized it.

The Chief Priests do not know where Jesus is or who he is. They expect that the faithful worshippers will come and testify or witness to them where Jesus can be found. In fact, one of them, Judas, does. One might infer from this that Judas is obedient to the religious authorities of his time. It is one of the many ironies in John that Judas knows where Jesus abides (i.e.: Judas is a disciple), but he is obedient to Jesus and the Temple priests. Thus, Judas "loses sight" of Jesus. He comes to Jesus in the darkness with those whose abiding place is in darkness (Jn. 1: 5; 18: 1-15). "Jesus asks, 'Τινα ζητειτε' *'Tina zateite'* 'Whom do you seek?' They answer, 'Jesus the Nazorean.' Jesus replies, 'Εγω ειμι.' *'Ego eimi'* 'I am.'[114] Judas, who betrayed him, was standing with them"(18:4, 5).

When Jesus provides a requested sign in 2: 18-19, saying that he will rebuild the Temple in three days, he is talking about his body as the new Temple (2: 21). In the narrative world of the Gospel of John, the Herodian Temple is no longer "*the* Temple," ("the House of God") but is "the house" of those who abide in darkness, the head of which is the legitimate (not the official) High Priest.

---

the ground), it bears much fruit (i.e.: brings forth new life, untouched by decay.)

[114]Not "I am he" (as in the NRSV), though such a translation is grammatically correct. The theological point is that Jesus identifies himself in the same way as God does to Moses from the burning bush. (Ex. 3: 14).

Caiaphas had the official role of High Priest because Herod had awarded it to him.[115] Annas, however, was secretly, among the Chief Priests, the "real" High Priest. Caiaphas was not a direct descendant of Aaron, as required by the Law (Nu. 3: 10; 18: 1-7), but "qualified" for the role through a female line of descent, i.e.: by his marriage to the daughter of Annas.[116] In other words, the official High Priest was legitimized to approach Israel's highest altar by his relationship to a woman, his wife, who happened to have political connections. Though women were usually prevented from approaching the altar themselves, this woman provided access to it for Caiaphas. History does not record her name. This is but one of the

---

[115]Gottlob Schrenk, "αρχιερευσ," Theological Dictionary of the New Testament, op. cit., vol. III, pp. 265-283, esp. p. 268. "The Herodian-Roman period brought decisive changes. Anointing was abandoned and consecration was only by investiture -- a significant loss of prestige. Herod destroyed the Hasmoneans. The hereditary and permanent character of the office was disregarded by the political rulers, and arbitrary depositions and appointments followed. The rights of the Zadokites were ignored. Representatives of other priestly families were accepted. In the 106 years between 37 B.C. and 70 A.D. 28 high priests discharged the office, and 25 of these were of non-legitimate priestly families."

[116]Ibid. pp. 270-272. "It is inconceivable that a book so knowledgeable in Jewish matters as John's Gospel should be suggesting that the High-Priesthood was a yearly office. . . Annas (6-15 A.D.) had been replaced at the time of Jesus (by Caiaphas c. 18-37 A.D.), but he was still influential, Lk. 3: 2; Ac. 4: 6; Jn. 18: 13, 24. Apart from his son-in-law, five of his sons and his grandson, Mattias (65 A.D.), held the office. He was thus the head of a *genos arxieratikon* . . . (which) denotes membership of the legitimate priestly nobility (in the strictest and most proper sense, the Zadokites) . . . this priestly aristocracy occupied the higher priestly posts . . . and was socially distinct from the ordinary priesthood. Wealth contributed no little to their success."

many ironic circumstances by which the Jews indict themselves from the perspective of the Gospel.[117]

The house of the High Priest is the Herodian Temple. That the gate to this house is guarded by a woman indicates that the courtyard to which Peter is given access (Jn. 18: 15-18) is the Court of the Women, and the charcoal fire by which those who wait in this courtyard warm themselves, is the fire prepared for use in the Temple. Jesus appears before the Sanhedrin, which convenes in the Court of the Israelites, just beyond the Nicanor gate.[118]

In summary, John sprinkles signs about historical time and place liberally in the setting for our pericope. The time is six days before the Passover Festival begins. The place is outside of the Herodian Temple. The signs say, "This is a story about the time when the disciples were set apart, so that they could become new priests in the Temple of Jesus."

---

[117]Ibid., "Speculation concerning the High-priest in Philo," p. 272f. Schrenk considers the *logos* link between the roles of Moses and Aaron. In Jn., the presence of two persons in the role of High Priest is not only not an error, but an important sign: that the *logos* was no longer the link between the two in the High Priest's position. By this time, the link was the political power of Herod.

[118]See Comay's <u>Plan of the Second Temple</u> in the Appendix.

Chapter 8
A Setting in Cosmic Time

Cosmic Time

Consideration of historical time, however, does not
adequately address the use of time as a setting in the Fourth
Gospel. The more important perspective, hinted in the
prologue, is that of cosmic time, an unfolding of the eternal
order, in contrast to the temporal succession of events. The
writer uses cosmic time[119] to place the reader[120] in a position
to "see" the signs in the Gospel, which lead to deeper
theological and Christological reflection. Cosmic time is an
intentional didactic tool, intended to prompt a growth in
faith.

---

[119]See Culpepper, op. cit., pp. 20-49, who suggests that the
writer's psychological point of view is omniscient (p. 20), spacial point of
view is omnipresent (p. 26) and ideological point of view is reliable and
stereoscopic (p. 32). He deals with the concept of narrative time, but does
not use the term "cosmic time."

[120]Ibid. Culpepper provides a valuable and apparently
comprehensive survey of the importance of the reader of a narrative in
literary criticism. After a careful analysis, he draws the following
conclusions, "If the intended audience (of the Gospel) is not Christian, it
is certainly familiar with Christian beliefs and the Christian story." (p.
223) "Readers found their identity in the Gospel story and through it they
could rise from their present struggles to hear their values and views
reaffirmed, to hear again reassuring words from Jesus, to glimpse the
mystery of the world above, and find themselves, or at least their ideal, in
the figure of the Beloved Disciple, whose witness was true and whose
'place' was the bosom of the Lord." (pp. 226-227); Brown, Community,
op. cit., pp. 191-192, says, "Discipleship is the primary Christian category
for John, and the disciple par excellence is the Disciple Whom Jesus
Loved."

In the Fourth Gospel, there is only one hour, one day, one period of three days, one Sabbath (seventh day), one season, and one year. History is measured in relationship to these singular moments in cosmic time (*kairos,* that is, time measured by meaning, not *chronos,* time measured mechanically). It cannot limit such divinely appointed times. These cosmic moments in time, rather, limit history.

Hour

In the Gospel of John, there are twenty-four references to the word "hour."[121] Each one of them is in relation to the signal hour of Jesus, the hour when he must go to the cross, when he says, "My hour has come," which he announces to the disciples (Jn. 16: 32) and in prayer he acknowledges to God (Jn. 17: 1), i.e.: to himself as *Logos*, "I Am."

Each hour marks a separation point in the Gospel, which is written as a theological, Christological textbook for Christian disciples seeking a closer relationship with Christ. It appears that every time an hour is mentioned, the disciple is supposed to stop reading and contemplate the sign or signs that have been revealed since the last hour was given.[122] In this way, the disciples may work their way through the Gospel, using this integrated system of locators.

---

[121]See Jn. 1:39; 2:04; 4:06; 4:21; 4:23; 4:52(a); 4:52(b); 4:53; 5:25; 5:28; 7:30; 8:20; 12:23; 12:27(a); 12:27(b); 13:01; 16:02; 16:04; 16:21; 16:25; 16:32; 17:01; 19:14; 19:27. (Written as digital clock settings.)

[122]Contrary to C.H. Dodd, Fortna and others, there are far more than seven signs in the Gospel.

With this structure in mind, it is not difficult to imagine a Johannine teacher[123] asking a group of students, in a manner consistent with rabbinical teaching, "Who can tell me the signs in the first hour?" At this point a student may expound upon the symbolic, theological and Christological content of all that occurs in the Johannine version of the Jesus story (the Gospel of John) within the parameters defined by the holy textbook as "the first hour (probably Jn. 1: 1-39)."[124]

Day

Though there is only one hour, there is yet a full day. The entire gospel is told in the cosmic sense as though it were one day. It is the day that the disciples may spend with Jesus, the beginning of which is marked at Jn. 1: 39 (the first hour). Two disciples of John the Baptist hear his witness and are the first fruits of it. They follow Jesus. Jesus asks the first Rabbinical question. "Whom do you seek?" They respond appropriately by addressing him by his title and answering with a question. "Rabbi, where do you abide?"

---

[123]R. Alan Culpepper, The Johannine School: An Evaluation of the Johannine School Hypothesis Based On An Investigation of the Nature of Ancient Schools, Scholars Press for the Society of Biblical Literature, Missoula, (1975). (Originally printed as the author's Ph.D. thesis at Duke University in 1974). It proves the hypothesis that the Gospel of John came from and probably was written by students in a school.

[124]Note that this text identifies this time as "about the tenth hour" which is about 4 O'clock in the afternoon. In other words, the cosmic hour of Christ approaches before the "new day" begins (at sundown).

Imagine now the Johannine school. The teacher announces "It is about the tenth hour (translated in the NRSV as about four O'clock in the afternoon). What time is it?" The correct answer to the question is "It is time to seek Jesus!" In that same session the teacher might ask each student "Whom do you seek?" The catechism implied by this interpretation of the Gospel would suggest that the right answer to this question is "I seek Jesus." "Where does Christ abide?" the teacher continues; answer: "Christ abides in me."

Admittedly this reads a lot into the forms of language used in the Gospel, but these conclusions produce similarly pleasing results no matter which hour is chosen throughout the text. It is difficult to believe that such a didactic use of the text is not intentionally woven into it. If so, the Gospel of John may be the oldest textbook in Christian dogmatics.

The "day" of the Fourth Gospel is also inferred by the opening line to the Prologue. "In the beginning . . ." points the student to the familiar opening lines of the Torah, a logical starting place for students learning to study the Bible. Here, too, is the model for marking passages of scripture at the end of the unit of meaning. "And there was evening and there was morning, the first day."(Gn. 1: 5, 8, 13, 19, 23, 31b.)

The passage of time in Genesis is marked by the intersection of darkness and light. In this intersection, God can be "seen." God actively and passively separates the light from the darkness. God *is* between the darkness and the light. God is visible when the darkness of the world comes into contrast with the light of God's presence (epiphany).

The pattern of creation in Gn. 1 is the Word of creation followed by a name, identifying whatever is being created. The symbolism is that of birth, followed by the granting of a name by which to proffer a cosmic, spiritual identity upon that which has been born. Jesus implies knowledge of this same power when he teaches Nicodemus to consider baptism as an act of re-birth, implying that a new identity is necessary for him (Jn. 3: 1-21).

In the Exodus story, God is visible as a dark pillar of cloud by day and as a light pillar of fire by night. God is visible because of the contrast, a concept that is both consistent with a cosmic view of creation and an enlightening one for those seeking to gain spiritual vision through which to "see" Christ in a world filled with spiritual darkness.

"In the beginning was the Word . . ." The language in the Prologue is similar to that in the creation story because it infers the foundation of the Christology of the Johannine community, namely, that Jesus is the Word, pre-existent with God at the time of creation.

In Gn. 1: 2, the breath of God moving over the darkness initiates the creation. In Jn. 20: 22-23, Jesus breathes on the disciples and directs them to receive the Holy Spirit, through which authority to grant or withhold forgiveness is given. The implication is that God is continuing the act of creation, now on a specifically spiritual plain. The importance of this continuing process of creation is explained briefly in the Prologue. "The law indeed was given through Moses; grace and truth came through Jesus Christ (Jn. 1: 17)." The identity of God is

in this creative power, the Author of Existence, "I am."[125]
This is the identity, the awesome transcendent, yet
omnipresent, identity of Creator God, that the evangelist
sees in Jesus, and it is John the Baptist who sees and
announces this identity first. He opens the eyes of two of
his own disciples, who become disciples of Jesus.

The one day that these two disciples spend with
Jesus is the day of cosmic birth, the day of light in the
midst of darkness, the day of life overcoming death. In
God's time, there is but one day, repeated over and over
again. It is the eternal day, the Day of the Lord. While
the hour is the moment of death, the day is the moment of
creation -- life.

Three Days

Jesus is dead for three days after his "hour" has passed.
This three-day period is prophesied by Jesus in response to
a request for a sign of his authority (Jn. 2: 13-23). Jesus
promises to "rebuild the Temple" (his own body) in three
days after it is torn down.

---

[125]The phrase "I am," used to identify God in Ex. 3: 14 and used
repeatedly in the Old Testament (651 times), is used 80 times in the Fourth
Gospel, compared to 22 in Matthew, 13 in Mark and 25 in Luke. See
Friedrich Buchsel, "ειμι," Theological Dictionary of the New Testament,
op. cit., vol. II, p. 399. re: Jn. 8: 24, 28, 58; 13: 19. "The verse (8: 58)
ascribes to Jesus consciousness of eternity or supra-temporality." See also
Ethelbert Stauffer, "εγω ειμι," Theological Dictionary of the New
Testament, op. cit., vol. II, pp. 352-354 "The central passage is Jn. 8: 24-
29. . . Life and death decision is decision for or against Christ (v. 24) . .
. It is thus plain that the εγω of Jesus is the point where there is the Yes
of belief or the No of unbelief. This is the critical point on which the
waves of world history break."

When Jesus approaches the tomb of Lazarus (Jn. 11: 39) Martha reminds him that Lazarus has already been dead four days.[126] The story underscores the authority of Jesus over death, not merely sleep, as Jesus himself declares (Jn. 11: 11, 14).

The Seventh (Sabbath) Day

In the Torah the seventh day is separated from the other six days in each week, to cause those in covenant with God to remember God's role in creation (Ex. 20: 8-11; Dt. 5: 12-15). As we have learned, the semeiotic pattern of separating and remembering is transferred in the Gospel According to John in terms of seeing and believing. Passages set in the context of the Sabbath in John focus on the fact that the temple authorities ("the Jews") refused to see Christ in Jesus and believe (Jn. 9: 1-41; 7: 19-25). Jesus replaces the Sabbath (Jn. 5: 1-18), declaring, "My Father is still working, and I also am working." Jesus is continuing the work of creation each time he performs a healing.

The period leading to the Sabbath (six days) is significant in Jn. 12: 1 as a time of purification. As a holy day, the Sabbath is replaced by the first day (Jn. 20: 1, 19), the day of resurrection, the new day of creation.

---

[126]C.K. Barrett, The Gospel According to St. John, Westminster, Philadelphia, (1955, 2nd ed. 1978), p. 401. See Jn. 11: 6, 17 (The timing of four days was intentional on the part of Jesus.) Quote Herodotus II, 89 re: 'to be four days dead.' "A state of death beyond the third day meant, from the popular Jewish point of view, an absolute dissolution of life. At this time the face cannot be recognized with certainty; the body bursts; and the soul, which until then had hovered over the body, parts from it." (Eccl. R. 12. 6; Lev. R. 18. 1)

Season

The seasons of the Jewish calendar were marked by sacred
festivals during which sacrificial offerings were made to
God. In the Fourth Gospel Jesus systematically replaces
each one of these festivals, before replacing the sacrifices
that go with them all at once. Thus, the "hour" of Jesus is
a "season" to itself. In the cosmic perspective offered by
the Gospel, this "season" is the pivotal point of all history,
the singular event that defines all time. As we shall see, in
this Gospel Jesus systematically replaces every one of the
prescribed festivals, broadening and deepening the original
meaning and identifying his own sacrifice as the fulfillment
of each festival's purpose.

Year

The fact that there are references to three Passover festivals
(Jn. 2: 13, 23; 11: 55) suggest to some scholars that the
Gospel covers a period of about three years or that the
writer is perhaps reusing traditional material because the
setting is so unimportant that it does not warrant writing a
new introduction.[127] This disregards the oracular nature of
much of the material in the Gospel, and that, in turn, leads
the reader to miss yet another sign. In the Fourth Gospel,
there is only one Passover, though Jesus, an eternal being,
may repeat his appearance at it three or even four times.
The Passover festival (not the Passover meal as in the

---

[127]Barrett, op. cit., p. 409; "This Passover is the third named by
John; if the unnamed feast of 5: 1 is a Passover, it is the fourth of the
ministry." (p. 410); See also n. 102 re: Brown's comp. of 11: 55 and 7:
11,13.

Synoptics) during which Jesus is arrested, tried, and
crucified, has a cosmic significance. It is that Passover
festival to which John refers.

At each one of these festivals, except those
connected with the harvest, animals are sacrificed. In some
cases, as in the ordination of the High Priest or the
completion of a Nazirite vow, several animals are
sacrificed. On the big feast days like Passover, thousands
of animals are sacrificed in the Temple. These sacrifices,
both of grain and of blood, are replaced by the Eucharist,
observed in remembrance of the sacrifice of Jesus.

Summary

Since the Fourth Gospel presents a cosmic perspective of
time, the events described in it are not arranged in a
chronological fashion. The objective is to grant seekers an
insight into the symbolic power and cosmic meaning of
each event in the traditions of both the Old and New
Covenants, rather than to focus on the maintenance of a
schedule of worship.

Chapter 9
Understanding a Sign Called Bethany

The House of Ananiah

The place setting of the trilogy is a δειπνον (*deipnon*) supper in Bethany "οπου ην Λαζαροσ" (*opou an Lazaros*) i.e.: "where Lazarus *is,*" not "the home of Lazarus." Lazarus abides in Bethany. Bethany gets its name from the same root word "Beth-" (house) as in the first part of Bethel, which has already been defined as "House of God." Among several theories[128] as to the origin and location of Bethany, one is particularly interesting, namely that it is derived from "Beth Ananiah" meaning "House of Ananiah." Neh. 11: 32 mentions Ananiah in the same context as Bethel as the abiding place of priests and Levites. The house of Ananiah is specifically mentioned in Neh. 3: 23. "Bethany" is a sign.

The book of Nehemiah is the chronicle of an exiled Levite priest, who, having become a slave, secures permission from his master to return briefly (for 12 years) to Jerusalem to rebuild the gates to the Temple, and the walls that had separated it from the city. They were in ruins. This destruction of the Temple was a source of great trouble and shame for the faithful remnant (Neh. 1: 3) Nehemiah organizes crews of priests and faithful people for this task, including persons identified with Ananiah.

---

[128] See Rainer Riesner, "Bethany" and "Bethany Beyond the Jordan," The Anchor Bible Dictionary, ed. Noel Freedman et. al, Doubleday, New York-London-Toronto-Sydney-Auckland, (1992), vol. 1 A-C, pp. 702-705.

Bethany is a place identified with the gates of the Temple. In John, it is a sign indicating that Jesus is about to enter the Temple (through the gate).

John mentions two locations for Bethany. In Jn. 1: 28, it is mentioned as a location across the Jordan where John the Baptist prepares the faithful through baptism with water and announcing (to the priests and Levites who ask him who he is), "Among you stands one whom you do not know, the one who is coming after me; I am not worthy to untie the thong of his sandal." John the Baptist and the baptisms he provides, is a gate to the new Temple, Jesus. John considers himself unworthy to untie Jesus' sandals. Such work was done by a slave or a member of the family, but not by a disciple.[129] Though he precedes and does not follow Jesus, John considers himself to be one of Jesus' disciples. Disciples are gates to the Jesus Temple, as is baptism.

The Role of John the Baptist

In fact, the writer of the Gospel defines the terms for disciple in the witness of John the Baptist. Jn. 1: 7 introduces John the Baptist this way: "He came as a witness to testify to the light, so that all might believe through him." A disciple of Jesus is a witness (who "sees") to the light (God in the world) and testifies (speaks the Word) so that all might believe (live in relationship, abide) in Jesus.

---

[129]Daube, op. cit., "Offices of a Disciple," pp. 267, 268. "In Talmudic utterances, whenever a slave's services are illustrated, these two -- carrying the master's things before him to the bathhouse and taking off his shoes (when he comes home) -- are listed together. . . . R. Joshua ben Levi (Rabbi Joshua, son of Levi) held that a disciple should do for his teacher anything a slave would do -- except take off his shoes."

John's own words reveal that this ability to "see" is not of his own making, but a consequence of the revelation given to him by God. His witness serves as a model for all disciples: seeing Christ in Jesus and testifying to that truth.

"I myself did not know him; but I came baptizing with water for this reason, that he might be revealed to Israel . . . I myself did not know him, but the one who sent me to baptize with water said to me, 'He on whom you see the Spirit descending and abiding is the one who baptizes with the Holy Spirit.' *And I myself have seen and have testified that this is the Son of God"*(Jn. 1: 31f).

By definition, John the Baptist is the first disciple of Jesus, since he has both "seen" and "testified" as to the cosmic identity of Jesus. This alone justifies calling the Gospel "The Gospel According to John." The John in the title is John the Baptist. This is not to suggest that the author is John the Baptist. The model for discipleship is John the Baptist's witness. Formation of disciples according to that model appears to be the purpose of the Gospel.

John the Baptist is important not just because of his role in providing the gateway of baptism into relationship with Jesus, but because he sets the standard for what it means to *see Christ* in Jesus. In the same context, a definition is also provided for what it means *to believe* in Jesus. "To all who received him, who believed in his name, he gave power to become children of God, who were born, not of blood or the will of the flesh or of the will of man, but of God" (Jn. 1: 12f.).[130]

---

[130]See also Jn. 3: 1-21, the dialogue with Nicodemus; Jn. 10: 1-18, the entire Good Shepherd passage.

The first Bethany, "Bethany beyond the Jordan," was where John the Baptist baptized the children of God (Jn. 1: 28). Baptism by a disciple is a gateway to Jesus, who is, himself, a gateway to the true Temple (Jn. 10: 1-10). The location of the second Bethany, the second gate, is a suburb of Jerusalem (Jn. 11: 1, 18; 12: 1). The fact that there are two locations for Bethany in the Gospel According to John is an important sign. It has to do with the degree of proximity of each of these locations to the Herodian temple. One was near to the temple (Bethany) and one was further away (Bethany beyond the Jordan).

The Gates of the Temple

The floor plan of the Herodian Temple,[131] had numerous gates, but two stand out. The principle gate by which worshippers entered was called The Beautiful Gate. It opened onto the Court of the Women. The Gospel writer(s) carefully associate Bethany with Mary and Martha, hinting that Bethany was a gate through which women could enter. The Gospel identifies two Bethanies, however, the other being "Bethany across (or beyond) the Jordan" (Jn. 1: 28).

To get to the Beautiful Gate, a worshipper was required to climb from the streets of Jerusalem up the steps of the temple mount. Primarily through the Beautiful Gate, all but the priests entered the Court of the Women. The priests could enter the Court of the Priests by a number of smaller gates.

---

[131]See Nehemiah or Comay, op. cit., p. 99-101, for the story of the restoring the temple gates.

Once inside the Court of the Women, devout Jewish men faced Nicanor's Gate. Depending upon whether one looks toward the sanctuary from outside of the Court of the Women or toward the Court of the Women from the Sanctuary, these two gates can be identified, just as Bethany is, as the near gate or the far gate. Note that the design of the Temple implies that women may not come as near to God as men can come. In John, the design of the Temple of Jesus clearly changes that.

To get to the inner gate, Nicanor's Gate, faithful Jewish men had to cross the Court of the Women and climb another set of steps.[132] There at the Court of the Israelites they stopped. Beyond that court was the Court of the Priests where only priests were allowed.   Thus,   after Jesus entered (or passed through) Bethany, he had to climb to get to where the sacrifice would be made. Note that the shape of the Court of the Women is that of a cross with the Beautiful Gate at its base (foot) and the Nicanor gate at its top (head).   The Beautiful Gate is furthest from the Sanctuary. The semi-circular steps leading to Nicanor's Gate might easily be associated with a halo, the sign of the Shekinah light of holiness emanating from the head of this cross-shaped area. Is it a coincidence that Jesus had to climb to the cross?

The symbolism of the Temple gate is repeated three more times in Jn. 10: 1-10 by Jesus. In Jn. 10: 1-5, Jesus seems to be saying that those who belong to the family of God, God's children/lambs/sheep can trust the shepherd who walks into the fold through the gate. That is, he comes into the Temple to lead those who seek God, by walking through the same gates they walk through (birth

---

[132]See the Plan of the Second Temple in the Appendix.

and death). He does not come in by one of the "service entrances" where the firewood or the oil or the livestock are brought in (by the Levites). Those who enter by such passageways are not there to lead the sheep out into the world, but rather are there to take from the sheep. They are strangers; their voices frighten the sheep. A Levite brings a sheep into the Temple for only one purpose: to sacrifice it. No sheep can expect to leave the Temple alive, but Jesus, the Good Shepherd, calls to his sheep and leads them out into the world.

In Jn. 10: 7-10, Jesus identifies himself as the gate. He is the one through whom a seeker must pass to find God. Such seekers may enter the Temple, then leave it again. They will find pasture, that is, they will be fed, nourished, not sacrificed. They will not be taken or killed, but given abundant life. Jesus carries this sign further in Jn. 10: 11-19, when he makes it clear that the gate through which he will pass will be the gate of death, a gate he willingly passes through because as the Good Shepherd, he gives his life for the lives of the sheep, as opposed to the "hired hand" (priests who are placed in the Temple by Roman authority for political and military reasons) who will scatter the sheep (Jn. 11: 52, 16: 32). When the hired hand sees the wolf (death) coming he runs away.

Thus Bethany is an important sign. It represents the gateway to the Temple, the way to the house of God. The residents of Bethany, identified as Lazarus and his two sisters, Martha and Mary, may be identified as gatekeepers in the house of the Lord. They are all key characters in the trilogy of stories, linked together to describe in detail how Jesus ordained his disciples.

Chapter 10
The Characters of the Trilogy

Lazarus, the Silent Priest

The location of the action for the trilogy in Bethany is tied carefully to the identity of one of the principle characters in that action. It is where Lazarus "abides." Actually, it would be more accurate to say that it is where Lazarus *should* abide. As we learn in Jn. 11: 11-14, Lazarus is dead. In Jn. 11: 43-44, Jesus calls Lazarus to come out of the tomb, and he does come out, but Lazarus may as well have stayed dead, because he never speaks.

Like the time and the place, the characters, for this pericope in the Fourth Gospel, while historic, real people,[133] were also symbolic figures.[134] Lazarus appears only in one other Gospel (Lk. 16: 19-31) and there only as a character in one of the parables of Jesus. Notably in Luke the need for the resurrection is expressed by the rich man, Dives, but Father Abraham explains that it would not convince those who already have the Law and the Prophets, even if Lazarus came back to life.

Whether Lazarus is a historical figure or not is a less important question than what his symbolic identity is in John's Gospel. His symbolic identity is what points to the truth. We know very little about him. In fact, all that we know is contained in the 11th and 12th chapters of the Gospel story. Lazarus is one of three disciples that Jesus loved (Jn. 11: 5), the other two being his sisters, Mary and

---

[133]Brown, op. cit., Community, pp. 191-192.

[134]Culpepper, op. cit., p. 140 f.

Martha (Jn. 11: 1). Lazarus dies and Jesus commands him to come forth from the tomb (Jn. 11: 1-44).

The names used to describe characters in John's gospel are important. Names are signs of the identities of these characters, not only in John's gospel, but in the Old Testament as well, especially in the Torah, by which many of John's signs can be decoded. The name Lazarus is an abbreviation of the name Eleazar, which is the name of the third son of Aaron (Ex. 6: 23) of the second generation of High Priests in the Temple.

While this may not be enough to convince us of the symbolic identity of Lazarus, such a role seems more likely when we add it to the second hidden sign regarding Lazarus: he never speaks. This is significant because John reports that a great crowd of Jews came to see Lazarus as well as Jesus (Jn. 12: 9). This is understandable. Here is a man who has died, has been buried for four days (Jn. 11: 39) and has been called out of the tomb by Jesus. Here is a chance to get a first-hand witness about what that experience is like. The High Priests plot to kill Lazarus as well as Jesus because they fear the kind of conversions[135] that the witness of Lazarus could promote (Jn. 12: 10, 11). As a disciple, by definition, Lazarus must speak, yet he does not speak. His witness, indeed his identity, is that he does not speak. The clue as to why he is silent lies in a story from the Septuagint.

---

[135] John uses the term *upagon* which the New Revised Standard Version of the Holy Bible translates as "desertions." It literally means "they were going away." "Desertions" is consistent with the military mentality of the Chief Priests implied earlier.

The Message of Silence

The story of Nadab and Abihu, two of the four ordained sons of the High Priest, Aaron (10: 1-3) tells why Aaron becomes silent. It is linked to the Gospel (Jn. 18: 18) by a sign that we have considered before: the coals for the holy fire kindled in the Temple to turn sacrifices into smoke and an aroma that is pleasing to God.

"They (Nadab and Abihu) each took a censer, put fire in it and laid incense on it and offered unholy fire before the Lord, such as he had not commanded them.[136] And fire came out from the presence of the Lord (i.e.: from the altar) and consumed them, and they died before the Lord. Then Moses said to Aaron, "This is what the Lord meant when he said, 'Through those who are near me I will show myself holy, and before all people I will be glorified.'[137]

---

[136]Jacob Milgrom, Leviticus 1-16: A New Translation with Introduction and Commentary, (The Anchor Bible, v 3), Doubleday, New York, etc., (1991), p. 598 suggests that Nadab and Abihu's sin involved using "unauthorized coals" (es zara) that is, from outside of the temple, to offer their incense.

[137]Milgrom, Ibid., p. 635, refers to four works of Philo of Alexandria (Laws 2. 57-58; Somniis 2. 6-6; De Fuga et Inventione 59; Her. 309) in which Nadab and Abihu are singled out for praise. This first century philosopher/ theologian's works are frequently cited in reference to the use of the term "logos" in John's prologue, suggesting that John knew Philo's works. Milgrom suggests that Jesus' prayer "Father, glorify your name." (John 12: 28) infers that "the glorification of the Lord through the death of Nadab and Abihu may have served as a model (for John) for the crucifixion and resurrection of Jesus."

This passage end with an extraordinarily important assertion: *And Aaron was silent*" (Lv. 10: 1-3).[138] It goes on to say that neither Aaron, nor his other two sons, Eleazar and Ithamar, were permitted to mourn the deaths of their brothers. They were not to dishevel their hair or tear their garments, as was customary as a sign of mourning, nor to leave the Temple or consume wine or strong drink.[139]

"And the Lord spoke to Aaron: Drink no wine or strong drink, neither you nor your sons, when you enter the tent of meeting, that you may not die; it is a statute forever throughout your generations. You are to distinguish between the holy and the common, and between the unclean and the clean; and you are to teach the people of Israel all the statutes that the Lord has spoken to them through Moses" (Lv. 10: 8-11).

Aaron explained to an upset Moses why Aaron, Eleazar, and Ithamar did not eat the priest's portion of the sacrifice on the altar at the time of the deaths of Nadab and Abihu.

"See, today they (Nadab and Abihu) offered their sin offering and their burnt offering before the Lord; and yet such things as these have befallen me (*i.e.: the deaths of my two sons whom I cannot mention because I am not*

---

[138]Milgrom, Ibid., p. 604, suggests that Aaron's silence was due to terror (See Ex. 15: 16) and that his silence contrasts with Lev. 9: 24 "Fire came out from the Lord and consumed the burnt offering and the fat on the altar; and when all the people saw it, they shouted and fell on their faces."

[139]See Nu. 6. re: Nazirite standards: do not cut your hair or drink wine, avoid contact with corpses.

allowed to mourn for them!) If I had eaten the sin offering today, would it have been agreeable to the Lord?   And when Moses heard that, he agreed" (10: 19,20).

Aaron cannot speak because if he opens his mouth to speak, he might mourn the deaths of his two sons, and to mourn in the Temple would defile the holy office of the High Priest. Neither he nor his remaining two sons can eat their portion of the sacrifice because it has been defiled by being in the presence of the two corpses. In other words, the inappropriate actions of two priests have virtually destroyed the Temple and its sacred function. Moses is at first upset, because it appears that the High Priests have failed to provide for the maintenance of the covenant through the prescribed rituals for the sacrifices. Aaron explains that precisely because of the meaning of those sacrifices, neither he nor his sons can eat the holy food (nor, except for this explanation, can Aaron speak).

The silence of Lazarus is a serious sign. It is an indictment against the Temple priests. They are spiritually as dead as he. Their holiness has been defiled by their actions as they stand before God as priests. Their Temple is but a glorified tomb. God is not there. The holy coals glow in the dark, and those who abide in that dark, cold place huddle in vain around them seeking warmth. The Word does not come from them; they are mute.

Lazarus is called forth from this tomb, but when he appears at the gate/ door where the great stone has been moved, his head, hands, and feet remain bound by grave cloths. It remains for the Beloved Disciples, Mary and Martha, his sisters, to remove the outward and visible signs of the death of the priesthood, to take away the grave cloths, the vestments of a dead priesthood.

The violation of the holy role of priest by the Temple priests has bound their heads. That is, their own holiness is shrouded in grave cloths. They cannot speak because their mouths are bound by their lack of holiness. Though they "stand" upon the altar of the Temple, their feet are no longer holy. When they "climb" the Temple steps, they are not coming closer to God. Their hands, too, are bound by their spiritual deaths. The sacrificial rituals they perform, the rites of the sacred festivals of Israel, no longer enable the children of God to reconcile themselves to God.

The Temple priests have defiled themselves and God's Temple by virtue of their subservience to Herod, who, himself, is subservient to the Caesar of Rome. Political alliance, rather than holiness in the sight of God, has become the way to the priesthood. The Temple has been defiled by virtue of the unholy sacrifices being made there. It has become a place of death, rather than a place of reconciliation.

Martha, the Deacon

Jesus has the power to return the priesthood to life. Martha and Mary know it. Each of them testifies of their faith in this truth. Martha says, "Lord, if you had been here, my brother would not have died. But even now I know that God will give you whatever you ask of him" (Jn. 11: 21f).

Martha believes that the priesthood can be restored. Jesus can call it back to life. Jesus affirms that the priesthood can be restored in those who believe in him (i.e.: restored in his disciples) because he is the resurrection and the life. Martha replies that she believes that he is the

Christ, the Son of God, the One coming into the world. This is Martha's confession of faith. She has been examined by Jesus for ordination, and her confession of faith while facing death, his death, and the death of the priesthood as well as the death of her brother priest, qualifies her for ordination with the other disciples.

Martha's identity can now be more clearly seen. She is a sister in the Johannine community, an equal to her brothers and sisters (disciples) in the community. She is a disciple who (by John the Baptist's definition) sees God in Jesus and has testified that Jesus is the Son of God. Jesus has examined her and found her qualified for ordination.

In Jn. 11: 2, Martha's part in the *Habdurah* meal being served for Jesus in Bethany is described in two words: "Martha served." She is a deacon, one who serves at table, like those who had served the wine at the wedding feast (Jn. 2: 5, 9).[140] She delivers the elements of the Eucharist to the disciples, who, like her, are priests in the Temple (church) of Jesus (see Jn. 12: 26).

This sign is a hard one to accept, because our historical minds interrupt us to point out that the Last Supper has not yet occurred. Martha cannot be serving a sacrament that has not yet been established! However, as we have shown above, the historical argument does not discount the validity of this sign. The Gospel of John does not provide a historical record of the words of institution at the Last Supper, but it clearly recognizes and uses the powerful symbols of the eucharistic meal. Jesus provides the wine in Jn. 2: 1-11, the first of his signs, at the

---

[140]See Hermann W. Beyer, "διακονεω , διακονια, διακονοσ," Theological Dictionary of the New Testament, op. cit., vol. II, pp. 81-93.

wedding feast in Cana. Jesus provides the bread and the fish in Jn. 6: 1-14, when he feeds five thousand people with two barley loaves and five fish. In Jn. 15: 1-11; 6: 22-58 during the course of an extensive soliloquies, Jesus speaks words of institution that would be quite appropriate at a Eucharist. "Abide in me as I abide in you. . . . I am the vine, you are the branches" (Jn. 15: 4a, 5a). "Those who eat my flesh and drink my blood abide in me, and I in them" (Jn. 6: 56), and, "I am the living bread that came down from heaven. Whoever eats of this bread will live forever; and the bread that I will give for the life of the world is my flesh" (Jn. 6: 51).

The eternal meaning of the elements of the sacraments is clearly of greater importance in the Gospel than is the form of the liturgy. In Jn. 4: 23, Jesus speaks to another disciple, a woman from Samaria, saying, "The hour is coming and now is here, when the true worshipers will worship the Father in spirit and truth, for the Father seeks such as these to worship him. God is spirit, and those who worship him must worship in spirit and truth." (Jn. 4: 23, 24) The Spirit or spiritual meaning of the Eucharist, that is, the truth conveyed to the seekers who receive it, is what is important -- not the liturgical form.

The omission of the traditional words of institution for the Eucharist is one that qualifies, in Raymond Brown's words, as "terms which John could hardly have omitted accidently."[141] The importance of those words and the traditional formulation they are given in the synoptic gospels will be considered later. For now, it is important to assert that the sacramental meal is not only not missing from the Gospel of John, it is woven throughout the

[141]See note 90.

Gospel, from beginning (the wedding at Cana) to the end (the resurrection appearance by the lake). The absence of an exact copy of the synoptic account does not negate the sign, simple as it is, that Martha was a deacon. She is the ideal model of the servant-disciple.

The Disciples of Jesus: Priests of the New Temple

There were other characters beside Lazarus and Martha at the anointing of Jesus' feet. The pericope in Jn. 11: 55 - 12: 11 does not specifically state that the disciples were present, but their presence is inferred. Barrett[142] points out that εποιησαν (*epoiasan*) "they made" in Jn. 12: 2 has no antecedent. It isn't clear who "they" are. It may be inferred that "they" are the disciples or, with Barrett, it may be inferred that Mary, Martha and Lazarus are hosting (i.e.: "making" the dinner). Judas, in Jn. 12: 4 is identified as "one of his disciples." It would seem unnecessary to make that distinction if other disciples were not present, especially since a further identification is given about him ("the one who was about to betray him.") Jesus, in response to Judas, uses the second person plural in Jn. 12: 8 εχετε μεθ εαυτον (*exete meth eauton*) "you have with you." This may simply be the language of the scripture passage he is quoting (Dt. 12: 11) or it could be a formal way of addressing Judas. However, usually Jesus addresses his disciples ("his own") in the second person singular or by name. The final possibility is that he is addressing all of the disciples who are present, and that seems the most likely case.

---

[142]Barrett, op. cit., p. 411.

While the lack of any names or other descriptions beyond Lazarus, Mary, Martha and Judas leaves the reader uninformed as to the identities of the disciples, gathered at the time of the anointing, the Gospel as a whole has listed a considerable list of persons who qualify by the standards set by John the Baptist (i.e.: that they (1) see Christ in Jesus and (2) witness this truth to others. By those two standards, the disciples are:

* John the Baptist (Jn. 1: 34)
* John's disciples (including the "other disciple" and Andrew) (Jn. 1: 40-42)
* Philip (Jn. 1: 45)
* Nathaniel (Jn. 1: 49) (We learn from Jn. 21: 2 that he is from Cana.)
* Nicodemus (Jn. 3: 1; 7: 50)
* A Samaritan woman (Jn. 4: 25, 29)
* Samaritans (Jn. 4: 39) (an indeterminate number with no other identity)
* A man who sees because of Jesus, though he was born blind (Jn. 9: 31-33)
* A Roman official[143] and his household (Jn. 4: 53, see Jn. 4: 48)
* A man who walks because of Jesus, though he once was lame (Jn. 5: 15)
* Mary of Bethany[144] (Jn. 11: 32)

---

[143]Compare 4: 49 "The official said (to Jesus) 'Sir, come down before my little boy dies.'" with 11: 21 "Martha said to Jesus, 'Lord, if you had been here my brother would not have died.'"

[144]See 19: 25, 26. Clopas is not mentioned anywhere else. Could this Mary be the same Mary as Mary of Bethany? If so, might this not provide direct evidence that Mary is the Beloved Disciple? Given that the writer's perspective is cosmic, not historical, it would seem consistent

* The Beloved Disciple (Jn. 13: 23) AKA "other disciple" (Jn. 1: 37, 40)
* Martha of Bethany (Jn. 11: 21)
* Many Jews AKA Great Crowd of Jews (Jn. 6: 14; 7: 31, 40f; 11: 45; 12: 11, 17)
* Some Greeks (Jn. 12: 21f.)
* Thomas (Jn. 21: 21; 20: 24-29)
* The Sons of Zebedee (Jn. 21: 2)
* Pontius Pilate (Jn. 18: 33, 35, 37, 38; 19: 9, esp. Jn. 19: 19)[145]
* Simon Peter (Jn. 21: 2)

Also of interest is the list of those who are *not* disciples:

* Jesus' brothers (Jn. 7: 5)
* Some of the people of Jerusalem (Jn. 7: 25-27)
* Some Jews (Jn. 11: 46) A.K.A. "the crowd" (Jn. 12: 37f, 34)
* Pharisees (Jn. 9: 16, 28)
* Chief Priests (Jn. 19: 16)

Then there are those who aren't sure:

* The crowd because they do not understand "lifted up" (Jn. 12: 34) and

---

to introduce the mother of Jesus as Mary's sister, because in 19:26 Jesus makes his mother a member of the family of disciples who are led by the Beloved Disciple. Brown, op. cit., suggests that this is the meaning (sign) of this verbal direction by Jesus.

[145]Compare Jn. 19: 9 "(Pilate) entered (the praetorium) again and asked Jesus, 'Where are you from?'" with Jn. 1: 38 "(Two of the disciples of John the Baptist) said (to Jesus) 'Where are you staying?'"

    * Philip (Jn. 14: 8)
    * Thomas (Jn. 14: 5)
    * Judas (not Iscariot) (Jn. 14: 22)

These last three all have doubts, and they all become disciples in spite of their doubts. The questions they ask are similar. Thomas said, "Lord, we do not know where you are going. How can we know the way?" and "Unless I see the mark of the nails in his hands, and put my finger in the mark of the nails and my hand in his side, I will not believe." Philip said, "Lord, show us the Father, and we will be satisfied." Judas (not Iscariot) said, "Lord, how is it that you will reveal yourself to us and not to the world?"

Compare Jesus' response to the discipleship of Thomas (Jn. 20: 29) with his response to the discipleship of Nathaniel (Jn. 1: 50). "Have you (Thomas) believed because you have seen me? Blessed are those who have not seen and yet have come to believe." "Do you (Nathaniel) believe because I told you I saw you under the fig tree? You will see greater things than these." Jesus recognizes and accepts doubt among his disciples.

Perhaps because there are doubters among his disciples, Jesus gives those who walk in darkness, but act as if they know who he is, two chances to change their minds and "see."

"So Judas brought a detachment of soldiers together with police from the Chief Priests and the Pharisees, and they came there with lanterns and torches and weapons (signs of people who walk in darkness). Then Jesus, knowing all that was to happen to him, came forward and asked them, 'Whom do you seek?' They answered, 'Jesus of Nazareth.' Jesus replied, 'I am.' Judas, who betrayed him, was standing with them. When Jesus said to them, 'I am,' they stepped back and fell to the ground (genuflecting!). Again (Jesus) asked them 'Whom do you seek?' And they said, 'Jesus of Nazareth.' Jesus answered, 'I told you that I am, so if you are seeking me, let these men go" (Jn. 18: 3-8).

On the other hand, those who believe and yet deny their belief get three chances to reaffirm that belief.[146] Even after such a reaffirmation, Jesus has to tell Peter twice to "follow me." Notably this has to do with his attitude toward the Beloved Disciple, whose identity as Mary of Bethany lends fresh insight into the nature of the conflict between Jesus and Peter in the closing verses of the Gospel.

The disciples as depicted in the Fourth Gospel were a very mixed group of people. There were many more than twelve. They came from at least four different cultures (Hebrew, Roman, Samaritan, and Greek) and many faced serious consequences for confessing their belief in Jesus. The Jews faced excommunication from the synagogue (9: 34) for their belief. Pilate faced a charge of treason (See Jn. 19: 15). The Samaritan woman faced exile from her faith community (Jn. 4: 20) and Nicodemus faced probable expulsion from the Sanhedrin (Jn. 7: 50f) or even death by stoning (Jn. 8: 59, 10: 31). Compare this last point with Jn. 8: 6b-9, where Jesus challenges those who would condemn a woman accused of adultery.

"Jesus bent down and wrote with his finger on the ground. When they kept on questioning him, he straightened up and said to them, 'Let anyone among you who is without sin be

---

[146]Compare Peter's denials (Jn. 18: 17, 25, 27) with Jesus' reordaining grace (Jn. 21: 15-19)

the first to throw a stone at her.' And once again he bent
down and wrote on the ground. When they heard it, they
went away, one by one, beginning with the elders; and
Jesus was left alone with the woman standing before him.
Jesus stood up and said to her, 'Woman, where are they?
Has no one condemned you? She said, 'No one, sir.'
Jesus said, 'Neither do I condemn you. (absolution) Go
your way (mission language), and from now on do not sin
again (penance).'"

If Jesus was training his disciples to be priests for
the outcasts of the cultures of his time, then his teaching
was as much a model of behavior as it was verbal
instruction, because he provided the services of a priest to
those who were to become priests. Those who followed
Jesus were priests-in-training, and Jesus was the High Priest
who not only trained them to be priests and supervised
them, but modeled true priesthood for them.

Deacons and Elders Among the Disciples

With so many disciples, also called "children of God," was
there any hierarchy in this community? Against Brown and
Culpepper, I would argue that such a hierarchy appears to
have existed, at least in regard to the separation of liturgical
and leadership functions. We have already established that
Martha was a deacon. If the "them" in Jn. 2: 7 refers to
the disciples in Jn. 2: 2 (one of whom may have been
Nathaniel), then there were other disciples who served as
deacons, for they served the wine in Cana at a wedding
party (a wonderful sign of the kind of celebration that
should be held when a new covenant is made as it is in the
Eucharist). Matched with the story of the feeding of the

five thousand in Jn. 6: 1-15, esp. 12, 13, both the bread and the wine of the sacramental meal are represented in the Gospel as being available to huge crowds of people. Deacons were clearly necessary.

So, it would seem, were those authorized to preside in the place of Jesus (Jn. 2: 7, 8; 6: 11) when the meal was served. In the first-century church, such a person was called a πρεσβυτεροσ (*presbyteros*) an elder[147] or an επισκοποσ (*episcopos*) an "overseer" or bishop.[148]

Thomas, the Elder

We have considered what, symbolically, a Temple priest did when a sacrifice was being offered in the Temple. The priest must see and touch the injury to the feet and side of the animal being sacrificed. In the process of separating the parts of the animal for sacrifice, the priest must place

---

[147]See Gunther Bornkamm, "πρεσβυσ, πρεσβυτεροσ, (etc.)," Theological Dictionary of the New Testament, op. cit., vol. VI, pp. 651 - 683. In the Sanhedrin, the lay *presbuteros* were associated with and subordinate to the chief priests and the scribes, who were ordained scholars.

[148]See H. W. Beyer, "επισκεπτομαι, επισκοπεω , επισκοπη, επισκοποσ, αλλοτριεπισκοποσ," Theological Dictionary of the New Testament, op. cit., vol. II, pp. 599- 622. In the New Testament, "This title arises only where there are settled local congregations in which regular acts are performed. For these fixed leaders of congregational life the designations πρεσβυτεροι (*presbuteroi)* or επισκοποι (*episkopoi)*, (και διακονοι) (*and diakonoi*) quickly established themselves. In the first instance . . . the two words πρεσβυτεροι and επισκοποι did not imply any distinction, let alone antithesis (See Acts 20: 28)." "The congregational leaders came into their own when the missionary charismatics either moved on or died. (See Didache 15, 1).

his hand into the side of the animal. Thomas is invited to perform both of these steps on the body of Jesus. "(Jesus) said to Thomas, 'Put your finger here and see my hands. Reach out your hand and put it in my side.'" (Jn. 20: 27)

In the Old Testament the priest who stood before God to preside at the altar was responsible for recognizing the holiness of the sacrifice. In Jn. Jn. 20: 28, responding to Jesus' invitation to touch the broken body of Christ, Thomas says, "My Lord and my God!" He recognized the holiness of the sacrifice of Jesus. Compare this reaction to the holiness of the resurrected Christ with the reaction of Jacob to the holiness of Bethel (Gn. 28: 16-17). Similarly, compare the blessing offered by Jesus to all of the disciples in 20: 19-23 to the priestly benediction that concludes the Nazirite ordination (Nu. 6: 24-26). These similarities point to the identity of the disciples as priests in comparable epiphany stories.

Using the Mosaic *semeia* associated with the ritual of sacrifice, Thomas is identified in John as a priest, an elder authorized by Jesus to administer the elements of the sacrifice of his own body: the Eucharist.

Mary of Bethany: Beloved Disciple and Bishop

The role of the bishop involved the keeping of the tradition, both in maintaining the theological significance of the ritual and in educating the community as to that significance. In the Johannine community, the Beloved Disciple (B.D.) was probably the teacher of tradition, the community's authority on Jesus' teachings and guide in interpreting them.[149]

---

[149]Culpepper, Johannine School, op. cit., p. 267f.

"Discipleship is the primary Christian category for John, and the disciple par excellence is the Disciple whom Jesus loved. But John tells us in Jn. 11: 5 'Now Jesus loved Martha and her sister (Mary) and Lazarus.' The fact that Lazarus is the only male in the Gospel who is named as the object of Jesus' love . . . has led some scholars to identify him as the Beloved Disciple. So it is note-worthy that John would report that Jesus loved Martha and Mary, who seem to have been better known than Lazarus, whereas Lazarus is a peculiarly Johannine character (at least as a historical figure; See Lk. 16: 19-31) who is introduced into the Gospel by being placed in a family relationship to Mary and Martha."[150]

Brown concludes that Lazarus is not the Beloved Disciple, but fails to complete his study in that he did not consider Mary and/or Martha of Bethany for that role. Instead of concluding his book with a chapter focused on such a possibility, Brown provides an appendix with the title, "The Role of Women in the Fourth Gospel"[151] in which he provides ample food for thought to support the thesis that Mary or Martha could have been the Beloved Disciple. However, he does not draw that conclusion. Instead, he asserts his respect for Papal directives regarding the teachings of the Roman Catholic Church and announces that he will not take his scholarship beyond such boundaries.[152]

---

[150]Brown, op. cit., Community of the Beloved Disciple, pp. 191f.

[151]Ibid., pp. 183f.

[152]Ibid., p. 193 n.343. Contrast this with his earlier statement on p. 80, "Orthodoxy, then, is not always the possession of those who try to hold on to the past. One may find truer criterion in the direction toward

Following Brown's rationale, let us begin by suggesting that the Beloved Disciple, the hero of the Johannine community, came from among the followers of John the Baptist.[153] Brown dispenses with the idea that the B.D. was a fictional character because that would mean that "the author of Jn. 21: 20-23 was deceived or deceptive, for he reports distress in the community over the Beloved Disciple's death. The Disciple was idealized, of course; but the fact that he (sic) was a historical person and a companion of Jesus becomes all the more obvious in the new approaches to Johannine ecclesiology."[154]

The question of the historicity of the person who plays the role of the Beloved Disciple in the Gospel is of less concern than the symbolic meaning of that role and what it communicates to the reader who has the eyes to see that meaning. Brown correctly draws a connection between the high Christology of the Gospel, as revealed in the Prologue, and the role of the Beloved Disciple. That is why, from a literary point of view, the relationship of the mysterious "other disciple" (not Andrew) identified in Jn. 1: 35-42 is important.

"John the Baptist is the only one in the first chapter to understand Jesus by Johannine standards, since he does not use of Jesus the traditional titles of early Christian

---

which Christian thought has been trending, even if that direction suggests that past formulations of truth have to be considered inadequate to answer new questions."

[153]Ibid., p. 31, also see pp. 29f.

[154]Ibid. Brown assumes that the B.D. must be a man. Jn. 21: 20-23 and several other passages use the male pronoun when referring to the B.D. This study will address itself to this problem later.

preaching, as do the disciples, but acknowledges Jesus' pre-existence (Jn. 1: 15, 30). "[155]

    This "other disciple" is a disciple before Peter, both in terms of the chronological order of the beginning of their relationships with Jesus and in terms of their ability to perceive the true identity of Jesus. The Gospel is written from the point of view of this "superior" relationship, consistent with one who "oversees" the spiritual formation of disciples. This "other disciple" does not begin with such an exalted identity. Rather, this identity develops as the disciple herself develops, as her eyes open wider and she begins to see more and more clearly.[156]
    The Gospel contrasts this clearer insight and higher point of view to that of the leader of the apostolic community, Peter. Each time this contrast is made, the role of the Beloved Disciple is shown to be superior to that of Peter, the relationship more intimate.

(It is) "no accident that the Beloved Disciple makes his appearance by name only in the hour (Jn. 13: 1) when Jesus, having loved his own, now showed his love for them to the very end. This does not mean that this Disciple was not present during the ministry, but that he achieved his *identity* in a Christological context. During his lifetime, whether in the period of Jesus' ministry or in the post-resurrectional period, the Beloved Disciple lived through

---

[155]Ibid.

[156]Ibid., p. 33, See R.A. Culpepper, op. cit., Johannine School, p. 265 "The actual founder of the Johannine school is more likely to be found in the figure of the Beloved Disciple . . . the role of the B.D. is the key to the character of the community."

the same growth in Christological perception that the
Johannine community went through, and it was this growth
that made it possible for the community to identify him as
the one whom Jesus particularly loved."[157]

Brown adopts the identifiers of the Beloved Disciple
listed by Oscar Cullman:[158] (1)He is a former disciple of
John the Baptist. (2)He began to follow Jesus in Judea
when Jesus himself was in close proximity to the Baptist.
(3)He shared the life of his master during Jesus' last stay in
Jerusalem. (4)He was known to the High Priest. (5)His
connection with Jesus was different from that of Peter, the
representative of the twelve.

The first two of Cullman's identifiers have already
been established by Brown. What remains is to prove that
a woman or women in general, could have been followers,
even disciples, of John the Baptist. The language of the
Prologue offers a view of his ministry.

"There was a man sent from God, whose name was John.
He came as a witness to testify to the light, so that all might
believe through him. . . . The true light, which enlightens
everyone was coming into the world. . . . But to all who
received him, who believed in his name, he gave power to
become children of God, who were born, not of blood or
the will of the flesh or of the will of man, but of God." (Jn.
1: 6, 7, 9, 12)

[157]Ibid.

[158]Oscar Cullman, The Johannine Circle, Westminster Press,
Philadelphia, (1976), p. 87, is quoted by Brown, Ibid, pp. 33-34.

The language referring to those to whom John the Baptist addressed his witness is inclusive language, written at a time when few, if any, authors were sensitive the the need for it. Except for the phrase "will of man," which is arguably a generic term, all of the the language from this passage seems carefully chosen to communicate a universal thought. These references are made in order to make the point that the followers of the light were not male or female exclusively. This may have been the attitude of John the Baptist and his disciples or of the Johannine community.

If one accepts the contention that the "other disciple" in Jn. 1: 35f was a woman, accompanied by Andrew, then it is not too far a leap to consider the possibility that this woman could have been Mary or Martha of Bethany. We have already noted the connection between Mary and Martha and the symbolic location: Bethany. The setting for the movement of the two disciples of John the Baptist toward Jesus in Jn. 1: 35f can be found at Jn. 1: 28. "This took place in Bethany across the Jordan where John was baptizing." There is, at least, no indication that women were *excluded* from John's baptisms.

Cullman's third identifier also points to Mary and Martha. Jn. 11: 55 - 12: 8 is set in Bethany, and Mary and Martha are named as participants in the anointing that occurred there. Mary and Martha qualify as disciples who "shared the life of (their) master during Jesus' last stay in Jerusalem." Martha's role as a deacon may be seen in the extra-ordinary liturgy that takes place in Bethany. Mary's role is shown to be quite significant. She is anointing the new altar, the feet of Jesus. She is functioning as a priest. Indeed, she is fulfilling a role established for priests first by a partriarch: Jacob, and by Moses.[159]

Mary of Bethany as a Nazirite

Consider the insights that arise by placing Mary of Bethany in the spotlight offered by Cullman's fourth identifier, namely, that the Beloved Disciple was known to the High Priest. The Gospel makes it clear that Judas was known to the Chief Priests, because he led some of their servants and temple guards to where they could arrest Jesus (Jn. 18: 3, 10). Why, other than for Judas' purpose (betrayal), would a disciple of Jesus be known to the High Priest? One possible explanation could be that this disciple was a Nazirite.[160]

Let us look carefully at the mysterious behavior that describes some of the activities of the Beloved Disciple during the night after Jesus was betrayed.

---

[159]The language used in the Johannine epistles is very similar to that used in the Gospel According to John. There are several hints as to the identity of the Beloved Disciple in these short letters. We have already considered 2Jn. 1 "The elder to the elect lady and her children . . ." Look as well at 2Jn. 13 "The children of your elect sister . . ." Both may refer to the leader of the Johannine community, a woman. The repetitious use of the word "beloved" as a salutation (1Jn. 2: 7; 4: 1, 7; 3Jn. 2, 5, 11) used interchangeably with the salutation "children" sounds very much like a mother figure, a female head of the community.

[160]The Greek term "Nazarios" is variously translated "Nazirite" and "Nazarene." A Nazarene hails from the area of Nazareth. A Nazirite, as has been explained, was a holy person. Later we will consider a curse used extensively in first-century Jewish benedictions that was addressed to the "Nazarios" which is how they identified Jews who were followers of Jesus. Could it be that Jesus and his disciples all considered themselves to be Nazirites? Could that explain why later Jewish authorities called Christians "Nazarios?"

"Simon Peter and another disciple followed Jesus. Since that disciple was known to the High Priest, he went with Jesus into the courtyard of the High Priest, but Peter was standing outside at the gate. so the other disciple, who was known to the High Priest, went out, spoke to the woman who guarded the gate, and brought Peter in (Jn. 18: 15-16)."

Twice the narrator tells the reader that "another disciple" or "the other disciple" was known to the High Priest. Access to this "courtyard" suggests that a level of trust and respect existed between them, providing access for this disciple and for Peter to the High Priest's domain. The "other disciple" is apparently recognized by the female gate keeper and allowed to enter without question, while even with the Beloved Disciple's intercession, Peter is questioned before he is admitted. "The woman said to Peter, 'You are not also one of this man's disciples are you?' He said, 'I am not'"(Jn. 18: 17).

The language in this exchange is fascinating. "You are not *also* one of this man's disciples . . ." implies that at least one other person, known by the gate keeper to be a disciple, has passed through the gate. Does this imply that the "other disciple" actually acknowledged her relationship to Jesus when seeking entrance to the High Priest's courtyard? Does it infer that she was admitted in spite of that relationship because the relationship with the High Priest was sufficiently important to overlook such an extraordinary confession? What could that relationship have been? I suggest that the "other disciple" could have been a Nazirite, even a Nazirite scheduled to complete her vow. The setting, as we have seen, is not the courtyard of an official's residence, but the Court of the Women in the temple itself. The gate being guarded by this female gate keeper could be either the Beautiful Gate or the Nicanor Gate. The High Priest would be holding court inside the Nicanor gate, the location wherein the Council of the Sanhedrin was usually convened, and the place before God where the Nazirite vow must be completed.

Why does the narrator not identify this location as the Temple? The high Christology of the Gospel has, by this time, established that Jesus *is* the Temple. The place where the High Priest abides is a dark and cold place, a tomb, a place of death.

"Now the slaves and the police had made a charcoal fire because it was cold, and they were standing around it and warming themselves. Peter also was standing with them and warming himself." (Jn. 18: 18)

In the narrative world of the Fourth Gospel whenever the word "stand" is used in the context of the temple, the one who does the standing is being identified as a priest.[161] In the LXX God stands at Horeb (Ex. 17: 6); Abraham stands before God (Gn. 18: 22; 19: 27); Moses and the Lord stand together (Ex. 34: 5); the congregation of Israel stands before God when Aaron's priesthood is inaugurated (Lv. 9: 5).

In John, Jesus stands in the Temple (Jn. 7: 37); John the Baptist recognizes Jesus standing (1: 26); John the Baptist stands before Jesus (Jn. 1: 35; 3: 29); many Jews (priests) stand in the Temple (Jn. 11: 56); Judas stands with the Jews (Jn. 18: 5); Peter stands with the Jews (Jn. 18:

---

[161]See Walter Grundmann, "στηκω , ιστημι," Theological Dictionary of the New Testament, vol. VII, pp. 636-653.

18); three Marys stand before the cross (Jn. 19: 25); Mary
Magdalene stands before the resurrected Jesus (Jn. 20: 11,
14); the resurrected Jesus stands among his disciples (Jn.
20: 19; 21: 4).

To "stand" with another priest, is to participate in
the ritual and share in the holiness (or lack thereof) of that
priest. For Peter to "stand" with the "slaves and the
police," of the High Priest, places him, symbolically in the
same relationship to Jesus as Judas was in the garden of
Gethsemane, when he (Judas) "was standing with them
(soldiers and police from the Chief Priests)." Peter, at this
moment, abides in darkness. He stands with the High
Priest's people, seeking warmth from a charcoal fire that
cannot provide warmth. It is here that Peter twice more
denies that he even knows Jesus. He separates himself
from "I am" by stating emphatically, "I am not."

Where is the "other disciple?" "Since that disciple
was known to the High Priest, he went with Jesus into the
courtyard of the High Priest"(Jn. 18: 15). This disciple
was with Jesus, at the side of Jesus, standing with Jesus,
abiding with Jesus. Unlike the Synoptic Gospels, this
Gospel does not say that all of the disciples abandoned
Jesus in the last hour. This one says that one disciple, the
Beloved Disciple, remained with him to the very end. In
this passage, it says that the "other disciple" went into "the
courtyard of the High Priest" with Jesus. The Court of the
Priests, near the sacrificial altar, is where they went.

Could the Beloved Disciple Have Been a Woman?

The other Gospels say that "some women who had come with (Jesus) from Galilee"[162] remained with Jesus at the cross. Jn. 19: 25-27 offers some of the identities of these otherwise anonymous women. That fact, alone, suggests that the writer of the Gospel held individual women, and women in general, in higher esteem than did any of the authors of the Synoptic Gospels.

"Meanwhile, standing near the cross of Jesus were his mother, and his mother's sister, Mary the wife of Clopas, and Mary Magdalene. When Jesus saw his mother and the disciple whom he loved standing beside her, he said to his mother, 'Woman, here is your son.' Then he said to the disciple, 'Here is your mother.' And from that hour the disciple took her into his own home."

Even the Gospel According to John establishes first of all that those who were "standing near the cross of Jesus" (i.e.: in the position of priests standing before the altar) were his mother and his mother's sister, Mary the wife of Clopas, and Mary Magdalene. We might debate whether the phrase "his mother's sister, Mary the wife of Clopas" suggests one woman or two, but clearly all who are named are women, women named "Mary." There is a mention of a man named Cleopas in Lk. 24: 18, but no other mention of anyone named "Clopas," nor of his wife in any of the Gospels. No name is given to "his mother's sister," (unless it is Mary the wife of Clopas) and we are not told whether this sister is a biological sister, Jesus'

---

[162]See Matt. 27: 55-56; Mark 15: 40; Luke 23: 27-31, 55-56.

biological aunt, or whether this "sister" is a close friend to Mary, the mother of Jesus. What follows provides reason to believe that this latter identity could be identifying Mary of Bethany. It tells us two things: that the Beloved Disciple was present, and that Mary, the mother of Jesus, became one of that disciples' "own."

"When Jesus saw his mother and the disciple whom he loved standing beside her..." would seem inconsistent if "the disciple whom Jesus loved" were not a woman, since only women have been listed. Yet there are the words of Jesus to his mother, "Woman, here is your son." More than one scholar has looked at this passage and quickly concluded that the Beloved Disciple must be a man, because Jesus is telling his mother to look upon that disciple as her son. There is another way to hear these words.

When Jesus says, "Woman, here is your son," he is clearly addressing his mother, as he has before, using that same term "Woman" in Jn. 2: 4. If we consider that all who were standing before him were women, who, then, is he referring to as her son? Was Jesus referring to the Beloved Disciple or to himself? Could he be saying to his mother, "Woman, here (on this cross) is your son." Why would he say such an obvious thing? He *is* her son.

The code book for this entire Gospel is the Pentateuch. At the very beginning of the Pentateuch (Gn. 3: 15), God addresses the serpent, who has tempted the woman (who is not named Eve until later -- Gn. 3: 20). God says to the serpent, "I will put enmity between you and the woman, and between your offspring and hers; and he will strike your head, and you will strike his heel."

Once again the symbolism of head/hand/foot emerges. From the Johannine theological perspective, Gn. 3: 15 would be appropriately interpreted to be an oracle meaning that the offspring of Woman would strike against the holiness (the head) of the Serpent, represented by the temple leaders, "the Jews," while those same offspring of the Serpent would strike against the temporal life (the heel) of the truely holy one, Jesus. Put more simply, the son of Woman will strike a deadly blow to those who falsely claim holiness, while those who falsely claim holiness will strike out at the temporal life of Woman's offspring (her son).

The mother of Jesus is treated in this Gospel as the archetype Woman, not as a particular woman. She is invited to behold her son, who, though a blow has been struck against his heel (his incarnation), has ended the life of those who falsely claim to be holy. The Evangelist offers three incidents in which heads are assaulted. In Jn. 18: 10 Peter draws a sword and strikes at one of the high priest's slaves, cutting off his ear. In Jn. 18: 22 one of the temple police strikes Jesus on the face, apparently believing that Jesus has insulted the High Priest's holiness. Then in Jn. 19: 2 the crown of thorns is thrust down upon Jesus' head. The battle for holiness is fought on the heads of representative persons.

The next sentence is often translated to mean that the Beloved Disciple took the mother of Jesus to "his home." Jesus, identifying himself as "the good shepherd" in Jn. 10: 1f, uses the expression "take unto his own," meaning that a shepherd takes sheep under his care; they become "his" even though he doesn't "own" them or "take them home."[163] Use of this language suggests that the Beloved Disciple understood what Jesus intended: that Mary become one of that disciples' "own," part of *her* (Mary of Bethany's) flock.

---

[163]See Jn. 10: 13; 13: 1; 15: 19.

There is another passage that some scholars have cited in their conclusion that the Beloved Disciple could not have been a woman. Charlesworth, for example, builds much of his thesis contending that Thomas is the Beloved Disciple on this passage.

In Jn. 21, which many scholars consider an appendage to the original Gospel, some disciples, including Simon Peter, Thomas called the Twin, Nathanael of Cana in Galilee, the sons of Zebedee, and two others, went fishing on the Sea of Tiberias, but they didn't catch anything. Jesus appears, instructs them to cast their nets on the other side of the boat and they catch more fish than they can haul into the boat. No women are mentioned in the list of disciples on the fishing party, unless one were to consider that either or both of the un-named "two others" might be women. It seems unlikely that women of that time would have climbed into the fishing boat with at least five men to do what was traditionally a male activity, especially when one considers that apparently Peter stripped himself naked to do the work. Peter was clearly uncomfortable in the presence of the Beloved Disciple (Jn. 21: 20-22). It hardly seems likely that Peter would strip naked in the presence of a female disciple. These rationales are enough to convince most scholars that no females were present at this event. The Beloved Disciple, however, was present, informing Peter that the one standing on the shore was the Lord (Jn. 21: 7).

Note, however, what Peter does when that message is given to him. First, he puts his clothes back on, then jumps into the water and wades the hundred yards to shore. Now it could be that Peter got dressed out of respect for the Lord, or it could be that there is a symbolic meaning behind the fact that he had dis-robed as Jesus did at the foot washing, thereby removing the symbol of his identity as a disciple.   Perhaps upon realizing that he was in the presence of the resurrected Lord he chose to re-assume his role as a disciple.

Could it not also be that Peter got dressed because the Beloved Disciple was present, not in the boat, but on the shore? The Beloved Disciple or "the other disciple" or "the disciple whom Jesus loved" is always found in the presence of Jesus.   Could it not be that the Beloved Disciple is on the shore with Jesus?

Consider the form of address that Jesus uses to speak to the disciples in the boat. "Children, you have no fish, have you?" This same appelation is used only in the Johannine epistles (1Jn. 2: 1, 18; 3: 2, 18; 2Jn.: 4, 13; 3Jn.: 4). Jesus does not use it in any other passage either in John or any of the synoptic gospels. It is in the prologue (Jn. 1: 12), but not as a quotation of Jesus. Does this not sound like the language of the Beloved Disciple?   In Jn. 11: 28 Martha announces to Mary of Bethany that "The Teacher is here and is calling for you." There is no record of Jesus asking Martha to convey that message, yet Martha, as a disciple, calls Mary to discipleship just as Andrew called Peter, and just as Philip called Nathanael. Was Jesus actually calling these people? They each heard his voice when someone else called them to him. Is it possible that the Beloved Disciple was actually the one who suggested that the fishermen cast their nets on the other side of the boat? Is it possible that the Beloved Disciple, when Peter and the other disciples still didn't understand that the resurrected Christ was speaking through her, was compelled to give them a little hint (Jn. 21: 7)?

The other disciples joined Peter and Jesus on shore at the charcoal fire where fish and bread had been prepared.

The charcoal fire is an important *semeion* representing true worship, and fish and bread were the elements of the meal that fed five thousand people. This was a Eucharist. Jesus says to them, "Come and have breakfast." In Jn. 1: 28 Jesus invites the two disciples of John the Baptist (Nathaniel and, I suggest, the Beloved Disciple, Mary of Bethany) to "Come and see." He was responding to their inquirey about where he lived. At this point, after the resurrection, Jesus abides in the Beloved Disciple and shares in the fellowship of disciples through the Eucharist. For the disciples to be invited to "come and have breakfast" was to be invited into the presence of the resurrected Jesus.

"Now none of the disciples dared to ask him, 'Who are you?' because they knew it was the Lord" (Jn. 21: 12b). Compare that with the reaction of the disciples in Jn. 4: 27. "Just then the disciples came. They were astonished that he was speaking with a woman, but no one said, 'What do you want?' or 'Why are you speaking with her?'" This Samaritan woman then brings other Samaritans to Jesus, to become his disciples. Could it be that the Beloved Disciple, Mary of Bethany, a woman, had followed the other disciples to the Sea of Tiberias, called instructions to them from the shore, then served them the Eucharist once they reached the shore, and they dared not ask who she was, because they knew it was the Lord, who was actually speaking to them *through her*?

What happens next is even more extraordinary. Jesus Christ re-ordains Peter. We will see that when she is ordained in 12: 8, Jesus authorizes Mary to "keep the tradition of my death." As keeper of the Jesus tradition, she has the authority to re-instate Peter to the role which he abandoned in the courtyard while Jesus was under trial (Jn. 18: 17, 25, 27). By posing questions in what we have learned to recognize as the Beloved Disciple's language, she in whom Christ abides asks him three times, "Peter, do you love me?" After each affirmative response, Peter is raised to another level of responsibility among the disciple/priests of Jesus. First, instructed to "feed my lambs," he is a servant, a deacon. He will carry *The Meal* to the children of God. Then as one who "feeds my sheep" he becomes an elder who is authorized to celebrate the Eucharist. Finally, as one who "tends my sheep" he becomes a bishop, overseeing the other disciples.

Peter has been ordained by the resurrected Christ, who was abiding in the Beloved Disciple at that moment in historical time. Now Peter turns to question the Christ he sees so clearly about the one he had seen before when he looked at Mary of Bethany, the one who is always following Jesus. "Lord, what about him?" Jesus says, pointedly, to Peter, "If it is my will that he remain until I come, what is that to you? Follow me!" Peter had difficulties with the idea that Mary of Bethany was a disciple, but Jesus did not have such difficulty. He intended that Peter would follow his example and accept her.[164]

Could the Beloved Disciple have been a woman? Could this female disciple have taken her "sister" Mary, the mother of Jesus, into her own community? Could a woman have prepared a meal for a group of tired fishermen, called to them from the shore and served them communion? Could Peter have been instructed by the resurrected Christ, abiding in Mary of Bethany, to accept her? I think that the Gospel says yes to all of these.

---

[164]We will consider the problem of the male pronouns in this passage and others later.

Remember that the model for the sacrifice of atonement was that *two* goats were brought before the Lord. One was sacrificed on the altar; the other was *cast out* of the camp. In the ritual of the consecration of a Nazirite vow, the sacrifice that parallels the rite of atonement provides that one of these two animals is a *female*. Could the Beloved Disciple have been *the scapegoat*? Wasn't Miriam?

The Meaning of the Name Sign: Mary

It is no accident that all of the women who are named as being at the feet of Jesus when he is on the cross are named Mary. Just as Woman is an archetype, so is Mary. The role of Mary, viewed from a cosmic perspective, is set, once again, in the Pentateuch.

In Nu. 12, Aaron and his sister, Miriam,[165] are set apart by God because they have dared to question the authority of Moses to speak for God. Motivated, it would seem, by jealousy because Moses has married a Cushite (Ethiopian?) woman, Aaron and Miriam say, "Has the Lord spoken only through Moses? Has he not spoken through us also?" (Nu. 12: 2). God hears this and calls Moses, Aaron and Miriam to the Tent of Meeting.

"Then the Lord came down and stood at the entrance of the tent and called Aaron and Miriam; and they both came forward. And he said to them, 'Hear my words: When there are prophets among you, I the Lord make myself

---

[165] In Greek, *Mariam*, also *Maria*. See E.P. Blair, "Mary," The Interpreter's Dictionary of the Bible: An Illustrated Encyclopedia, Abingdon Press, Nashville-New York, vol. 3., (1962), p. 288f.

known to them in visions; I speak to them in dreams. Not so with my servant Moses; he is entrusted with all my house. With him I speak face to face -- clearly, not in riddles; and he beholds the form of the Lord" (Nu. 12: 5-8a).

Aaron and Miriam appear to understand themselves as equals to each other and together as equals to Moses, their brother. This understanding is corrected by God, who makes it clear that Moses has a direct, face-to-face relationship with God, not like prophets whose understanding comes through dreams and *ainigmaton*, riddles, enigmas, the forms in which prophesies and oracles are given.[166]

In Ex. 15: 20 Miriam is "the prophet Miriam, Aaron's sister." As a prophet, she is an equal to Aaron. Aaron receives revelations from Moses (who receives them directly from God); it follows from Nu. 12: 5-8a that Miriam receives and professes her knowledge of God in the form of *ainigma*, oracles (though there is no record of her prophesies or oracles).

What is significant about this passage is not just that Miriam is an equal to Aaron or that she speaks through oracles. What is significant is that the jealousy that she and Aaron shared results in what appears to be a severe penalty, visited upon her alone by God.

---

[166]See Gerhard Kittel, "αινιγμα," Theological Dictionary of the New Testament, op. cit., vol. I, p. 178. "Since the mysterious elements in religious utterances can also be interpreted and understood as riddles, there is a material link between the concept and oracular or prophetic pronouncement... Among both Greeks and Jews, the essence of prophetic utterance is thus speaking in riddles in the sense of saying things which require elucidation."

"And the anger of the Lord was kindled against them, and he departed. When the cloud went away from over the tent, Miriam had become leprous, as white as snow. And Aaron turned towards Miriam and saw that she was leprous. Then Aaron said to Moses, 'Oh, my Lord, do not punish us (Hebrew: do not lay sin upon us) for a sin that we have so foolishly committed. Do not let her be like one stillborn, whose flesh is half consumed when it comes out of its mother's womb.' And Moses cried to the Lord, 'O God, please heal her.'" (Nu. 12: 9-13)

Aaron does as a High Priest should do: he speaks for himself and Miriam. He seeks atonement for her sin and for his own. He pleads with Moses not to "lay sin upon us." Perhaps by addressing himself to Moses instead of God, Aaron is acknowledging that the relationship between Moses and God is, after all, greater than, not equal to, his own relationship with God. Aaron interprets Miriam's leprosy as a sign that she is "like one stillborn." Could this be a vague reference to a priesthood that has only just begun? Moses speaks directly to God in a straight-forward way, pleading for Miriam's healing. God hears these prayers, and exiles Miriam from the camp for seven days, using an odd rationale.

"But the Lord said to Moses, 'If her father had but spit in her face, would she not bear her shame for seven days? Let her be shut out of the camp for seven days, and after that she may be brought in again.' So Miriam was shut out of the camp for seven days; and the people did not set out on the march until Miriam had been brought in again." (Nu. 12: 14-15)

This account is easily interpreted as a curse of God against Miriam for having dared to consider herself equal to Moses. Yet Aaron is not cursed, and he committed the same offense. On closer examination, several things come to light. First, notice that Aaron's appeal is to Moses, not to God, and that it is that Moses not "lay sin upon us" (translated as "punish us"). Who has sinned? Is Aaron pleading with his brother to tell God not to hold him and his sister responsible for their jealousy? Or is he imploring with his brother not to sin by using the power that God has given to Moses against their sister? If the latter is the correct understanding of this passage, then is Aaron not successful when Moses pleads directly with God to heal Miriam?

If we assume, as most readers do, that Miriam has sinned, and the leprosy is her punishment for that sin, then why must she be exiled as well? What is the meaning of the reference to her father spitting in her face? Perhaps we could say that God is agreeing to withdraw the punishment, but slowly, so that Miriam will suffer. Is this divine justice?

Consider this passage another way. Consider the possibility that it is Moses who is sinning. Remember that God grants to Moses the power to place his hand inside of his bosom and withdraw it again "white as snow" with leprosy (Ex. 4: 6-8). Is it this power that Aaron entreats Moses not to use? If so, then God's reply to Moses' urgent appeal for Miriam's healing makes more sense. Miriam can be healed from this sin which has been laid upon her, but Moses must understand that he cannot simply impose and then withdraw such powerful signs at a whim. She must at least go through the same rite of purification that would be required if her father (or, it might be said, her brother) had spit on her!   Moses has offended her, his protector since infancy.   It would seem more appropriate that he be purified, yet Miriam's role, even when Moses was an infant, was to "(stand) at a distance and see what would happen to him" (Ex. 2: 4).   Nothing more is recorded about Miriam until she dies and is buried (Nu. 20: 1).   In John's Gospel, she returns as Mary.

Earlier in the Septuagint, as we have seen, Aaron suffers vicariously in silence because his two sons have died as a consequence of their sins.   In this passage from Numbers Aaron, Moses and the entire community suffer vicariously because Miriam has been sent "out of the camp."   The community does not move without her. Miriam must return before the children of God can proceed to fulfill God's plan of salvation.   Miriam's exile is for seven days.   Mary of Bethany is completing a seven-day period of purification as our study begins.   She is returning to her own, no longer exiled as a consequence of the sin of Moses' abuse of divinely granted power, returning as a priest, an equal to Aaron.

The Rite of Purification

The seven-day period of purification is required of anyone who is cleansed of leprosy.   According to Lv. 14: 1-32, this ritual must take place outside of the camp.   The priest makes an examination of the formerly diseased person.   If the disease is healed, then two clean living birds are brought out to the cleansing site.   One of them is slaughtered over fresh water in an earthen vessel.   Then the other bird, along with some cedarwood and crimson yarn and a branch of hyssop,[167] is dipped in the first bird's blood. Then the one who is to be cleansed is sprinkled seven times with this blood and pronounced clean. The living bird is released, and the one being cleansed shaves off all of his (or her) hair, bathes and returns to the camp, living outside of her (or his) tent for seven days. On the seventh day she /he again shaves all of her/his hair, washes his/her clothes, and bathes.

On the eighth day, the one who has been purified takes two male lambs without blemish and one ewe yearling lamb without blemish, and a grain offering of choice flour mixed with oil, and a log of oil to the priest, who brings him to stand with his offerings before the Lord at the entrance to the Tent of Meeting. One lamb is offered, along with the oil, as a guilt offering by the priest and raised as an elevation offering before the Lord. This lamb and oil are the priest's portion.

The priest takes some of the blood from this offering and puts it on the lobe of the right ear of the one being cleansed, and on that person's right thumb and right big toe. (i.e.: head, hand, and foot.) The priest pours some of the oil into his own left hand, dips his right finger into that oil and sprinkles it seven times before the Lord (i.e.: on the altar). Then the priest puts some of that oil on the lobe of the right ear, the thumb of the right hand, and the big toe of the right foot, on top of the blood of the guilt offering. The rest of the oil in the priest's palm is then placed on the (bald) head of the one being cleansed. Next, to make atonement for the cleansed one's sins, the priest offers a sin offering, a burnt offering and a grain offering

---

[167]See Jn. 19: 29; Ex. 12: 22 Jesus' sacrifice is the gateway (door) to salvation.

on the altar. Provisions are made for the possibility that the one to be cleansed may not be able to afford such expensive offerings: two turtledoves or pigeons may be substituted for one male lamb and the ewe lamb, but there still must be at least one lamb for a guilt offering, and the liturgy must follow the same procedure.

This ritual is almost identical to the ritual for the ordination of a High Priest and the completion of a Nazirite vow. The Nazirite's earlobe, thumb, and toe are not anointed like the High Priest's, and the High Priest is not required to shave off all of his hair, like the Nazirite. Otherwise, the rituals are nearly identical and quite extraordinary and expensive.

If, in the narrative world of the Gospel of John, Mary of Bethany represents Miriam, who has been exiled from the camp, then she must go through this prescribed ritual in order to return to the camp. Mary completes Miriam's archetypal role, going through a rite very similar to the Nazirite ritual and the High Priest's ordination ritual, to return to the camp.

Mary of Bethany was known to the High Priest because she was a Nazirite, ready to complete her vow on the night before Passover. She had completed a period of purification and was expected at the Temple, where the High Priest would perform the ritual.

The Beloved Disciple and Jesus

Cullman's fifth identifier is that the Beloved Disciple's connection with Jesus was different from that of Peter, the leader of the twelve. In the narrative world of the Gospel of John, Peter represented the apostolic church, the orthodox Christian community of the first-century. The

Gospel of John is a subversive Gospel which tells a truth that could not be told in an orthodox way in the first-century. Brown elaborates on Cullman's fifth criteria.

"In five of the six passages where he is mentioned, the Beloved Disciple is explicitly contrasted with Peter: (1) in Jn. 13: 23-26, the Beloved Disciple rests on Jesus' chest, while Peter has to signal to him for information; (2) in Jn. 18: 15-16, the Beloved Disciple can accompany Jesus into the High Priest's palace, while Peter cannot enter without his help. In Jn. 18: 15 John speaks simply of αλλοσ (*allos*) another disciple without further identification, while ο αλλοσ (*ho allos*) the other disciple of Jn. 20: 2 is specifically identified as the Beloved Disciple. (3) in Jn. 20: 2-10, the Beloved Disciple outruns Peter to the tomb, and only he is said to believe on the basis of what he sees there; (4) in Jn. 21: 7, the Beloved Disciple recognizes Jesus standing on the shore of the Sea of Tiberias and tells Peter who it is; (5) in Jn. 21: 20-23, when Peter jealously inquires about the Beloved Disciple's fate, he is told by Jesus, "Suppose I would like him to remain until I come, how does that concern you?"[168]

Each of these five points contains the kernel of a valuable argument that favors the thesis of this study, though that was not Brown's original intention.[169]

---

[168] Raymond E. Brown, The Community of the Beloved Disciple, Op. cit, pp. 82-83. (parenthetical Greek alliteration is mine.) Brown notes "That 18: 15 also refers to the Beloved Disciple is convincingly shown by F. Neirynck, ETL 51 (1975), pp. 115-51." Brown assumes that the B.D. is a man referred to as "he."

[169] Confirmed through personal correspondence.

(1) The reference in Jn. 13: 23-26 uses language εν
τω κολπω (*en to kolpo*) "in his bosom" to describe the
relationship between the Beloved Disciple and Jesus.[170] The
same expression is used to describe the relationship between
Jesus and the Father in Jn. 1: 18. "God no one has seen at
any time; the only begotten Son, who is in the bosom of the
Father, he declared (him)."[171]

Meyer[172] suggests essentially two meanings for the
term "in his bosom" may be found in the LXX. In Dt.
13: 6; 28: 54, 56 it refers to the intimacy between a
husband and a wife. In Gn. 16: 5, it is used to describe
the intimacy into which Sarah gave her maidservant,
Hagar, to Abraham. In Nu. 11: 12, Moses asks God, "Did
I conceive all this people (Israel)? Did I give birth to them,
that you should say to me, 'Carry them in your bosom, as
a nurse carries a suckling child,' . . ."

The term is used here to describe a close family-like
intimacy, the intimacy between a husband and a wife (or
surrogate wife) and a husband. The figurative use of the
term by Moses to describe his relationship with the people
of Israel suggests that Moses is challenging God by
suggesting that such a close relationship should not exist

---

[170]See Luke 16: 19-31, esp. vss. 22-23. Lazarus is carried away
by angels "into the bosom of Abraham."

[171]Lit. trans. fr. George Ricker Berry, Ph.D., The Interlinear Literal
Translation of the Greek New Testament, Zondervan, Grand Rapids, (1977 -
19th Printing), p. 241.

[172]Rudolf Meyer, "κολποσ," Theological Dictionary of the New
Testament, op. cit., vol. III, pp. 824-826. Meyer lists Greek references to (a)
"lap," "mother's womb - motherly love," "at a meal, the guest of honor,
hence fig. to express an inward relationship." "The κολποσ (*kolpos*) of
mother earth is the grave. (b) the "fold" of a loose garment used as a pocket;
it can also be used to hide things . . ."

between Moses and God's people; that such a relationship rightfully is between God and Israel.

As we have seen, In Ex 4: 6, God answers Moses concerning the possibility that the people of Israel will not believe that God has sent Moses to them by instructing Moses, "Put thine hand into thy bosom; and he put his hand into his bosom, and his hand became as snow."[173] Meyer suggests that "into thy bosom" refers to a fold in the clothing of Moses. It means much more.

Symbolically, Moses is instructed to insert his own hand into his own body. This is the gesture of a priest, inserting his hand into the sacrifice. That his hand emerges from his bosom "as snow," is usually interpreted to mean that his hand becomes leprous, and this is clearly understood to be a sign of God's close relationship with Moses. Later God instructs Moses to replace his hand into his bosom, then to withdraw it, and it is healthy.

This same pattern is used with Miriam. She becomes "as snow" and is required to leave the camp (i.e.: withdraw from the bosom of Israel). After a period of seven days for purification, she is allowed to return to the camp (the bosom of Israel) and she is whole.

The use of the phrase *en to kolpo* (in his bosom) in Jn. 13: 23-26 identifies the Beloved Disciple in terms usually reserved for a level of intimacy shared only between a husband and a wife or at least by a parent for a child. When applied to Jesus in Jn. 1: 18, it describes the relationship Jesus has with God. In addition, it refers to a sign with which we are already familiar which is used to identify a female character in the LXX: Miriam.

---

[173]Lit. trans. from The Septuagint Version of the Old Testament, Zondervan, Grand Rapids, (1970).

In the Fourth Gospel there is more than a temporal meaning behind the description of the relationship between the Beloved Disciple and Jesus. It is intended to convey the message that Miriam (Mary) is back in the family of God. She shares a relationship with Jesus on a level of intimacy equal to that between Jesus and God! She is the oracle in the ephod of Jesus the High Priest. Her identity as a priest, an intermediary between God and God's children, should no longer be in question. Mary of Bethany is the Beloved Disciple.

(2) In Jn. 18: 15-16, the Beloved Disciple is able to secure access to "the High Priest's house" for Peter. By reading the signs that make it clear that the courtyard of the "High Priest's house" was in fact the Court of the Women of the Herodian Temple, and by reading the signs that suggest that Bethany, a dual location clearly identified with Mary and Martha, and representing the very set of gates on either side of the Court of the Women, we may conclude that Mary and Martha were not only known to the gatekeepers; they perhaps were, themselves, gate keepers in the Temple before the events we are about to describe.

(3) In Jn. 20: 2-10, the Beloved Disciple outruns Peter to the empty tomb, but waits for Peter to enter first. Perhaps, if it could be inferred that the Beloved Disciple recognized Peter's superior authority, such deference would be expected; but in the Fourth Gospel, the Beloved Disciple is clearly superior to Peter. This deference might be better explained by virtue of custom: women did not customarily precede men into any room. In the male dominated Hebrew culture, a woman's place was always in deference to a man.

The sign that identifies Mary most clearly in this passage, however, is not that she deferred to Peter by waiting for him to enter the empty tomb first. It has more to do with the contrast between the reactions of each to what they both saw in the tomb. The Beloved Disciple arrives at the tomb first and looks in (Jn. 20: 5). Then Peter arrives and enters the tomb and sees the linen wrappings lying there, the cloth that had been on Jesus' head being in a separate place from that of the other cloths, rolled up in a place by itself (Jn. 20: 6-7). Now the Beloved Disciple enters the tomb and sees the cloths again and believes. Peter sees the cloths once and has no apparent reaction.

(4) The Beloved Disciple sees the sign in the cloths. She looks twice and believes. The Beloved Disciple is the one who can see the meaning of these cloths and who recognizes their value as an element of faith, while Peter does not.

What is the significance of the cloths? The most significant thing in this passage is that the cloth that covered the head of Jesus has been separated from the cloth that covered his body. The Mosaic *semeia* tell us the meaning of this: that which is holy about Jesus has been separated from his body. In the passage that follows this one (Jn. 20: 11-18), Mary Magdalene sees two angels dressed in white, sitting where the body of Jesus had been lying, one at the head and the other at the feet (Jn. 20: 12). Jacob's ladder has been reestablished. The angels now may ascend and descend between heaven and earth because of the sacrifice of Jesus. This is what the Beloved Disciple sees in the separated cloths. This is what she understands and believes (Jn. 20: 8), even though as yet neither she nor anyone else fully understands the meaning of the resurrection (Jn. 20: 9).

(5) There remains one problem regarding the identity of the Beloved Disciple as Mary of Bethany. Brown's fifth identifier is the only one that argues against our thesis. All of the pronouns used to refer to this disciple are male. Why, if the Beloved Disciple is a female, doesn't the author of the Gospel tell us that, or at least refer to her as "she?"

Until recently, even in English, "he" was thought to be a universal pronoun, equally applicable to males and females. "He" could mean "she" in Greek, but there are more complex and compelling reasons for it to be used in John to hide Mary's identity.

The political repercussions in the Jewish, Christian, and Greek cultures, if Mary's identity had been revealed, would have likely meant that this gospel would never have been circulated, and certainly would have been suppressed. Karen Jo Torgesen has show that women did hold leadership positions, even the role of bishop, in the first-century church, and that such leadership was rejected by the established leaders in all three cultures.[174]

The Gospel itself tells of a bias against the Beloved Disciple's role and authority, a bias shared by two men: Peter and Judas (Jn. 12: 4-6; 20: 20-22). The Gospel writer or writers have characterized leaders of the institutional church, concerned with money and power, as antagonists to the Beloved Disciple, whose concern is spiritual truth. The intentional blindness of such authority figures is well presented in the story of the healing of a blind man (Jn. 9: 13-34). Clearly, the author or authors

---

[174]See Karen Jo Torgesen, When Women Were Priests: Women's Leadership in the Early Church and the Scandal of Their Subordination in the Rise of Christianity, Harper, San Francisco, (1993).

were well acquainted with those whose ecclesiastical power in Jewish and Christian circles could be used to suppress the truth, even when it conflicted with the will of Jesus!

Summary

Lazarus is a symbolic character representing the dying priesthood of Israel. Martha is one of the deacons in the Johannine community. The disciples of Jesus are identified by their ability to see the Christ in Jesus and their readiness to give witness to what they see, and there are many more of them than twelve. Thomas is one of the elders in the community. Mary of Bethany is the Beloved Disciple, a bishop in the Johannine community, the source of the Gospel of John, probably a Nazirite who served as a temple gate keeper.

Chapter 11
The Ordination Trilogy: Act 1, Scene 1
The Examination of Martha and Mary

Mary, Martha, and Lazarus Identified

"Now a certain man was ill, Lazarus of Bethany, the village of Mary and her sister Martha. Mary was the one who anointed the Lord with perfume and wiped his feet with her hair; her brother Lazarus was ill" (Jn. 11: 1-2).

Ην δε τισ ασθεν ω ν Λαζαροσ απο Βηθανια, εκ τησ κωμησ Μαριασ και Μαρθασ τησ αδελφησ αυ τησ. ην δε Μαρια η αλειψασα τον κυριον μυρω και εμαζασα τουσ ποδασ αυτου ταισ θριζειν αυτησ, ησ ο αδελ φοσ Λαζαροσ ησθενει.

(Now there was a certain [man] sick, Lazarus of Bethany, of the village of Mary and Martha her sister. It was and Mary who anointed the Lord with ointment and wiped his feet with her hair, whose brother Lazarus was sick.)[175]

As the action begins on the first act of the trilogy, the reader is to see two people and a place. (a) We see a man named Lazarus, whose identity is linked to Bethany. (b) We have learned that the place, Bethany, represents the gates of the Temple and is linked to Mary and Martha. (c) We see a woman named Mary, who is identified in terms that will not become clear until later in the Gospel, yet the

---

[175]Gk. and lit. trans. fr. Barry, op. cit., p. 277.

writer assumes that readers will recognize who she is. She is the one who anoints the feet of Jesus and wipes his feet with her hair. This unique behavior identified her to those for whom the Gospel was originally written.

The placement of this identifier is not an indication that an editor has erred in arranging the sequence of events. It is intended to link the liturgy, which we will soon consider as the second act of the trilogy, to the event involving Lazarus, the first act of the trilogy. What occurs in the context of the raising of Lazarus from death is directly tied to what happens when Jesus, Mary, Martha, Lazarus, and the other disciples are gathered for the evening meal, the setting for the second and third acts of the trilogy.

These first words of our study sound a lot like soliloquy at the beginning of a play, an introduction to the audience, just before the characters appear on stage.

The Message

"So the sisters sent a message to Jesus, 'Lord, he whom you love is ill.'" (Jn. 11: 3)

απεστειλαν ουν αι αδελφαι προσ αυτον λεγουσαι, Κυριε, ιδε ον φιλεισ ασθενει.

(Sent therefore the sisters to him, saying, Lord, lo, he whom thou lovest is sick.)[176]

The first oracle in this part of the Gospel is a literal message, sent by the sisters to Jesus. The obvious

---

[176]Gk. and lit. trans. fr. Barry, op. cit.

meaning of this message is that someone that Jesus loves is
ill, but we have learned to look for a deeper meaning. The
message is addressed, not to a friend or a teacher (rabbi),
nor to any of the names previously used by any of the
disciples,[177] but to *Kurie* "Lord." No one except Peter,

---

[177]See Jn. 1: 19-51. John the Baptist denies being: Messiah,
Elijah, the prophet. Compare Lk. 9: 18: John identifies Jesus as : the
Lamb of God, Son of God. The disciples address or refer to Jesus as:
Rabbi, Messiah (translated **Anointed**-- Jn. 21: 30), **Jesus, son of Joseph
from Nazareth, King of Israel**. Jesus predicts that the disciples "will see
heaven opened and the angels of God ascending and descending upon the
Son of Man (Himself. See also Jn. 8: 28, 9: 35-37, 13: 31). Nicodemus
calls Him **"Rabbi"** (Jn. 3: 2); the Samaritan woman calls Him **"a Jew,"**
"Sir," and **"a man,"** and Jesus responds to her faith statement: "I know
that the Messiah is coming" with **"I am he."** (Jn. 4: 25-26). The lame
man who was healed told the Jews that is was **"Jesus"** who healed him
(Jn. 5: 15). Likewise the Greeks ask to see **"Jesus."** (Jn. 12: 20) Jesus
seems to call Himself **"the Son"** (Jn. 5:19f, 17: 1f) and **"Jesus Christ"**
(Jn. 17: 3). The crowd that wanted to crown Him their king called him a
prophet (Jn. 6: 14) and **Rabbi** (Jn. 6: 25). Jesus calls Himself **The
Bread of Life** (Jn. 6: 35) and **"The Light of the World"** (Jn. 8:12, 9: 5).
The Jews refer to Him as **"a good man"** and as **"a man who is deceiving
the crowd"** (Jn. 7: 12), as **"this man"** (Jn. 7: 15; 11: 47), as **"the man"**
(Jn. 7: 25), as **"one man"** (Jn. 11: 50)," and as **"Teacher"** (Jn. 8: 4). In
response to the Jews who call Him "a Samaritan (with) a demon," (Jn.
8: 48) Jesus says, "Very truly, I tell you, before Abraham was, **I am**."
(Jn. 8: 58). Jesus calls Himself **The Gate** (Jn. 10: 9), **The Good
Shepherd** (Jn. 10: 11), **"God's Son"** (Jn. 10: 36), **"The Resurrection
and the Life."** (Jn. 11: 25), **"The True Vine"** (Jn. 15: 1f), **"A Friend"**
(by inference) (Jn. 15: 14). Judas and company, when asked "Who do
you seek?" say twice **"Jesus of Nazareth,"**(Jn. 18: 5, 7) and Jesus says
twice **"I am."**(Jn. 18: 6, 8). "They" (the Jews) refer to Jesus as "a
criminal" (Jn. 18: 30). Pilate asks Him if he is **"King of the Jews."** (Jn.
18: 33, See Jn. 19: 3, 19f., also 6: 14). Jesus responds, "You say I am
a king. For this I was born . . . to testify to the **Truth**." Jesus calls
Himself **"The Way, The Truth and The Life,"** (Jn. 14: 6) and **"The
Resurrection and The Life"** (Jn. 11: 25). Mary Magdalene calls him

who identifies Jesus as "The Holy One of God" (Jn. 6: 68-69) and a man healed by Jesus of blindness (Jn. 9: 38), had called Jesus "Lord" in this gospel before this message is sent.[178]

From this point forward, only the disciples (Jn. 11: 12; 20: 25), Martha (Jn. 11: 21, 27, 39), and Mary (Jn. 11: 32), "they" (Mary and Martha) (Jn. 11: 34), Mary Magdalene (Jn. 20: 18), Peter (Jn. 13: 6, 9, 36, 37; 21: 15, 16, 17, 20, 21) and "that disciple whom Jesus loved" (Jn. 21: 7) use this title.

Jesus acknowledges that "Lord" is an address used only by his disciples when addressing or referring to him. He says to the disciples in Jn. 13: 13. "You call me Teacher and Lord -- and you are right, for that is what I am." In John, *Kurios* is used only by those who "see" the divine nature of Jesus. It is a name sign from the LXX.

In the LXX, $Kυριοσ$ *(Kurios)* is used as "an expository equivalent for the divine name" (YHWH) of God.[179] It derives from the Song of Moses, found in Ex. 15: 1-18 sung after the pursuing Egyptian army drowns in the Red Sea. In this song Moses declares,

---

"**Rabbouni**" (**Teacher**) (Jn. 20: 16). "**The Lord**" is used in John when quoting the Old Testament (Jn. 1: 23) by the narrator (Jn. 6: 23). (Titles in bold).

[178]The translators of the NRSV apparently consider Jn. 5: 4, which refers to "an angel of the Lord" a gloss. (It is printed in a footnote). The NRSV also translates Kurie as "sir" instead of "Lord" at Jn. 8: 11.

[179]Gottfried Quell, "$Kυριοσ$: The Old Testament Name for God: the Name for God in the LXX," Theological Dictionary of the New Testament, vol. III, pp. 1058 f.

"I will sing to the Lord, for he has triumphed gloriously; horse and rider he has thrown into the sea. The Lord is my strength and my might, and he has become my salvation; this is my God, and I will praise him, my father's God, and I will exalt him. The Lord is a warrior; *the Lord is his name.*"(Ex. 15: 1-3)

Miriam's song, which follows in Ex. 15: 20-21, repeats some of Moses' words. "Then the prophet Miriam, Aaron's sister, took a tambourine in her hand; and all the women went out with her with tambourines and with dancing. And Miriam sang to them: 'Sing to the Lord, for he has triumphed gloriously; horse and rider he has thrown into the sea.' "

The Greek meaning of the term translated as Lord (*Kurios)* in the LXX indicates how those who translated the sacred Hebrew text into Greek intended it to be used.

"At the time when the specifically Hellenistic usage was first emerging, *Kurios* denoted the one who has lawful power of disposal. The element of legality is to be emphasized . . . This affirmation (the legal Lordship of Yahweh) can be based on the historical fact of the election of Israel. He who redeemed Israel from the "iron furnace" of Egypt had thereby a right to this people. But the affirmation can also be based on the fact that God is Creator. He who has made the universe and men is their legitimate Lord."[180]

---

[180]Werner Foerster, "Lord in Later Judaism: the Choice of the Word *Kurios* in the LXX," Theological Dictionary of the New Testament, op. cit., vol. III, pp. 1081-1082. (Parentheses are mine for clarification.)

In Palestine in the days of Jesus, the Hebrew term for Lord had almost disappeared from ordinary speech. It was used occasionally along with a title for a king or for the High Priest by persons who respectfully considered themselves to be servants, slaves or subjects.[181]

"The lordship of God is absolute, but still concealed . . . 'Blessed art thou, O Lord, King, great and mighty in thy greatness. Lord of all the creation of heaven, King of kings and God of the whole world. Thy power, dominion and greatness remain to all eternity, and thy lordship throughout all generations; all heavens are thy throne to eternity, and the whole earth is always the foot-stool of thy feet. For thou hast created all things and dost rule all things.'"[182]

The use of the term "Lord," then, is intended to provide those with eyes to see a clue as to the relationship between Jesus and the disciples. They recognized his divinity and addressed him privately in a way otherwise restricted to indirect references to God.   Mary   and Martha, authors of this message, saw themselves as servants of God. They were addressing One with legal authority, the One who had assured Nathaniel and Philip that "you will see heaven opened and the angels of God ascending and descending upon the Son of Man."[183] They were addressing the Son of Man, the legitimate Temple of God. They were his servants, the "footstools of (his) feet," the earth-bound end of Jacob's ladder.

---

[181]Ibid., "'Lord' in Rabbinic Judaism," p. 1084.

[182]Ibid., p. 1085, See Jub. 9: 4f.

[183]Jn. 1: 51; See also Gen. 28: 12 (Jacob's ladder); Jn. 6: 62, 20: 17 (Jesus refers to His ascending).

The message sent by Mary and Martha to the Lord is very simple. "The one whom you love is ill." The obvious reference is to Lazarus, whom we already know is ill. (Jn. 11: 1) Given that Lazarus represents not a single personal friend of Jesus, but the priesthood of the Jerusalem Temple, what does this message mean on a deeper level? If Lazarus is not "the disciple whom Jesus loved," then how is the reader to understand the message?

The answer is provided in Jn. 14: 15f., esp. 15: 9-10, where Jesus says to his disciples,

"If you love me, you will keep my commandments . . . As the Father has loved me, so I have loved you; abide in my love. If you keep my commandments, you will abide in my love, just as I have kept the Father's commandments and abide in his love."

This relates to the second commandment.

"You shall not make for yourself an idol whether in the form of anything that is in heaven above or that is on the earth beneath, or that is in the water under the earth. You shall not bow down to them or worship them, for I the Lord your God am a jealous God, punishing children for the iniquity of parents to the third and fourth generation of those who reject me, but showing steadfast love to the thousandth generation of those who love me and keep my commandments (Dt. 5: 8-10; See Jn. 14: 23-24)."

The disciple, any disciple, whom Jesus loves, is the one who keeps God's commandments. The disciple whom Jesus/God loves, but who is ill, is anyone, up to the third and fourth generation, who has rejected God. In the Fourth Gospel, those who do not know where God abides are those who have rejected the very God for whom they serve as priests: the Chief Priests of the Temple, including the High Priest, those called "the Jews." This spiritual blindness defiles the Temple. The Temple has become a gilded idol.

The Chief Priests later condemn themselves on this charge and on a charge of violating the first commandment as well, when Pilate asks them, "Shall I crucify your King?" "The Chief Priests answer, 'We have no king but the emperor.'" (Jn. 19: 15)

Mary and Martha have assessed the state of the spiritual health of the Temple priests. They send a coded message to the Holy One of God, the One with authority to cleanse the Temple, the One with the authority to return the priesthood to a condition of holiness. Their message says, simply, "Lord, he whom you love is ill."[184]

That Jesus has the power to heal the sick has already been established in Jn. 5: 1-15 when Jesus heals a lame man on the Sabbath and in 9: 1-41 when Jesus heals a man who has been blind since birth. In the latter passage, the relationship between sickness and sinfulness is explored, and it becomes clear that the Pharisees who refuse to see the truth, who claim to see, but do not see, are the sick ones, full of sin. They are "stumbling."

---

[184]See Gustav Stahlin, "ασθενασ," Theological Dictionary of the New Testament, op. cit., vol. I, pp. 490-493. "In the LXX means 'to stumble,' 'to be weak.' The cause of sickness in the NT: the work of spirits or the penalty of sin. There is an ασθενεια προσ θανατον (astheneia pros thanaton - sickness unto death) Jn. 11: 4; also an αμαρτια προσ θανατον (amartia pros thanaton -- sinfulness unto death) 1 Jn. 5: 16.

**"But when Jesus heard it, he said, 'This illness does not
lead to death; rather it is for God's glory, so that the
Son of God may be glorified through it.'"** (Jn. 11: 4)

Ακουσασ δε ο Ιησουσ ειπεν, Αυτη η ασθενεια
ουκ εστιν προσ θανατον, αλλ υπερ τησ δοζησ
του θεου, ινα δοζασθη ο υιοσ του θεου δι
αυτησ.

(But having heard Jesus said, This sickness is not unto
death, but for the glory of God, that may be glorified the
Son of God by it.)

The illness, sickness, weakness, whatever it is that
causes the "stumbling" of he whom Jesus loves appears to
be minimized at first by Jesus. The illness is not God's
punishment for the loved-one's sins, but God's way of
bringing glory to the Son of God.

John's Gospel once again returns to the LXX for the
oracular material with which to tell the Jesus story. The
correlation between death and glory is made in Lv. 10, the
story of Nadab and Abihu, the eldest sons of Aaron,[185] who
carried "unauthorized coals" to the altar fire, producing an
unholy fire in the Temple.

"And fire came out from the presence of the Lord and
consumed them, and they died before the Lord. Then
Moses said to Aaron, 'This is what the Lord meant when he
said, 'Through those who are near me I will show myself
holy, and before all the people I will be glorified.'" (Lv.
10: 2-3)

---

[185]See Jacob Milgrom, op. cit., "The Tragic Aftermath," p. 598.

Jacob Milgrom provides a detailed exegesis of this passage, in which it becomes clear that Nadab and Abihu had to be standing in the Tabernacle court when they were struck down by God's consuming fire. They died "standing" before the Lord, i.e.: while performing the rites assigned to them as priests, but they died because they defiled those rites by using "unholy coals." Moses understands the meaning of the deaths of these two Chief Priests. Then Moses speaks God's words of warning: "Through those who are near me (i.e.: priests)[186] I will show myself holy and before all the people I will be glorified." A priest who encroaches upon the holiness of God, by being or acting in a manner that is not specifically prescribed, will die by God's hand, because priests represent God, and they *must be holy*.

Milgrom defines what it means for God to be glorified, that is, treated as holy.

"The deaths of God's intimate priests, Nadab and Abihu, perform the function of sanctifying God -- providing awe and respect for his power to all who witness the incident or who will subsequently learn of it."[187]

The primary role of priests and Levites is to serve as intermediaries between the people of God and God, to maintain boundaries between the sacred and the profane.

---

[186]Ibid., p. 600-601. "Those who are near me" (are defined as) an official who can have access to his sovereign directly, without resorting to an intermediary, a group of officials . . . close to, in intimacy with someone, the inner circle of the royal court, Israel's priests 'who are close to the Lord,' . . . a sense that is only applicable to Israel's priesthood."

[187]Ibid., p. 601-603.

"Priests and Levites share the custody of the sanctuary, the priests guarding within (and at the entrance, Nu. 3: 38) and the Levites guarding without (Nu. 3: 23, 29, 35). All priests and Levites are responsible if disqualified priests or Levites encroach upon the sancta . . . The penalty priests and Levites pay for failure to prevent encroachment is that of Nadab and Abihu- death by divine agency (Nu. 18: 3)."[188]

In response, Jesus says, "This illness does not lead to death; rather it is for God's glory, so that the Son of Man may be glorified through it." Jesus declares a word of grace for the encroaching priests. The just consequence of their defilement of all that is holy in Israel is death, but rather than consume them with fire, as God did with Nadab and Abihu, Jesus declares that God will be glorified by the Son of Man, whose glory the reader knows comes about through the crucifixion death and resurrection of Jesus.[189]

"Accordingly, though Jesus loved Martha and her sister and Lazarus, after having heard that Lazarus was ill, he stayed two days longer in the place where he was."(Jn. 11: 5-6)

Ηγαπα δε ο Ιησουσ την Μαρθαν και την αδελφην αυτησ και τον Λαζαρον. ωσ ουν ηκουσεν οτι ασθενει, τοτε μεν εμεινενεν ω ην τοπω δυο ημερασ.

---

[188]Ibid., p. 602.

[189]See Jn. 15: 8. "My Father is glorified by this, that you bear much fruit and become my disciples."

(Loved now Jesus Martha and sister her and Lazarus. When therefore he heard that he is sick, then indeed he remained in which he was place two days.)[190]

"Now Jesus loved Martha, and her sister, and Lazarus. When he had heard therefore that he was sick, he *abode* two days still in the same place where he was" (Jn. 11: 5-6 KJV).

Where does Jesus abide? He abides two days longer in the place where he was. Where was he? With the disciples. The disciples abide with Jesus for one day (Jn. 1: 38-39). Jesus abides with them for two: their historical day and his cosmic, eternal day.

Jesus knows what it is that concerns Martha and Mary: the illness of the priesthood, indeed, the decaying stench of the dead priesthood, defiling the Temple and all that was holy in Israel. He cares about this concern and those who carry it, but he chooses to abide a little longer with his own before embracing the hour in which he will be glorified.

"Then after this he said to the disciples, 'Let us go to Judea again.' The disciples said to him, 'Rabbi, the Jews were just now trying to stone you, and are you going there again?" (Jn. 11: 7-8)

επειτα μετα τουτο λεγει τοισ μαθηταισ, Αγωμεν εισ την Ιουδαιαν παλιν. Λεγουσιν αυτω οι μαθηται, Ραββι, νυν εζητουν σε λιθασαι οι Ιουδαιοι, και παλιν υπαγεισ εκει;

---

[190]Gk. and lit. trans. Berry, op. cit., p. 278.

(Then after this he says to the disciples, Let us go into
Judea again. Say to him the disciples, Rabbi, just now
were seeking thee to stone the Jews, and again goest thou
thither?)[191]

　　　The literal translation of "just now trying to stone
you" is "seeking you to stone." The Jews (temple
authorities) seek Jesus, not for Life, but so that they might
stone him to death. The disciples do not seem to
comprehend the manner of the approaching death of Jesus,
but they do understand the risk he takes by returning to
Jerusalem.

**"Jesus answered, 'Are there not twelve hours of
daylight? Those who walk during the day do not
stumble, because they see the light of this world. But
those who walk at night stumble, because the light is not
in them.'"** (Jn. 11: 9-10)

Απεκριθη ο Ιησουσ, ουχι δωδεκα εισιν ωραι τησ
ημερασ; εαν τισ περιπατη εν τη ημερα, συ
προσκοπτει, οτι το φωσ του κοσμου τουτου
βλεπει εαν δε τισ περιπατη εν τη νυκτι,
προσκοπτει, οτι το φωσ ουκ εστιν εν αυτω .

(Answered Jesus, Not twelve are there hours in the day? If
anyone walk in the day, he stumbles not, because the light
of this world he see; but if anyone walk in the night, he
stumbles, because the light is not in him.)[192]

---

[191] Gk. and lit. trans. fr. Berry, op. cit., p. 278
[192]Ibid.

The disciples have been spending the day with
Jesus. They need not worry about their walk, their spiritual
life. They will not stumble, because they can see the Light
of the World. They can see and believe. It is those who
abide in darkness for whom Jesus has concern. They
stumble because the Light is not in them. They are weak,
sick, not whole or wholesome. They do not abide in
Christ, therefore they walk in darkness; they fail to see God
in the new light being offered by Jesus the Christ.

**"After saying this, he told them, 'Our friend Lazarus
has fallen asleep, but I am going there to awaken him.'
The disciples said to him, 'Lord, if he has fallen asleep,
he will be all right.' Jesus, however, had been speaking
about his death, but they thought that he was referring
merely to sleep."(11: 11-13)**

Ταυτα ειπεν, και μετα τουτο λεγει αυτοισ,
Λαζαροσ ο φιλοσ ημων κεκοιμηται αλλα
πορευομαι ινα εξυπνισω αυτον. Ειπον ουν οι
μαθηται αυτου, Κυριε, ει κεκοιμηται σωθησεται.
Ειρηκει δε ο Ιησουσ περι του θανατου αυτου
εκεινοι δε εδοζαν οτι περι τησ κοιμησεωσ του
υπνου λεγει.

(These things he said; and after this he says to them,
Lazarus our friend has fallen asleep; but I go that I may
awake him. Said therefore his disciples, Lord, if he has
fallen asleep he will get well. But had spoken Jesus of his
death, but they thought that of the rest of sleep he
speaks.)[193]

---

[193]Ibid.

Jesus is speaking about his own death, which will be a sacrifice to glorify God and recreate all that is holy. Sleep is an obvious metaphor for death, but in John's Gospel its use is even more significant than the metaphor first implies. It is in sleep that dreams occur,[194] and the dream that immediately springs to mind regarding the Temple is Jacob's ladder dream (Gn. 28: 10f).

Sleep (or the lack of it) is also a factor in motivating the covenant between Jacob and his father-in-law, Laban[195] and (the approaching sleep of death) in motivating Jacob to ask his son to swear that he would carry him out of Egypt to the burial place of his ancestors.[196] Jacob refrains from sleeping so that he can maintain the covenant, and even in the sleep of death sustains the dream, but now Jesus must "awaken him," literally "take sleep (the dream) from him (from Israel)." The sleep of "Lazarus" will not lead to "his" death, but to the death of Jacob's dream: the Temple.

---

[194]Horst Balz, "υπνοσ," Theological Dictionary of the New Testament, op. cit., vol. VIII, pp. 545-556, esp. p. 550. "In LXX Gk. the word almost always used for dream . . . which as a development from the stem expresses the connection with sleep."

[195]See Gen. 31: 36- 32: 2, esp. 31:40 Gilead (Hebrew for "Heap of Witness") is the name of the holy place (temple?) where stones were gathered and a pillar (Hebrew: "Mizpah" -- "Watchpost") erected to witness the covenant: "The Lord watch between you and me, when we are absent one from the other." (31: 49)

[196]See Gen. 47: 27f, esp. vs. 30; 49: 29-33.

"Then Jesus told them plainly,[197] 'Lazarus is dead. For your sake I am glad I was not there, so that you may believe. But let us go to him.'" (Jn. 11: 14-15)

τοτε ουν ειπεν αυ τοισ ο Ιησουσ παρρησια, Λαζαροσ απεθανεν και χαιρω δι υμασ, ινα πιστευσητε, οτι ουκ ημην εκ ει   αλλ αγωμεν προσ αυ τον .

(Then therefore said to them Jesus plainly, Lazarus died. And I rejoice on your account, in order that ye may believe, that I was not there. But let us go to him.)[198]

Now Jesus chooses not to speak in metaphor or oracle.[199] The priesthood is dead. "For your sake," he says to them, "I am glad that I was not abiding there (with

---

[197]See Jn. 16: 29-30 "His disciples said, 'Yes, now you are speaking plainly, not in any figure of speech! Now we know that you know all things, and do not need to have anyone question you; by this we believe that you came from God.'

[198]Gk. and lit. trans. fr. Berry, op. cit.

[199]See Heinrich Schlier, "παρρασια, παρρασιαζομαι ," Theological Dictionary of the New Testament, op. cit., vol. V., pp. 871-886, for an extensive consideration of the term translated in the NRSV as "told them plainly." The Greek term in the political sphere indicates an openness to truth along with a resistance to concealment; in the private sphere it indicates a sign of friendship, unafraid to censure a friend.(p. 873) In the LXX it is used as the mark of a free person as distinct from δουλοσ (doulos) "slave" (Lev. 26: 13). "The LXX goes beyond the Hellenistic senses in passages where it is stated that God gives the people παρρασια and that divine σοφια (sophia) has παρρασια." (p. 875). "In the Johannine writings (parrasia) is distinctively linked with the work of Jesus and has a place in the Johannine dialectic of the (public) revelation of Jesus." (See Jn. 18: 20) In Jn. 11: 14 its use "means concretely to 'speak non-figuratively,' 'openly,' 'without concealment.'

the priests who are dead to me), so that you may believe
(by seeing the priesthood revived)." The time[200] for
waiting is past; the time has come to go to the (Temple)
tomb where Lazarus is.

The double entendre (metaphor) of sleep as it is
used here has four meanings: real sleep, figurative sleep
(death), the death of the Temple dream, and the real death
of Jesus. Real sleep, the sleep of Jacob, gives rise to
Jacob's dream. It is from this dream that Jesus must
awaken Israel. Figurative sleep (death) is the temporary
state of the priesthood. This sleep occurs while Jesus is not
abiding in the Jerusalem Temple, so that the disciples can
see the contrast (life) that Jesus brings to it. The death of
the Temple dream is the real end of a sacred tradition.
Jesus' own real death is to be the cost of this "awakening."

**"Thomas, who was called the Twin, said to his fellow
disciples, 'Let us also go, that we may die with him."**
(Jn. 11: 16)

Ειπεν ουν θωμασ, ο λεφουμενοσ Διδυμοσ, τουσ
συμμαθηταισ, Αφωμεν και ημεισ ινα αποθανωμεν
μετ αυτου .

(Said therefore Thomas, called Didymus, to the fellow-
disciples, Let go also us, that we may die with him.)[201]

Thomas' Greek name, "Didymus" (twin), would
call to mind for any seafaring Greek, the twin figures
Castor and Pollux, the Gemini twins, third sign of the

---

[200]*Kairos*, cosmic time, God's timing.
[201]Gk. and lit. trans. fr. Berry, op. cit.

zodiac, which were carved as figureheads on many Greek ships because they were a sign of good luck.

"They were saviors, who looked down from their celestial positions and saved those in peril on the sea. They might even show themselves in the form of St. Elmo's fire, the glow accompanying the brushlike discharges of atmospheric electricity appearing as a tip of light on the ends of pointed objects such as masts of ships, during storms."[202]

Thomas was an elder among the disciples, a figurehead on the ship that represented the early church, a little point of light, an overseer (Bishop) in the Johannine community. He is prepared to die with Jesus and encourages the other disciples to follow Jesus to death.[203] The concern of the disciples is the death of Jesus, not the death of Lazarus.

Arriving at the Temple

"When Jesus arrived, he found that Lazarus had already been in the tomb four days." (Jn. 11: 17)

Ελθων ουν ο Ιησουσ ευρεν αυτον τεσσαπασ ημερασ ηδη εχοντα εν τω μνημειω.

---

[202]F.D. Gealy, "Twin Brothers," The Interpreter's Dictionary of the Bible, op. cit., vol. 4, pp. 719-720. See also in the IDB: E.P. Blair, "Thomas," vol. 4, pp. 631-632; Also see E.P. Blair, "Didymus," vol. 1, p. 843; Also B.H. Throckmorton, Jr., "Figurehead," vol. 2, p. 268.

[203]Thomas, not Peter, shows this courage. See Mt. 26: 35 = Mk. 14: 31.

(Having come therefore Jesus found him four days already having been in the tomb.)[204]

The priesthood has no spiritual vitality left in it. God has waited until there is no sign of life in the Temple before the *Logos* "arrives" to redeem it.

"Now Bethany was near Jerusalem, some two miles away . . ." (Jn. 11: 18)

ην δε η Βηθανια εγγυσ τω ν Ιεροσολυμων , ω σ απο σταδιων δεκαπεντε

(Now was Bethany near to Jerusalem, about off furlongs fifteen . . .)[205]

Again we are reminded of the special significance of Bethany beyond the Jordan. This location represents an entry gate to the Temple, through the Court of the Women. Here in Jerusalem, on the site of the first and second Temple, cosmic time and chronological time will, for the second time since creation, intersect. Here Jesus, the Logos, will confront the power of those who abide in death: those who do not accept his authority and will not accept the light he offers them. Here God will be glorified and Jesus will become the last sacrifice ever to expiate the sins of the people of God.[206]

---

[204]Gk. and lit. trans. fr. Berry, op. cit.

[205]Ibid.

[206]See Eduard Lohse, "Zion-Jerusalem in the New Testament," Theological Dictionary of the New Testament, op. cit., vol. VII, pp. 327f, esp. 332-333. "Jerusalem is repeatedly the place where Jesus manifests

"And many of the Jews had come to Martha and Mary to console them about their brother." (Jn. 11: 19)

και πολλοι εκ τω ν Ιουδαιων εληλυθεισαν προσ τασ περι Μαρθαν και Μαριαν , ινα παρα μυθησωνται αυ τασ περι του αδελφου αυτων.

(and many of the Jews had come unto those around Martha and Mary, that they might console them concerning their brother.)

At first glance, this appears to be an account of sensitive friends dropping by at the wake for a deceased relative. "The Jews" (Chief Priests), however, are never otherwise depicted as "friends" in John's gospel.[207] The literal Greek version says that these men had come "προ σ τασ περι Μαρθαν και Μαριαν " *(pros tas peri Marthan kai Marian)* i.e.: to those around (close to)[208]

His glory and must contend with the representatives of the unbelieving cosmos *(Ioudaioi)* the Jews."

[207]Unless exceptions are made for Nicodemus (3: 1-21, 19: 39) and Joseph of Arimathea (19: 38), who were disciples. "The Jews oppose Jesus as Jews when to their eyes he seems to reject the temple. For them the temple is the place of God's presence. Hence their opposition arises from their essential Jewishness, from their attachment to the temple, 2: 18, 20." See 10: 31, 33; 5: 16, 18; 7: 1; 8: 48, 52, 57; 13: 33. See also Walter Gutbrod, "Israel: ii In John," Theological Dictionary of the New Testament, op. cit., vol. III, p. 378.

[208]William F. Arndt and F. Wilbur Gingrich, A Greek-English Lexicon of the New Testament and Other Early Christian Literature, a trans. and adapt. of Walter Bauer, Griecheisch-Deutsches Worterbuch zu den Schriften des Neuen Testaments und der ubrigen urchristlichen Literatur, University of Chicago Press, Chicago, (1957 - twelfth impression - 1969), p. 650-651 "peri: 2. w the ABC.- d. of persons who

Martha and Mary. This gives the impression that these
Jews were friends of the family or close friends of Martha
and Mary. It could also mean that Martha and Mary were
living near to the temple leaders who posed a threat to Jesus
(Jn. 11: 8).   The picture that this verse paints is at odds
with the impression given in the rest of the Gospel, which
suggests that this reference may be a sign. We have an
image of priests comforting and consoling two grieving
sisters. That is an appropriate role for a priest, one which
reflects God's compassion and comfort, but "the Jews" in
John's Gospel do not abide in God, so this would be "out
of character" for them.

It is conceivable that some of the priests were
grieving with Martha and Mary for the same reason that the
sisters were grieving: they perceived the death of their
institution, their sacred place and their sacred role in
maintaining the covenant between God and Israel.
However, neither the High Priest nor a Nazirite priest may
mourn in the Temple,[209] though lesser priests, under certain
circumstances (like the death of a close relative), could.

The consequence for violating the taboo against
grieving in the Temple is death by divine action. If the
Temple priests were indeed perceiving the absence of
spiritual life in their rituals and among their leaders, their
grief would have been of a personal nature, for they would
expect to die at God's hand. But it is not the High Priest,
nor a Nazirite priest, nor any of the Chief Priests or Levites
who is to die. The old Temple is dying; the dream of
Jacob is ending; a new Temple is about to take its place.

---

are standing, sitting, working or staying close to someone . . . *pros tas
peri Marthan kai Marian* Jn. 11: 19."

[209]Lev. 21: 10, See 10: 6-11; Nu. 6: 6-8.

The first Temple was constructed on a threshing floor by Solomon on a site selected by his father, David.[210] The Herodian Temple was built over the site of the first Temple. Before David had chosen that site, however, another event of great significance for the people of God whose descendants were to worship in the Temple, occurred on a similar (symbolically the same) threshing floor. Jacob, who dreamed of a place where heaven and earth could meet, died and was carried to a threshing floor beyond the Jordan.[211]

"When they came to the threshing floor of Atad, which is beyond the Jordan, they held there a very great and sorrowful lamentation; and he (Joseph) observed a time of mourning for his father seven days. When the Canaanite inhabitants of the land saw the mourning on the threshing floor of Atad, they said, 'This is a grievous mourning on the part of the Egyptians.' Therefore the place was named Abelmizraim (*mourning meadow of Egypt*); it is beyond the Jordan. Thus his (Israel's) sons did for him as he had instructed them. They carried him to the land of Canaan and buried him in the cave of the field at Machpelah, the field near Mamre, which Abraham bought as a burial site from Ephron the Hittite." (Gn. 50: 10-13; See Gn. 47: 27-31)

Just as one of the two locations for Bethany is "beyond the Jordan," so the threshing floor to which Father Israel's body was "carried up" after his death was located "beyond the Jordan." It was a place of great mourning,

---

[210]See 1 Chron. 21: 28 through 22: 1.
[211]See Gen. 49: 29 through 50: 14, esp. 50: 10-14.

bought as a burial site from a man named Ephron.   To understand how this is significant in the Gospel, we must jump ahead to when act one of the trilogy ends.

"Jesus therefore no longer walked about openly among the Jews, but went from there to a town called Ephraim in the region near the wilderness; and he remained there with the disciples." (Jn. 11: 54)

Ιησουσ ουν ουκ ετι παρρησια περιεπατει εν τοισ Ιουδαιοισ, αλλα απηλθεν εκειθεν εισ την χωραν εγυσ τησ ερημου , εισ Εφραιμ λεγομεν ην πολιν, κακει διετριβεν μετα τω ν μαθητων αυτου.

(Jesus therefore no longer publicly walked among the Jews, but went away thence into the country near the desert, to Ephraim called a city, and there he stayed with his disciples.)

The indictment against the Chief Priests is obvious in this passage. God had walked freely in the Garden (Gn. 3: 8). The people of God had followed the Tabernacle in the wilderness   (Nu. 9: 15-23).   John the Baptist had recognized the significance of the fact that Jesus had walked among the people (Jn. 1: 26f, esp. 36). Now he no longer walked openly among them. The inference is that he was still among them, but not publicly; the separation had begun.

The region identified with Ephron and the town or region called Ephraim are apparently the same.[212] The writer of the Gospel of John has carefully included references in this story that tie it to the story of the death of Jacob, the man who first dreamed of the ladder to connect heaven and earth. The death and burial of Jacob/ Israel, one whom God loved, and the grieving of the children of Israel, specifically represented by Ephraim, provide the Mosaic setting for the first act of John's trilogy. Though mourning was not permitted in the Temple, the death of the institution of the Temple, of the idea of the Temple as it had been known among the Jews, prompted mourning which could not be prevented.[213]

The words of the prophet, Hosea (esp. chapters 5 and 11) ring true to the theological import of Jn. 11.

"Hear this, O priests! Give heed, O house of Israel! Listen, O house of the king! For the judgement pertains to you; . . . I know Ephraim and Israel is not hidden from

---

[212]W.L. Reed, "Ephraim," Interpreter's Dictionary of the Bible, op. cit., vol. 2, pp. 119-121. One of the 12 tribes of Israel was named Ephraim after the younger son of Joseph (Gen. 41: 52; 46: 20) was adopted by Jacob along with Manasseh and treated as the firstborn (48: 1ff.) . . . "Ephraim" was used to designate Israel after the Syro-Ephraimite War (734-732). . . and endured when this remnant was made into the Assyrian province of Samaria ten years later; (also) "a town in the vicinity of Bethel (II Sam. 13: 23). II Chr. 13: 19 is probably concerned with the same geographical area in mentioning 'Bethel with its villages and Jeshanah with its villages and Ephron with its villages.' 'Ephron' may be the Chronicler's reading for 'Ephraim.'" Bethel, of course, means "house of God." Being in Ephraim, Jesus was not, in a cosmic sense, "out of the house" of God.

[213]Note also that "the tomb of Eleazar, the son of Aaron, could also be located in the hill country of Ephraim (Josh. 24: 33). Ibid., p. 120.

me; for now, O Ephraim, you have played the whore;
Israel is defiled. Their deeds do not permit them to return
to their God. For the spirit of whoredom is within them,
and they do not know the LORD. Israel's pride testifies
against him; Ephraim stumbles in his guilt; Judah also
stumbles with them. With their flocks and herds they shall
go to seek the LORD, but they will not find him; he has
withdrawn from them." "When Israel was a child, I loved
him, and out of Egypt I called my son." (Hos. 5: 1, 3-6;
11: 1)

This sheds new light on the meaning of the cryptic
message sent by Martha and Mary to Jesus: "He whom
you love is ill." It is Ephraim/Israel that is ill, stumbling,
defiled. The Chief Priests and the High Priest do not
know the LORD, their God. Jesus knows who the "he
whom you love" in the cryptic note is. He tells his
disciples that "those who walk at night stumble, because the
light is not in them" (Jn. 11: 10). Israel, Ephraim, and
Judah, all terms associated with the Hebrew nation, the
covenant people of God, descendants of Abraham, Isaac
and Jacob, are stumbling in pride and guilt. The people
bring their flocks and herds to the Temple for sacrifice,
seeking the LORD, but they will not find him there,
because he has withdrawn from them (Jn. 11: 15, 54).

"Arriving" at the Temple has a different meaning
for those who can read the signs in the Gospel than for
those who cannot. It is Martha and Mary who arrive at the
temple, that is Jesus. Jesus, the new temple, arrives at
what has been the temple; it has become a tomb, a cold,
dark place filled with the stench of decaying flesh, the
abode of those who do not know God, a place of heavy
grief for those who truly seek God.

Martha's Examination

"When Martha heard that Jesus was coming, she went and met him, while Mary stayed at home." (Jn. 11: 20)

η ουν Μαρθα ω σ ηκουσεν οτι ο Ιησουσ ερχεται, υπηντησεν αυτω Μαρια δε εν τω οικω εκαθεζετο.

(Martha therefore when she heard that Jesus is coming, met him; but Mary in the house was sitting.)[214]

"Martha . . . met him (Jesus), but Mary in the house was sitting." Since both had sent the message, why would one go out to meet Jesus and the other sit in the house? Mary was "sitting" in the "house" of the Lord; she was at worship. In the synagogue men stood, but women as well as the teacher and the leader sat to worship.[215]

---

[214]Gk. and lit. trans. fr. Berry, op. cit, p. 279.

[215]Carl Schneider, "καθαμαι, καθιζο , καθεζομαι," Theological Dictionary of the New Testament, op. cit., vol. III, pp. 440-444, esp. p. 443. Sitting is also a gesture of grief, a sign of mourning. Sitting is a gesture of religious mourning among women who bewail the gods of the mysteries; thus the mourning Isis sits, and so do the women who bewail Adonis.(Ez. 8: 14) The women who weep for Jesus also sit (Mt. 27: 61). Ez. 8 chronicles the abominations in the temple seen in a vision by the prophet. Among them is women sitting at the north gate of the house of the LORD weeping for Tammuz. (8: 14); See J. Gray, "Tammuz," Interpreter's Dictionary of the Bible, op. cit. vol. 4, p. 516. Tammuz is "the Sumerian deity of spring vegetation; known from the Gilgamesh Epic as the lover of Ishtar, goddess of love, who had betrayed him. The anniversary of her betrayal was the occasion of an annual wailing for the god on the fourth month, which was named for him. Ezekiel attests a local variation of this rite practiced by the women of

Mary was mourning in the "house" of the Lord,
mourning for the death of Israel, of the Temple, mourning
in anticipation of the death of Jesus, or perhaps praying in
order to avoid mourning.

Martha was a deacon, whose ministry was to receive
the host and bring it to those who were at worship. Mary's
role is to consecrate through prayer the elements for
distribution. Martha goes to receive Jesus. Mary
encounters God through prayer. The deacon reaches out
(seeks outwardly) for the Lord; the bishop reaches in (seeks
inwardly).

**"Martha said to Jesus, 'Lord, if you had been here, my
brother would not have died. But even now I know that
God will give you whatever you ask of him." (Jn. 11: 21-
22)**

ειπεν ουν η Μαρθα προσ τον Ιησουν, Κυριε, ει
ησ ω δε, ο αδελφοσ μου ουκ αν ετεθνηξκει.
αλλα και νυν οιδα οτι οσα αν αιτηση τον θεον,
δωσει σοι ο θεοσ.

(Then said Martha to Jesus, Lord, if thou hadst been here,
my brother had not died; but even now I know that
whatsoever thou mayest ask of God, will give thee God.)

Martha is affirming her faith in Jesus. She knows
that the reason that the priesthood has died is because Jesus

---

Jerusalem on the fifth day of the sixth month. The motif of a dying god
is suggested by the annual wilting of vegetation in the Near East, and has
sundry local variations - e.g., the cult of Adonis in Syria, Persephone &
Dionysus in Greece, Osiris in Egypt."

was not abiding in the Temple. If he had "remained"
there, Lazarus would not have died. She also believes that
Jesus can restore life to all that is holy. All he has to do
is ask that it be so. It will be if he will speak the word of
creation.

Martha has made her affirmation of faith. She sees
the power of Creator God in Jesus. She has witnessed
directly to Jesus what she believes. She is worthy to serve
as a priest, interceding between God and the people of God,
even the priests of God.

**"Jesus said to her, 'Your brother will rise again.'
Martha said to him, 'I know that he will rise again in
the resurrection on the last day.'"** (Jn. 11: 23-24)

Λεγει αυτη ο Ιησους, Αναστησεται ο αδελ φοσ
σου. Λεγει αυτω Μαρθα, Οιδα οτι αναστησεται
εν τη αναστασει εν τη εσχατη ημερα.

*(Says to her Jesus, Will rise again brother thy. Says to him
Martha, I know that he will rise again in the resurrection
in the last day.)*

Martha's faith is grounded in a belief in the
resurrection on the last day. It could be that she believes
that the death of the Temple means that the creation must
come to an end, since nothing can exist without God, and
without the Temple, the world cannot encounter God. Her
faith is that God will create a new covenant in a new
creation after the last day.

In contrast to this interpretation, which seems to
suggest that Martha's faith was somehow lacking, it may be
that we are to hear that Martha's statement of faith affirms

the cosmic order of creation. There is only one day in creation. The last day is the first day.[216]

Martha's faith is a resurrection faith. All things are possible through Jesus. Even the covenant can be reborn, just as those who worship in spirit and in truth are born anew.[217]

"Jesus said to her, 'I am the resurrection and the life. Those who believe in me, even though they die, will live, and everyone who lives and believes in me will never die.'" (Jn. 11: 25, 26a)

Ειπεν αυτη ο Ιησουσ, Εγω ειμι η αναστασισ και η ζω ν. ο πιστευω ν εισ εμε, καν αποθανη ζησεται και πασ ο ζω ν και πιστευω ν εισ εμε ου μη αποθανη εισ τον αιωνα.

(Said to her Jesus, I am the resurrection and the life: he that believes on me, though he die he shall live; and everyone who lives and believes on me, in no wise shall die forever.)

Jesus affirms Martha's faith with powerful words of comfort that no one needs to interpret to understand, then he poses the final examination question.

---

[216]This is easy for Christians to understand, because we worship God on the first day, not the last day of the week. We do not end the week with worship, we begin it with God. A first century Jewish Christian would have worshipped in the synagogue on Friday night (the beginning of the end of the week, the Sabbath), when Jesus was buried and again on Sunday morning, (the beginning of the week) when Jesus was resurrected.

[217]"Very truly I tell you, no one can see the kingdom of God without being born anew." Jn. 3: 3 (alt.).

'Do you believe this?' She said to him, 'Yes, Lord, I
believe that you are the Messiah, the Son of God, the
One coming into the world.'" (Jn. 11: 26b - 27)

πιστευεισ τουτο; Λεγει αυτω , Ν αι, κυριε εγω
τετιστευκα οτι συ ει ο χριστοσ, ο υιοσ του
θεου, ο εισ τον κοσμον ερχουνενοσ.

*(Believest thou this? She says to him, Yea, Lord; I have
believed that thou art the Christ, the Son of God, who into
the world comes.)*

Martha knows Who Jesus is and where he abides.
He abides in the world, among those who believe and those
who do not believe, walking both with those who walk in
the light and with those who stumble in the darkness.
Martha can witness to the presence of God in the world,
because she has seen Christ. She is ready for ordination.

Mary's Examination

"When she had said this, she went back and called her
sister Mary, and told her privately, 'The Teacher is here
and is calling for you.'" (Jn. 11: 28)

Και ταυτα ειπουσα απηλθεν , και εφωνησεν
Μαριαν την αδελφην αυτασ λαθρα, ειπουσα, Ο
διδασκαλοσ παρεστιν και φωνει σε.

*(And these things having said she went away, and called
Mary her sister secretly, saying, The teacher is come and
calls thee.)*

The reader is supposed to wonder at this point, "I didn't read where it said that Jesus was calling for Mary; did I miss something?" Jesus did call Mary, and the reader didn't miss anything.   Martha called her sister Mary. Where does Christ abide?   In Martha, now Christ's messenger.   The Christ in Martha called to her sister.

Christ is calling Mary, i.e.: she is called to him, she has a vocation because Jesus calls her.   Martha and Mary send a message seeking Jesus.   Martha seeks to receive Jesus.   Mary seeks to respond to Christ's call.   Again, this characterization is consistent with what we have already learned about the roles of Martha and Mary in the Johannine church.   The deacon brings the Word of the Lord to the bishop.

"And when she heard it, she got up quickly and went to him." (Jn. 11: 29)

Εκεινη ω σ ηκουσεν εφειρεται ταχυ και ερχεται προσ αυτον.

(*She when she heard rises up quickly and comes to him.*)

Mary heard the call, and her response was immediate; she went to him. Her response is characterized in the same way as that of other disciples as reported in the Synoptic Gospels (Mk. 1: 17f; =Mt. 4: 20f).[218]

---

[218]Comp. Dt. 9: 12. God says to Moses, "Get up. Go down quickly from here, for your people whom you have brought from Egypt have acted corruptly. They have been quick to turn from the way that I commanded them; they have cast an image for themselves." Also, See Jn. 13: 27 Jesus says to Judas, "Do quickly what you are going to do." Quick, immediate response is required of those who are called by God.

"Now Jesus had not yet come to the village, but was still at the place where Martha had met him." (Jn. 11: 30)

ουπω δε εληλυθει ο Ιησουσ εισ την κωμην ,
αλλ ην εν τω τοπω ο που υπηντησεν αυ τω η
Μαρθα.

(*Now not yet had come Jesus into the village, but was in the place where met him Martha.*)[219]

Mary, in other words, had to leave the Temple to go to Jesus. She found Christ abiding, not in the Temple worship, but in the witness of her sister, Martha.   She found him outside the village, or in Old Testament terms, "outside the camp." The parallel is found in Ex. 33: 7.

"Now Moses used to take the tent and pitch it outside the camp, far off from the camp; he called it the tent of meeting. And everyone who sought the LORD would go out to the tent of meeting, which was outside the camp."

The house of God is no longer in Jerusalem, but, like the Tabernacle, "outside the camp." Mary went to "the place" (τοποσ - *topos)[220]* where Martha had met Jesus.

---

[219]Gk. and lit. trans. fr. Berry, op. cit., p. 279.

[220]Helmut Koster, " τοποσ, " Theological Dictionary of the New Testament, op. cit., vol. VIII, pp. 193f., esp. 202, 195. This term, used as an adverb of place used with a relative pronoun in John "always indicates a Semitic foundation, (and) is only found elsewhere in the NT in OT quotations."   When used in re: to holy places, "we find in the OT a very ancient and perhaps original technical use of (the Hebrew form of τοποσ) esp. for the great Canaanite shrines which then played a role in the history of Israel: i.e.: Bethel." Gn. 28: 11-19; 35: 7,13,15

"The place" of significance for the Gospel of John, especially with regard to the Temple, is Bethel.

"(Jacob) came to a certain *place* and stayed there for the night, because the sun had set. Taking one of the stones of the *place*, he put it under his head and lay down in that *place*"[221]

Mary went to "the (new) *place*" where heaven and earth meet: to Jesus.

"The Jews who were with her in the house, consoling her, saw Mary get up quickly and go out. They followed her because they thought that she was going to the tomb to weep there." (Jn. 11: 31)

οι ουν Ιουδαιοι οι οντεσ μετ αυτησ εν τη οικια και παραμυθουμενοι αυτην, ιδοντεσ την Μαριαν οτι ταχεωσ ανεστη και εζηλθεν , ηκολου θησαν αυτη, λεγοντεσ, Οτι υπαγει εισ το μνημειον ινα κλαυση εκ ει.

(The Jews therefore who were with her in the house and consoling her, having seen Mary that quickly she rose up and went out, followed her, saying, She is going to the tomb that she may weep there.)[222]

The term translated "go out" is εζερχομαι (*exerxomai*). It is used in one other place in the context of the trilogy; it describes the action of Lazarus when he

---

[221]Gen. 28: 11, 12. Reread the entire account: 28: 10-22.
[222]Gk. and lit. trans. fr. Berry, op. cit.

194   The Examination of Martha and Mary

leaves the tomb (11: 44). Schneider's work[223] makes it possible to understand this text to mean that Mary was "going out" of the tomb that the Temple had become, leaving the place that had been her spiritual home. Her departure from the Temple was like a death and resurrection experience for her. She was leaving darkness and entering into light, going out from death and into life.

The Jews, Temple priests, who had been with Mary, consoling her, witnessed her actions and followed her! Why did they follow her? The text provides a few clues. It says specifically that the priests *said* (not thought) that she was going to the tomb to weep there.   We know that the Temple she is leaving *is* the tomb. Why is she weeping? The term κλαιο (*klaio* -- to cry, to bewail) is used in the New Testament to express grief at parting or strong inner emotion, especially shame or remorse, or weeping for the dead.[224]

"The term has theological significance in the NT only in a few materially related passages, (i.e.:, Lk. 6: 21, 25; 23: 28; Jn. 16: 20). "Very truly I tell you, you will weep and mourn, but the world will rejoice; you will have pain, but your pain will turn to joy." (Jm. 4: 9; 5: 1; Rev. 18: 9ff.) In all these it is used with reference to the present to

___

[223]Johannes Schneider, "εζερχομαι ," Theological Dictionary of the New Testament, op. cit., vol. II, pp. 678f. "To go out . . . The main sense in the NT is local. It serves especially to denote resurrection (Jn. 11: 31 ανεστα και εζηλθεν ; v. 44 εζηλθεν ο τεθνηκοσ). The word can also be used more generally for "to go out from a fellowship;" "to leave" it as a spiritual home." (See 1Jn. 2: 19; 4: 1; 2Jn. 7; 3Jn. 7)

[224]Karl Heinrich Rengstorf, "κλαιο, κλαυθμοσ," Theological Dictionary of the New Testament, op. cit., vol. III, p. 722f.

describe a typical attitude of men of God, or, when applied
to the future, to denote that which awaits the ungodly when
God manifests his right and rule to the whole world . . .
This kind of weeping arises when man recognizes his total
inadequacy in face of God and when he sees that he cannot
evade this, whether it be in respect to his life and its
duration, of his human powers and capacities, or of his
service to God, including the moral life. Thus, in weeping,
God is acknowledged as God and his sway is fundamentally
accepted. This secures to the κλαιοντεσ (klaiontes) God's
grace and fellowship in the future when God will manifest
himself as such. But for those who now set aside God's
claim, this self-revelation will mean the disclosure of their
lostness before him, and it will thus bring κλαιειν (klaiein)
and the more so the more confident they have felt."[225]

Rengstorf notes that κλαιο describes Jacob's
"striving" with God in Hos. 12: 4. "He strove with the
angel and prevailed, he wept and sought his favor; he met
him at Bethel, and there he spoke with him"(Gn. 32: 22).
This "weeping" is a prayer of supplication.
Mary weeps as she leaves the Temple, because she
understands what it means to those to whom she has been
close (the Jews) for Jesus to come in response to her
message. She is weeping with deep emotion for the priests
of the Temple and for the people of Israel whose encounter
with Jesus will leave them lost, spiritually homeless. She
leaves to strive with Jesus to cry out to him on behalf of
those whose souls are separated from God.
She also cries out for herself and all who will be
expelled from the synagogue, a threat that, though it did

---

[225]Ibid.

not begin until around 90 A.D., is clearly recorded in the
Gospel. In Jn. 9 Jewish authorities question the parents of
a blind man Jesus has healed.

" 'Is this your son, who you say was born blind? How then
does he now see?' His parents answered, 'We know that
this is our son and that he was born blind; but we do not
know how it is that he now sees, nor do we know who
opened his eyes. Ask him; he is of age. He will speak for
himself.' His parents said this because they were afraid of
the Jews; for the Jews had already agreed that anyone who
confessed Jesus to be the Messiah would be *put out of the
synagogue.*"

Schrage[226] notes the threat of total expulsion from
the synagogue was a powerful motivator used by Jewish
authorities to discourage heresy in the first and second
centuries.

"In the oldest Palestinian version of the 12th benediction of
the Prayer of Eighteen Benedictions, now known to us
through the findings in the Cairo Geniza, Nazarenes and
minim are mentioned together: 'May the Nazarenes and
heretics perish in a moment, be blotted out of the book of

---

[226]Wolfgang Schrage, *"αποσυναγογοσ,"* Theological Dictionary
of the New Testament, op. cit., vol. VII, p. 848f. See also Jn. 9: 22; 12:
42, "Nevertheless many, even of the authorities, believed in Him. But
because of the Pharisees they did not confess it, for fear that they would
be put out of the synagogue." In 16: 1-3 Jesus says, "I have said these
things to you (disciples) to keep you from stumbling. They will put you
out of the synagogues. Indeed, an hour is coming when those who kill you
will think that by doing so they are offering worship to God. And they
will do this because they have not known the Father or me."

life, and not be written with the just.' The introduction of
this benediction into the Shemone Esre and therewith into
the liturgy by Rabbi Gamaliel II c. 90 A.D. carried with it
a definitive breach between the Christian church and
Judaism. From then on cursing the Nazarenes became an
integral part of synagogue worship and the daily prayer of
every Jew. Precisely in this benediction every great care
was taken to see that the cursing of the minim was done
correctly and without abbreviation. Attending the
synagogue and taking part in its worship thus became
impossible for Christians. Complete separation resulted.
In future confession of Jesus Christ meant excommunication
and expulsion from Judaism. The Johannine statements
belong to this period."

Mary was casting herself out of the synagogue. She
cried as she did it, cried out to God with the passion of a
grief-stricken woman, knowing what it meant for herself,
for the Jews, for the children of Israel, and for the
followers of Jesus.[227]

Perhaps in a cosmic sense, *Marian* knows what it
means for female priests and prophets to be "sent out of the
camp." The picture in the Gospel of John is not of a
quietly weeping woman slipping out of her house to go
greet a beloved friend and teacher on the road in order to

---

[227]That this practice is anachronistic, i.e.: does not present an
accurate *historical* picture of the relations between Jews and Christians
during Jesus' time, but reflects upon the nature of these relations at the
close of the first century does not detract from its importance in the gospel
of John. The theology of John allows for meaning to be "read backwards"
into history, as long as the oracular message remained true to the OT and
the Jesus story as it was known (i.e.: from the synoptic gospels.) Truth is
from the cosmic, not historical, realm.

share her sorrow. It is of a respected member of the Temple community wailing in grief and pain as she throws herself out of the Temple.

The Jews followed her. Why? For Mary, especially Mary the Nazirite, to venture toward a tomb would have been to risk the defilement of her Nazirite vow. For the temple authorities to have followed to witness this does seem in character with the way they are presented in the Gospel. Knowing that the completion of her vow was only hours away, to see her running out of the Temple, obviously grieving, would present the prospect of a scene one didn't see very often, the desecration of a holy vow, and the consequences of it, including the public shaming of a holy woman by the unbraiding of her Nazirite hair and then watching her shaving her head bald! If she were to touch a corpse, or even a tomb, all of that theater would be forthcoming!

"When Mary came where Jesus was and saw him, she knelt at his feet." (Jn. 11: 32a)

Η ουν Μαρια ω σ ηλθεν οπου ην ο Ιησους, ιδουσα αυτον επεσεν εισ τουσ ποδασ αυ του

(Mary therefore when she came where was Jesus, seeing him, fell at his feet)[228]

The journey Mary makes at this moment in the Gospel story is not primarily a topographical one, but a spiritual one. She "walks" from the Temple to "where Jesus was." Where does Jesus abide? At this point, the

---

[228]Ibid.

question uppermost for her and for the reader is one that has been taken for granted throughout the Gospel, a question that must be asked alongside of the most basic question in Christology: "Where does Christ abide?"

A disciple must also be able to respond to the question, "Where do I abide?" Jesus makes it clear that the relationship he models with God is a reciprocal one. (Jn. 14: 10, 20) Mary must now define herself in relation to Jesus. She "sees" him and kneels at his feet; she is no longer a gate keeper. Now she is a humble footstool. She will be the guardian of the incarnate Word of God. At the feet of Jesus she takes her place. This is "the place" where she will encounter God, where she will "see" and "believe."

Mary has fulfilled another function as defined in the Mosaic tradition: she has brought people "out of the camp" to meet God. In Ex. 19: 17 "Moses brought the people out of the camp to meet God. They took their stand at the foot of the mountain."

"and said to him, 'Lord, if you had been here, my brother would not have died." (Jn. 11: 32b)

λεγουσα αυτω , Κυριε, ει ησ ω δε ουκ αν απεθανεν μου ο αδελφοσ.

(saying to him, Lord, if thou hadst been here had not died my brother.)[229]

Mary's first affirmation of faith is identical to her sister Martha's, though she was not a witness to Martha's

---

[229]Gk. and lit. trans. fr. Berry, op. cit.

confession of faith. This is her own confession. It has the same meaning as Martha's, though now it can be understood in greater depth.

"When Jesus saw her weeping, and the Jews who came with her also weeping, he was greatly disturbed in spirit and deeply moved. He said, 'Where have you laid him?' They said to him, 'Lord, come and see.' Jesus began to weep." (Jn. 11: 33-35)

Ιησουσ ουν ω σ ειδεν αυτην κλαιουσαν, και τουσ συνελθοντασ αυτη Ιουδαιουσ κλαιοντασ, ενεβριμησατο τω πνευματι, και εταραζεν εαυτον, και ειπεν, Που τεθ εικατε αυτον; Λεγουσιν αυτω, Κυριε, ερχου και ιδε. Εδακρυσεν ο Ιησουσ.

(Jesus therefore when he saw her weeping, and the who came with her Jews weeping, he groaned in spirit, and troubled himself, and said, Where have ye laid him; They say to him, Lord, come and see. Wept Jesus.)[230]

The phrase translated "groaned in spirit "ενεβριμησατο τω πνευματι" (*enebrimasato to pneumati*) is difficult to translate. *Ενεβριμασατο (enebrimasato)* is a form of εμβριμαομαι (*embrimaomai*), which means "deeply moved, indignant," but its etymology is more illustrative of its powerful intent. It means literally "to snort," and is used in the LXX to translate an image of a wrathful God snorting smoke from his

---

nostrils.[231] It was against this wrath that the Levites were to defend the congregation of the Israelites.[232]

For the writer of the Gospel to have used this term, reflecting a rare image of God, suggests that the reader is to recognize a reference to a LXX passage: Lam. 2.

"How the Lord in his anger has humiliated daughter Zion! He has thrown down from heaven to earth the splendor of Israel; he has not remembered his footstool in the day of his anger.(vs. 1) . . . The Lord has become like an enemy; he has destroyed Israel; he has destroyed all its palaces, laid in ruins its strongholds, and multiplied in daughter Judah mourning and lamentation. He has broken down his booth like a garden, he has destroyed his Tabernacle; the Lord has established in Zion festival and Sabbath, and in his fierce indignation ($\epsilon\mu\beta\rho\iota\mu\alpha o\mu\alpha\iota$) has spurned king and priest.   The Lord has scorned his altar, disowned his sanctuary . . . (vss 5-7a) The elders of daughter Zion sit on the ground in silence; they have thrown dust on their heads and put on sackcloth; the young girls of Jerusalem have bowed their heads to the ground. My eyes are spent with weeping; my stomach churns; my bile is poured out on the ground because of the destruction of my people (vss. 10-11b) . . . Your prophets have seen for you false and deceptive visions; they have not exposed your iniquity to restore your fortunes, but have seen oracles for you that are false and misleading. (vss. 14)"

---

[231]See 2 Sam. 22: 2f , esp. vss. 9, 16; Compare with Psalm 18.

[232]"But the Levites shall camp around the Tabernacle of the Covenant, that there may be no wrath on the congregation of the Israelites; and the Levites shall perform the guard duty of the Tabernacle of the Covenant" (Nu. 1: 53).

"The Jews," the leaders, the "elders" of Israel have been mourning with Mary. They follow her out of the Temple to the place where she falls to the ground before Jesus, as his footstool. The Jews have abandoned their post in the Temple (Nu. 1: 53). When Jesus "snorts" in indignation at the sight of the Jews grieving along with Mary, it is as a sign that God is abandoning his former "footstool." God is replacing the Temple with a new One.

Jn. 11: 33 says that Jesus was "deeply moved" a translation from εταραζεν (*etaraxen*), a form of ταρασσο (*tarasso*), which literally means, "shake together, stir up of water." Figuratively it means, in this context, "He was troubled or agitated."[233] Jn. 5: 2-4 provides a model for the use of this term as part of the description of the pool located near the Sheep Gate, where those who were ill or "stumbling" from infirmities came to be healed.

"Now in Jerusalem by the Sheep Gate there is a pool, called in Hebrew (*Aramaic*) Bethzatha (or *Bethesda* or *Bethsaida*), which has five porticoes. In these lay many invalids -- blind, lame, and paralyzed, *waiting for the stirring of the water; for an angel of the Lord went down at certain seasons into the pool, and stirred up the water; whoever stepped in first after the stirring of the water was made well from whatever disease that person had.*"

The NRSV places vs. 4 in a footnote (italics). It should not be removed from the main body of the text,

---

[233]Wm. F. Arndt and F.W. Gingrich, <u>A Greek-English Lexicon of the New Testament and Other Early Christian Literature</u>, Univ. of Chicago Press, licensed to Zondervan, (12th printing., 1969), pp. 812-813.

because it provides data that relates to other parts of the Gospel. That Jesus was "stirred," indicates that he was agitated like the waters in the pool by the Sheep Gate, named after one of the families who had covenanted with God for the healing of the broken Temple and covenant.

In the reference to "Bethzatha," Beth- means house. Zatha could be "Zattu," one of the lay families who signed a written covenant with God, following the re-building of the Temple (Neh. 10: 14, 28-39). "The rest of the people, the priests, the Levites, the gatekeepers, the singers, the Temple servants, and all who have separated themselves from the peoples of the lands to adhere to the law of God . . . We will not neglect the house of our God."[234]

Those who have eyes to see will understand that Jesus is deeply moved to bring healing to the Temple. Indeed, healing is needed for the entire religious system.

Now the writer of John reminds the reader that what is printed is a cosmic story, a story that is not confined to chronological limitations, but a story that supervenes history. The language of the following exchange comes directly from the well-known account of the first witness of the resurrection found in Jn. 20, the witness of another woman named Mary -- Mary Magdalene,[235] who comes to the tomb in the darkness, sees that the stone has been removed and, seeking Jesus, states twice **"we do not know where they have laid him"** and once **"tell me where you have laid him."** (Jn. 20: 2, 13, 15)

---

[234]See T.M. Mauch, "Zattu," The Interpreter's Dictionary of the Bible, op. cit, vol. 4, p. 936.

[235]The Hour of Jesus' Death functions as a cosmic mirror. All that occurs before it points to it. All that occurs after it points back at it. Jesus' relationship with "Mary" fits tightly on both sides of that mirror.

The first statement is a witness to Peter and the Beloved Disciple, the second is in response to two angels who ask Mary, "Woman, why are you weeping?" The third time the phrase is used is in response to Jesus, whom Mary does not recognize, who asks the same question as asked by the angels, "Woman, why are you weeping?" All of these have a theological importance of their own, but the point for consideration here is that the language[236] used in this portion of Jn. 11 appears to be the same as that used in Jn. 20. In Jn. 11: 34, the question is on the lips of Jesus, whereas in both of the two statements and the question in Jn. 20, the words are on the lips of Mary. Does Mary pattern her language after Jesus, or does Jesus prophesy what Mary will say? Since Jesus is a cosmic being, the answer is "both."

This language is resurrection language, theologically akin to the basic question posed throughout the Gospel: "Where does Christ abide?" It projects a theological challenge by the first-century Christian community (or at least the Johannine community) to the non-believing Jewish community. In each of the three verses of chapter 20 where the phrase in question is used, the inference is that someone ("they") have moved the body of Jesus. It is inferred that the crucified body of Jesus presents a problem to the Jews. Where does one lay the body of one considered by some to be God incarnate? If the Chief Priests ("the Jews") can kill God, then in what "place" do

---

[236] *"Pou tetheikate auton,"* Where have you laid him (11: 34). Compare to *"ouk oidamen pou ethakan auton,"* We know not where they laid him (20: 2) and *"ouk oida pou ethankan auton"* I know not where they laid him (20: 13) and *"pou auton ethakas"* where him you did lay (20: 15).

they put the body? From the Johannine perspective, if
Jacob's ladder has been taken down, either by the defiling
of the Temple by the Chief Priests or by God in response
to the priests' lack of holiness, or by the priests' plot to kill
Jesus, or by God's plan to make the final sacrifice, then
what do such faithless people do with that ladder, that is,
with the Temple building and with the body of Christ?
How can they abandon the Temple? How can they deny
the incarnation when the body of Christ exists in a tangible
form? How can they deny what their own eyes tell them is
true?

The question on the lips of Jesus in Jn. 11: 34 is not
"Where have *they* laid him," but "Where have *you* laid
him." Που τεθεικατε αυτον (*Pou tetheikate auton*).
Unlike Jn. 20: 2, which is in first person plural ("We know
not where they laid him"), or Jn. 20: 13, which is in first
person singular ("I know not where they laid him"), or Jn.
20: 15, which is in second person singular ("Tell me where
you laid him"), this phrase is spoken in second person
plural, the formal address, ("Where have you -- as in all of
you -- laid him?"). The question is not posed to Mary
alone. It is addressed at least to Mary and Martha. More
likely it is addressed to those who followed Mary to Jesus.

That more than one person responds to Jesus'
question is indicated by the voice correctly translated from
Greek in the NRSV, "*They* said to him, Lord, come and
see." Again the language is that of Jesus, replying to the
inquiry of the first disciples, "Where do you abide?" in Jn.
1: 38-39. Those who respond to the question in this
passage address Jesus as Lord, indicating that *they*
understand themselves as disciples. Either Mary and
Martha are replying, or those following Mary have
followed her all the way to faith in Jesus.

This presents the pathetic scene of self-deposed priests guiding Jesus to the Temple, which they now recognize as a tomb, escorting him to the place where his sacrifice must be made. Some have seen the light and are now disciples who know where it is that Christ abides and where his body is to be laid when the sacrifice is complete. Some are still filled with doubt, as is revealed in their verbal reactions to what Jesus does next.

"Jesus began to weep." (Jn. 11: 35)

Εδακρυσεν ο Ιησουσ

(Jesus wept.)

The waters within him are stirred. The healing begins. One passage in the Old Testament uses this word *dakruo* -- not *klaio* "to bewail" as Mary did when she left the Temple. It reveals the meaning of the tears of Jesus.

"On this mountain the Lord of hosts will make for all peoples a feast of rich food, a feast of well-aged wines, of rich food filled with marrow, of well-aged wines strained clear. And he will destroy on this mountain the shroud that is cast over all peoples, the sheet that is spread over all nations; he will swallow up death forever. Then the Lord God will wipe away the tears from all faces, and the disgrace of his people he will take away from all the earth, for the Lord has spoken." (Is. 25: 6-8)[237]

---

[237]The LXX version of this passage, used in the first century, is substantially different from the NRSV. (See vs. 5f:) "We were as faint-hearted men thirsting in Sion (sic), by reason of ungodly men to whom

"So the Jews said, 'See how he loved him!' But some of them said, 'Could not he who opened the eyes of the blind man have kept this man from dying?'" (Jn. 11: 36-37)

ελεγον ουν οι Ιουδαιοι, Ιδε πωσ εφιλει αυτον. Τινεσ δε εζ αυτω ν ειπον, Ουκ ηδυνατο ουτοσ ο ανοιζασ τουσ οφθαλμουσ του τυφλου ποιησαι ινα και ουτοσ μη αποθανη ;

(Said therefore the Jews, Behold how he loved him! But some of them said, Was not able this [man] who opened the eyes of the blind [man], to have caused that also this one should not have died?)[238]

      Some are moved to faith by the love of Jesus. His tears are a sign to them that he knows about the sacrifice and moves toward Jerusalem anyway. Others, though encouraged to believe by the healing of the blind man, wonder, if Jesus is God, why the Temple and all associated with it, could not have been kept alive. For them, the tears of Jesus may have appeared to be a sign of frustration over a circumstance that divine Jesus could not change, raising doubts as to his power and authority. If he could not

---

thou didst deliver us. And the Lord of hosts shall make a feast for all the nations: on this mount they shall drink gladness, they shall drink wine: they shall anoint themselves with ointment in this mountain. Impart thou all these things to the nations; for this is God's counsel upon all the nations. Death has prevailed and swallowed men up; but again the Lord God has taken away every tear from every face. He has taken away the reproach of his people from all the earth: for the mouth of the Lord has spoken it. "

[238]Gk. and lit. trans. fr. Berry, op. cit.

prevent the Temple and the priesthood and all that is holy in Israel from dying, then can he really be God? Unlike Mary's affirmation of faith, "Lord, if you had been here, my brother would not have died," these same words for some of the Jews, were stumbling blocks.

Ironically, the healing of the blind man did, indeed, provide evidence that Jesus could resurrect the priesthood, but those who refused to see that evidence were also blind to the power of creation in Jesus which allowed him to do what he was about to do.

Mary passes her examination, not only because of the meaning of her affirmation of faith, but because of her liturgical gesture in kneeling at the feet of Jesus, weeping and bringing with her those who had chosen to follow her from the Temple. She is more than a disciple who has led others to Christ. She has fulfilled some of the symbolic functions of Moses. Her faith is superior to that of some who are with her, but she does not claim a position of authority. Rather, she assumes the humble posture of a servant, willing to be nothing more than a footstool for Christ. Her deep and sincere humility endears her to a humble Jesus.

Chapter 12
The Ordination Trilogy: Act 1, Scene 2
The Raising of Lazarus

The Stone

"Then Jesus, again greatly disturbed, came to the tomb. It was a cave, and a stone was lying against it. Jesus said, 'Take away the stone.'" (Jn. 11: 38-39a)

Ιησουσ ουν παλιν εμβριμωμενοσ εν εαυτω ερχεται εισ το μνημειον. ην δε σπηλαιον, και λιθοσ επεκειτο επ αυτω. λεγει ο Ιησουσ, Αρατε τον λιθον.

(Jesus therefore again groaning in himself comes to the tomb. Now it was a cave, and a stone was lying upon it. Says Jesus, Take away the stone.)[239]

What Jesus is about to do disturbs him greatly. Though this disturbance will provide for the healing of the covenant, this is no mere healing miracle. He is about to destroy the Temple. The text says that he came to the tomb, which was a cave.

"Μνημειον (mnameion -- tomb) literally means 'memorial,' connected especially with the dead and can even mean the grave. In antiquity the grave is a lonely place to which one may withdraw and which can be in some sense a dwelling. This is particularly true of the

---

[239]Gk. and lit. trans. fr. Berry, op. cit.

Palestinian tombs hewn out of the rock, which can serve as hideouts. According to popular belief, however, the burial ground is a sinister (and unclean) place, for the souls of the dead wander there "[240]

    Jesus has come to the abode of the dead, the Herodian Temple. The text calls it a σπηλαιον *(spalaion -- a cave.)* Once again we turn to the Old Testament for this word's meaning.

"The word that came to Jeremiah from the Lord. Stand in the gate of the Lord's house, and proclaim there this word, and say, Hear the word of the Lord, all you people of Judah, you that enter these gates to worship the Lord. Thus says the Lord of hosts, the God of Israel: Amend your ways and your doings, and let me dwell with you in this place. Do not trust in these deceptive words: 'This is the Temple of the Lord, the Temple of the Lord, the Temple of the Lord.' For if you truly amend your ways and your doings, if you truly act justly one with another, if you do not oppress the alien, the orphan, and the widow, or shed innocent blood in this place, and if you do not go after other gods to your own hurt, then I will dwell with you in this place, in the land that I gave of old to your ancestors forever and ever. Here you are, trusting in deceptive words to no avail. Will you steal, murder, commit adultery, swear falsely, make offerings to Baal, and go after other gods that you have not known, and then come and stand before me in this house, which is called by my name, and say, 'We are safe!' - only to go on doing all

---

[240]O. Michel, "μναμα, μναμειον," <u>Theological Dictionary of the New Testament</u>, op. cit., vol. IV, pp. 679-681

these abominations? *Has this house become a den (spalaion) of robbers in your sight?* You know, I too am watching, says the Lord. Go now to my place that was in Shiloh, where I made my name dwell at first, and see what I did to it for the wickedness of my people Israel. And now, because you have done all these things, says the Lord, and when I spoke to you persistently, you did not listen, and when I called you, you did not answer, therefore I will do to the house that is called by my name, in which you trust, and to the place that I gave to you and to your ancestors, just what I did to Shiloh. And I will cast you out of my sight, just as I cast out all your kinsfolk, all the offspring of Ephraim. . . . Cut off your hair and throw it away; raise a lamentation on the bare heights, for the Lord has rejected and forsaken the generation that provoked his wrath." (Jer. 7: 1-15, 29)

The "cave" is the hide-out of those who dwell in darkness and death, a den of robbers, hewn out of Temple stones. Jesus must confront and cast out this generation of priests, cut them off, end their identity as holy priests. It will be for them as though their (holy) hair were to be cut off and thrown away (not offered for sacrifice as with Nazirites).

"The stone" has important theological significance for John's Gospel. This is not just any stone rolled or placed in front of a tomb. As readers who are by now attuned to the use of oracles in this Gospel, we know that if the "cave" is really the Temple, then the "stone" must be significant in relation to the Temple.

The Temple structure is built of huge stones, and we know from Jn. 2: 19 that the sign sought by the Jews to prove the authority of Jesus to cleanse the Temple was,

"Destroy this Temple, and in three days I will raise it up."
That would seem to imply that the huge stones of the
Jerusalem Temple would be pulled down before the
sacrifice and the resurrection of Jesus would be made to
"raise it (a new Temple) up." It is a historical fact that the
stones of the Temple were pulled down in 70 A.D., a fact
that would have been a matter of recent history to the first-
century Johannine community. The command that Jesus
gives, however, "remove the stone," implies that only one
stone must be removed.

The stone that signifies the Temple has already been
identified. It is the stone which Jacob anoints as the
"House of God" in Gn. 28: 10-22, the story of Jacob's
ladder dream. The removal of this stone theologically,
symbolically, destroys the Temple. Removing the stone of
Beth-el, the consecrated foundation stone that signifies the
base of Jacob's ladder, means that the Temple in Jerusalem
no longer serves its semeiotic function. The metaphor is
dead. Jacob's dream is no more.

The Stench

**"Martha, the sister of the dead man, said to him,
'Lord, already there is a stench because he has been
dead four days."** (Jn. 11: 39b)

Λεγει αυτω η αδελφη του τεθνηκοτοσ Μαρθα,
Κυριε, ηδη οζει τεταρταιοσ γαρ εστιν.

(Says to him the sister of him who has died, Martha, Lord,
already he stinks, four days for it is.)[241]

---

[241]Gk. and lit. trans. fr. Berry, op. cit.

Martha is more than "the sister of the dead man."
She is a disciple who has passed an examination by Jesus
for ordination as a priest. She is a sister in the Johannine
community, a priest whose relationship to the "dead man"
priests of Israel, is that she will take their place; she will
guard against encroachment upon the Temple's holiness.

The true Temple at this point in the Gospel is Jesus.
For Jesus to approach the Herodian Temple, the tomb of
the dead priests, will risk his defilement; it will risk an
encroachment upon his holiness because of the stench of
death that pervades it, since it is no longer protected by the
holy incense.[242]

Once the stone is removed, none of the rituals in the
Temple provide their *semeiotic* function, relating the
worshipper to God. The slaughter of livestock, especially
lambs at Passover, produces the stench of death. If the
message sent by Mary and Martha was sent on the day that
they perceived that the priests had abandoned their
responsibilities, including the placement of incense on the
altar of incense, then the day the message was sent, the two
days that Jesus chose to wait, and the day that he and the
disciples approached Jerusalem would have produced a
four-day period of defilement, leaving little doubt that the
Temple in Jerusalem could no longer be redeemed,
reclaimed, or cleansed.

Martha fulfills her proper role in warning Jesus of
the defilement that is possible. In addition to defiling him,
the risk exists as well for all who are holy in his sight, that
is especially herself and Mary. It would be particularly
important for Mary to avoid this defilement if she was a
Nazirite, since it could encroach upon her holy vow.

---

[242]See Houtman, op. cit., pp. 458-465.

The Glory of God

"Jesus said to her, 'Did I not tell you that if you believed, you would see the glory of God?'" (Jn. 11: 40)

Λεγει αυτη ο Ιησουσ, Ουκ ειπον σοι, οτι εαν πιστευσησ, οψει την δυζαν του θεον ;

(Says to her Jesus, Said I not to thee, that if thou shouldest believe, thou shalt see the glory of God ?)[243]

      Jesus told Martha "I am the resurrection and the life. Those who believe in me, though they die, will live, and everyone who lives and believes in me in no wise shall die forever" (Jn. 11: 25-26).[244] However, Jesus has told those who do not live in the spirit and do not believe,

"Very truly, I tell you, the hour is coming, and is now here, when the dead will hear the voice of the Son of God, and those who hear will live. For just as the Father has life in himself, so he has granted the Son also to have life in himself; and he has given him authority to execute judgement, because he is the Son of Man. Do not be astonished at this; for the hour is coming when all who are in their graves will hear his voice and will come out - those who have done good, to the resurrection of life, and those who have done evil, to the resurrection of condemnation."[245]

---

[243]Gk. and lit. trans. fr. Berry, op. cit.

[244] Literal trans. fr. Berry, op. cit., p. 279

[245] Jn. 5: 25-29 read on, esp. 39-43a; See also Jn. 1: 14; 8: 48-59; 11: 4; 12: 36-43; 17: 1-26

"So they took away the stone." (Jn. 11: 41)

Ηραν ουν τον λιθον ου ην ο τεθνηκωσ κειμενοσ.

(They took away therefore the stone where was the dead laid.)[246]

It is not clear who "they" are. It seems unlikely that "they" are Mary and Martha, because of Martha's concerns about defilement, yet they have proven themselves to be faithful disciples, and Jesus has just issued a command. It may well be that "they" include Mary and Martha as well as those Jews who had left the Temple with Mary and who chose to accept Jesus as Lord (i.e.: not all of those who were present, but some of them). We may infer that there were other (male) disciples present, though they are not specifically mentioned. As a metaphor, we need not be concerned about "who moved the stone." Jesus not only moved the stone, he *removed* the stone, and that is the important thing.

Those responding to the command of Jesus took the stone of Jacob's dream away from the Temple and placed it at Jesus' feet. Mary and Martha and the portion of the crowd from the Temple with them who now accepted and believed in Jesus, transferred their reverence, their allegiance, their loyalty, their devotion, from the Temple to Jesus. For them the Temple is no longer built upon the stone. Jesus is standing on it; Jesus *is* the stone.

---

[246] Lit. trans. fr. Berry, op. cit., p. 281 The KJV: "Then they took away the stone *from the place* where the dead was laid." The NKJV: "Then they took away the stone *from the place* where the dead man was lying."

The Resurrection

"And Jesus looked upward and said, 'Father, I thank you for having heard me." (Jn. 11: 41b)

Ο δε Ιησουσ ηρεν τουσ οφθαλμουσ ανω , και ειπεν, Πατερ, ευχαριστω σοι οτι ηκουσασ.

(And Jesus lifted eyes upwards, and said, 'Father, I thank thee that thou heardest me')[247]

Jesus is performing, or more accurately "celebrating" a liturgical act here. He is modeling the gesture of a priest, "standing" before a congregation and "standing" before God. He is their intermediary, the ladder between God and God's people. He "lifted his eyes upwards," or "looked upward," which is parallel to the description of his gesture in Jn. 17: 1, his priestly prayer: "After Jesus had spoken these words, he looked up to heaven and said, 'Father, the hour has come; glorify your Son so that the Son may glorify you."[248]

---

[247]Lit. trans. fr. Berry, op. cit., p. 280.

[248]See Roswell D. Hitchcock & Francis Brown, ed. & trans., Teaching of the Twelve Apostles, Charles Scribner's Sons, New York, (1885), pp. 16-21. re: pattern of Eucharistic prayers in the Didache: "Regarding the Eucharist. Give thanks as follows: First concerning the cup: 'We thank thee, our Father, Ευχαριστουμεν σοι, Πατερ ημον for the holy vine of David thy servant, which thou has made known to us through Jesus, thy servant; to thee be the glory forever σοι α δοζα εισ τουσ αιονασ. And concerning the broken bread: We thank thee, our Father, for the life and knowledge which thou hast made known to us through Jesus, thy servant; to thee be the glory forever. Now after ye are filled thus do ye give thanks: 'We thank thee, holy Father, for thy holy name which thou hast caused to dwell in our hearts, and for the knowledge

In John, the only other time Jesus offers thanks to God is when Jesus gives thanks for the bread in the story of the feeding of the 5,000 (Jn. 6: 11). This, too, is a liturgical setting, prefiguring the Eucharist. Though there is no indication in Jn. 11: 41 that a meal is about to be served, Act 2 of the trilogy (Jn. 11: 55ff) is clearly set as a meal, following this event. In offering this prayer, Jesus may be modeling the liturgy later used by the early church when celebrating the Eucharist: first giving God thanks, then giving God glory.

"I knew that you always hear me, but I have said this for the sake of the crowd standing here, so that they may believe that you sent me." (Jn. 11: 42)

εγω δε ηδειν οτι παντοτε μου ακουεισ αλα δια
τον   οχλον   τον   περιεστω τα   ειπον   ινα
πιστευσωσιν οτι συ με απεστειλασ.

(and I knew that always me thou hearest; but on account of the crowd who stand around I said [it], that they might believe that thou me didst send.)

The structure of this sentence suggests that it is not a reporter's record of a historical utterance. Jesus would hardly need to explain to God that he knew that God knew what he knew! Clearly the sentence is placed here as a message to the reader, explaining why Jesus was praying and what Jesus was praying.

---

and faith and immortality which thou has made known to us through Jesus, thy servant; to thee be the glory forever.

Once again the Gospel makes reference to those who "stand." Jesus is not merely referring to persons who are in an upright position and not moving. To "stand" in this gospel means "to stand before God," that is, as priests.[249] He is referring to the priests who have left the Temple with Mary. Jesus wants them to hear him. The Gospel writer is making it as clear as possible to the reader that Jesus is performing this act for the sake of those who are witnessing his actions. It is not his prayer alone that Jesus wants them to hear. He is about to bring them back to life spiritually, and his prayer is that they will hear and obey the command that he is about to give them.

Jesus is also praying that those who hear him will believe that God has sent him. The importance of this does not become apparent until Jn. 13: 20 when Jesus says, "Very truly, I tell you, whoever receives one whom I send receives me; and whoever receives me receives him who sent me." This is the beginning of apostolic succession. The *semeion* is the word αποστελοσ (*apostelos*) which means "sent." In Jn. 14: 26 Jesus promises, "The Advocate, the Holy Spirit, whom the Father will send in my name, will teach you everything, and remind you of all that I have said to you." In Jn. 15: 26 Jesus promises "When the Advocate comes, whom I will send to you from the Father, the Spirit of Truth who comes from the Father, he will testify on my behalf." Jn. 16: 7: "Nevertheless I tell you the truth: it is to your advantage that I go away, for if I do not go away, the Advocate will not come to you; but if I go, I will send him to you." In Jn. 17: 8, 18 the sermon reaches its climax. "The words that you gave to me I have given to them, and they have received them and

---

[249]See Lv. 9: 5f.; Ex. 17: 6; Jn. 1: 26; 7: 37.

know in truth that I came from you;   and they have believed that you sent me. . . . As you have sent me into the world, so I have sent them into the world." Finally in Jn. 20: 21 this Gospel's version of the Great Commission: "Peace be with you. As the Father has sent me, so I send you." He breathes on them, giving them new life, and says, "Receive the Holy Spirit."

'When he had said this, he cried out with a loud voice, 'Lazarus, come out!'" (Jn.11: 43)

Και ταυτα ειπων , φωνη μεγαλη εκραυγασεν , Λαζαρε, δευρο εζω.

(And these things having said, with a voice loud he cried, Lazarus, come forth.)

Εκραυγασεν   (*ekraugasen*), a strong form of κραζοω   (*krazo -- cried*)[250] conveys the sense that Jesus is making a loud pronouncement. Given the Prologue,[251] this

---

[250]Walter Grundmann, *"κραζω , "* Theological Dictionary of the New Testament, op. cit., vol. III, p. 901. (See Jn. 11: 43) "The strong verb κραυγαζειν, strengthened even more by the φονα   μεγαλα, is meant to express the greatness of the miracle. All resources have to be thrown in to rob death of its prey. The verb *krazein* occurs four times in John (Jn. 1: 15; 7: 28; 7: 37; 12: 44) and denotes a message which is declared in spite of contradiction and opposition. It is best rendered as crying in the sense of proclamation."

[251]See Gerhard Kittel, *"λεγω,"* Theological Dictionary of the New Testament, op. cit., pp. 131-132 for the connection between Genesis 1: 1 and the Prologue to the Gospel According to John.

is a divine utterance,[252] the voice of the Son of Man (Jn. 5: 19-29, esp. 28). Δευρο εζω (*deuro exo* -- come out) in this verse and εζηλθεν (*eksalthen*-- go forth) in the next are creation terms. The Greek term εζερχομαι (*ekserxomai*) may be used figuratively to mean "to issue from."[253] The same term is used at Jn. 11: 31 to describe the actions of Mary of Bethany and the Jews who followed her, when they "came out" of the "house" (Temple).

The difference between this phrase, "Lazarus, come out (or come forth)!" and the word of creation in Gn. 1: 3 "Come forth, light!" is that their order is reversed. In the creation story, the word of creation is followed by the name or identity of that which is created, prefiguring the process of birth, then the naming of the one who is born. In this passage, the identity of the created being is given first, then the command. In other words, the identity of "Lazarus" is already known. "Lazarus" has already been born (and has died.) Yet the command spoken by Jesus has the force of a word of creation. "Lazarus" is called into life again, "Lazarus" is recreated, resurrected, born anew (Jn. 3: 1-10. esp. vs. 3).

---

[252] "When Jesus with a loud voice summons Lazarus to come forth from the tomb in Jn. 11: 43, He anticipates the voice of the Son of Man that will pierce graves and summon the dead to life and judgement, Jn. 5: 28f" Otto Betz, "φωνεω," Theological Dictionary of the New Testament, op. cit., vol. IX, p. 295.

[253] Johannes Schneider, "εζερχομαι," Theological Dictionary of the New Testament, op. cit., vol. II, pp. 678- 679. The LXX uses the term for 16 Hebrew words. "Apart from the local significance, it is used fig. a. of fruit 'coming forth' out of the earth, and b. of what man 'produces,' whether the fruit of the body or of the lips. It is used esp. of the operations which 'proceed' from God. . . . The main sense in the NT is local. It serves especially to denote resurrection (Jn. 11: 31, 44; See Mt. 27: 53)."

"Lazarus" is the priesthood, represented by "the Jews" who "came out" of the "house" with Mary. The prophesy of Jesus in Jn. 5: 25f is now fulfilled.

"The dead will hear the voice of the Son of God, and those who hear will live . . . all who are in their graves will hear his voice and will come out- those who have done good, to the resurrection of life, and those who have done evil, to the resurrection of condemnation."

"The dead man came out, his hands and feet bound with strips of cloth, and his face wrapped in a cloth. Jesus said to them, 'Unbind him, and let him go.'" (Jn. 11: 44)

Και εζηλθεν ο τεθνηκωσ, δεδεμενοσ του σ ποδασ και τασ χειρασ κειριαισ, και η οψισ αυτου σουδαριω περιεδεδετο . λεγει αυ τοισ ο Ιησουσ, Λυσατε αυτον και αφετε υπαγειν .

(And came forth he who had been dead, bound feet and hands with grave cloths, and his face with a handkerchief bound about. Says to them Jesus, Loose him and let [him] go."[254]

The term translated "the dead man" or "he who had been dead" *o tethnakos* could as easily be translated, "the dead one" or, simply, "the dead." This one who had been dead is identified by the way in which his hands, feet, and head (face) were bound or wrapped. The *semeiotic* functions of a priest, the important roles for head, hands

---

[254]Gk. and lit. trans. fr. Berry, op. cit., p. 280.

and feet as signs of their intermediary role between God and the children of God, are still fettered, veiled, tied, bound. The resurrection of the dead priesthood is not complete. The dead priesthood is out of the Temple tomb, and there is now an indication that it is alive, yet it cannot function. The clothing that once gave it identity is now a grave cloth, a sign of death. To be released from such bindings, the trappings and vestments of the old priesthood must be removed.

The Gospel writer has used the term for "loose" λυο (*luo*) before. In Jn. 1: 27 John the Baptist says that he is not worthy to untie (*loose*) the thong of the sandals of the one who comes after him.

In Jn. 2: 19, Jesus gives a sign of his authority. "Destroy (*loose*) this Temple, and in three days I will raise it up." In Jn. 5: 18 the motive for the Jews seeking to kill Jesus is given. ". . . he was not only breaking (*loosing*) the Sabbath, but was calling God his own Father, thereby making himself equal to God." In Jn. 7: 23 Jesus defends his healing of a man on the Sabbath by pointing out ". . . if a man receives circumcision on the Sabbath in order that the law of Moses may not be broken (*loosed*), are you angry with me because I healed a man's whole body on the Sabbath?" In Jn. 10: 35, Jesus defends his authority with these words, "If those to whom the word of God came were called 'gods' -- the scripture cannot be annulled (loosed) - can you say that the one whom the Father has sanctified and sent into the world is blaspheming because I said, 'I am God's son?'" Clearly the use of this term denotes the sense 'to break up,' 'to destroy,' 'to dismiss.'[255]

---

[255]F. Buchsel, "Λυο ," Theological Dictionary of the New Testament, op. cit., vol. III, p. 336.

Jesus commands Martha and Mary, apparently, to remove the grave clothes from Lazarus. They are to remove the vestments of the Temple priests,[256] thereby removing, destroying, dismissing, breaking up the priesthood, stripping it of its authority and power. The dead are reborn, but not as Chief Priests of the Herodian Temple. They shall live as believers in Jesus, not in the manner and with the kind of authority and power they presumed to have while serving in the Herodian Temple, but as disciples.

"Many of the Jews therefore, who had come with Mary and had seen what Jesus did, believed in him." (Jn. 11: 45)

Πολλοι ουν εκ τω ν Ιουδαιων οι ελθοντεσ προσ την Μαριαν και θεασαμενοι α εποιησεν ο Ιησουσ, επιστευσαν εισ αυτον.

(Many therefore of the Jews who came to Mary and saw what did Jesus, believed on him.)[257]

As Jesus prophesied (Jn. 5: 28-29), some of the Jews believed and became disciples of Jesus. Jesus' prophesy says that "All who are in their graves will hear his (the Son of Man's) voice and will come out -- those who have done good, to the resurrection of life, and those who have done evil, to the resurrection of condemnation."

The Greek words translated by the NRSV as "resurrection of life" and "resurrection of condemnation"

---

[256]See Lv. 8: 13; Ex. 28: esp. 28: 40.

[257]Gk. and lit. trans, fr. Berry, op. cit. p. 280.

are found exclusively in Isaiah's prophetic oracle of judgement against corrupt rulers, priests, and prophets.[258] It refers to the "raising up" of a cornerstone, by inference the erection of a new wall or building (a Temple), which would serve to cause the unjust to stumble. This image is included in Psalm 118 which was traditionally recited (or sung) at the Passover observance.[259] It is used as a term for resurrection in Is. 26: 19-21a.

"Your dead shall live, their corpses shall *rise*. O dwellers in the dust, awake and sing for joy! For your dew is a radiant dew, and the earth will give birth to those long dead. Come, my people, enter your chambers, and shut your doors behind you; hide yourselves for a little while until the wrath is past. For the Lord comes out from his place to punish the inhabitants of the earth for their iniquity . . . "

---

[258]See Isaiah 28, esp. 28: 14f.; See also Albrecht Oepke, "αναστασισ, εζαναστασισ," and "ανισταμι, εζανισταμι," Theological Dictionary of the New Testament, op. cit., vol. I, pp. 368-372. *anastasin*, which means "raising up" applies to the installation by God of "a foundation stone, a precious cornerstone, a sure foundation." (Is. 28: 16). In Is. 8: 14-15, God addresses the nation called Immanuel through the prophet, warning them not to fear anyone but the Lord of hosts. "He will become a sanctuary, a stone one strikes against; for both houses of Israel will become a rock one stumbles over - a trap and a snare for the inhabitants of Jerusalem. And many among them shall stumble; they shall fall and be broken; they shall be snared and taken." This same symbol is quoted in Ps. 118: 22, 23. "The stone that the builders rejected has become the chief cornerstone. This is the Lord's doing; it is marvelous in our eyes." "Otherwise the term is used exclusively of the resurrection (of Christ) from the dead."

[259]See also Mt. 21: 42-44; Mk. 12: 10-11; 13: 1-2; Lk. 20: 17-18; Acts 4: 11; Rom. 9: 33; 1 Peter 6: 2-8.

This passage reads differently in the LXX than it does in the NRSV of the Bible.

"The dead shall *rise*, and they that are in the earth shall rejoice: for the dew from thee is healing to them: but the land of the ungodly shall perish.   Go, my people, enter into thy closets, shut thy door, hide thyself for a little season, until the anger of the Lord (has) passed away. For behold, the Lord is bringing wrath from his holy place upon the dwellers on the earth . . ." (Is. 26: 19-21a LXX).

The resurrection, viewed from the Septuagint version of this Isaiah passage, is a manner of judgement. God "comes out" in wrath not against individual priests, as with Nadab and Abihu in Lv. 10, but against all iniquity on the earth from *"his holy place,"* healing the dead with dew, and allowing "the land of the ungodly" to perish.

From the perspective of the Gospel of John, the wrath of God tears down the stone which has been raised up as the Temple, but has become the dwelling place of those who abide in death, and replaces it, raises it up or resurrects it, with a new Temple, which brings healing and rebirth to those in the world who have been dead in the spirit by applying "God's dew," the waters of life, baptism.[260] Judgement comes upon those who choose to live in the world without God, in the land of the ungodly, for they shall perish.

---

[260]Rudolf Bultmann, *"ζαω,"* Theological Dictionary of the New Testament, op. cit., vol. III, p. 840 n. 63. "Belief in the divine power of flowing water, which derives from (Semitic) nature religion, led to the idea of a fount of life in the heavenly world and also to belief in the lifegiving power of sacramental water, whether as a drink dispensing immortality or as baptism."

"But some of them went to the Pharisees and told them what he had done." (Jn. 11: 46)

τινεσ δε εζ αυτω ν απηλθον προσ τουσ Φαρισαιουσ και ειπον αυτοισ α εποιησεν ο Ιησουσ.

(but some of them went to the Pharisees and told them what did Jesus.)[261]

Jesus' prophesy in Jn. 5: 28-29 says that some who have done good will come out in response to his voice, to "the resurrection of life," while those who have done evil will come out "to the resurrection of condemnation." The Greek (*anastasin kriseos*) literally says "a resurrection of judgement."

The words translated judgement κρινο , κρισισ, κριμα (*krino, krisis, krima*) are used frequently and in a way that is distinctive in the Gospel of John.[262] It occurs at the moment that any person chooses to believe or not to believe in Jesus. It separates those who will live eternally from those whose life is terminal. The resurrection of

---

[261]Gk. and lit. trans. fr. Berry, op. cit, pp. 280-281.

[262]See Freidrich Buchsel, *"κρισισ,"* Theological Dictionary of the New Testament, Op. cit., vol. III, p. 941. "In the NT it is the "decision of the judge," the "judgement." This may be either divine or human, and it is mostly penal judgement. The word is rare in Pl. but common in Jn. and the Catholic Epistles. In Jn. *krisis* is the world judgment of Christ, originally future, 5: 28f and 1 Jn. 4: 17, but also present already, 3: 18-21; 5: 24f, 30; 12: 31; 16: 11. The sense of decision or separation is hinted here. But this does not mean that for Jn. *krisis* is not judgment. World judgement always entails separation, See Mt. 25: 31-46, esp. 25: 32. See also Buchsel, *"κρινο ,"* Ibid. pp. 938-939, including n. 69, p. 939.

judgement is the final moment of those who reject eternal
life through faith in Christ. In John those who belong in
this group are identified as "the world." They are people
who choose to live without faith and, therefore, without
God. They are, therefore, dead.

Jn. 11:46 fulfills the prophesy of Jn. 5: 28-29 by
identifying some of those who had heard the resurrection
command of Jesus as persons who chose to ally themselves
with the Pharisees, who are characterized as those who
abide in darkness. They have chosen the resurrection of
judgement. This judgement is not only against themselves;
it is against Jesus. By rejecting Jesus as God, they reject
God, and they condemn themselves.

The witness of these who separate themselves from
Jesus is not about what they have seen, (i.e.: a dead man
being raised to life), but about "what Jesus had done." He
had commanded them to be reborn (Jn. 3: 3). In
communicating this to the Pharisees, they served as
evangelists, passing the Word of God to the other Chief
Priests and Pharisees.

The Judgement

**"So the Chief Priests and the Pharisees called a meeting
of the council, and said, 'What are we to do? This man
is performing many signs. If we let him go on like this,
everyone will believe in him, and the Romans will come
and destroy both our holy place and our nation." (Jn.
11: 47-48)**

συνηγαγον ουν οι αρχιερεισ και οι Φαρισαιοι
συνεδριον, και ελεγον, Τι ποιουμεν; οτι ουτοσ ο
ανθρωποσ πολλα σημεια ποιει. εαν αφωμεν

αυτον ουτωσ, παντεσ πιστευσουσιν εισ αυτον, και ελευσονται οι Ρωμαιοι και αρουσιν ημων και τον τοπον και το εθνοσ.

(Gathered therefore the Chief Priests and the Pharisees a council, and said, What do we? for this man many signs does. If we let alone him thus, all will believe on him, and will come the Romans and will take away from us both the place and the nation.)[263]

     The Chief Priests[264] and the Pharisees[265] considered themselves separate and superior to the general population of Israel. Since they knew God's laws and most other people didn't,[266] it was incumbent upon them to protect the people of God from any influence which might cause the

---

[263]Gk. and lit. trans. fr. Berry, op. cit.

[264]Gottlob Schrenck, "αρχιερευσ," Theological Dictionary of the New Testament, op. cit., vol. 3, p. 270. "The Chief Priests seem to be an established college with oversight of the cultus, control of the temple, administration of the temple treasury, and supervision of priestly discipline. They have a seat and voice in the Sanhedrin." See the entire article, pp. 265-283; see also Schrenck, "ιερευσ," Ibid., pp. 257-265.

[265]Rudolf Meyer, "Φαρισαιοσ," Theological Dictionary of the New Testament, op. cit., vol. IX, pp. 11-35, (A: "Pharisaism in Judaism") esp. pp. 12, 15. See also H.F. Weiss, "Φαρισαιοσ," Ibid, pp. 35-48 ("B: Pharisees in the New Testament"), esp. p. 41 "Materially related to the observance of the priestly rules of purification are the characteristic attempts of the Pharisees to separate themselves from the 'people who knoweth not the law' (Jn. 7:49), i.e.: the 'Am ha-' Ares." See pp. 43-45 "II. The Pharisees in John's Gospel."

[266]See Rudolf Meyer, "οχλοσ," Theological Dictionary of the New Testament, op. cit., pp. 588-590.

children of Israel to violate the Law.[267]   They were powerful enough to call a meeting of the Council of the Sanhedrin, where their consternation previously expressed in Jn. 7: 32f is carried to a new extreme. The council is confused, since it does not know how to interpret the signs that Jesus offers. They fear both the religious and the political consequences of failing to maintain the law.[268]

Ironically, Jesus has already destroyed the Temple. Their holy "place" is already gone. Nothing that the council can do at this point can restore its holiness. Their confusion and paranoia reflect their inability to discern God's presence or absence in this situation.

In Jn. 7: 50f., Nicodemus reminds the Council that they are bound to act according to the Law, but in Jn. 11: 49f., the High Priest brings the proceeding to its conclusion.

"But one of them, Caiaphas, who was High Priest that year, said to them, 'You do not understand that it is better for you to have one man die for the people than to have the whole nation destroyed.' He did not say this

---

[267]See Jn. 7: 45 - 52. The Chief Priests and Pharisees reflect the attitude that the crowd "does not know the law," and therefore cannot know what is best for Israel and cannot know God. Note that Nicodemus, a Pharisee, debates with his colleagues regarding their condemnation of Jesus.

[268]Eduard Lohse, "συνεδριον ," Theological Dictionary of the New Testament, op. cit., vol. VII, pp. 860-871, esp. 862-866. The Council of the Sanhedrin was comprised of 70 aristocratic priests (called Chief Priests, Sadducean in sympathy) and elders (Pharisaic scribes) of Israel, and led by the High Priest. Lohse chronicles the violations of Sanhedrin law that occurred when Jesus was tried and condemned to die (p. 868).

on his own, but being High Priest that year he prophesied that Jesus was about to die for the nation, and not for the nation only, but to gather into one the dispersed children of God." (Jn. 11: 49-52)

Εισ δε τισ εζ αυ τω ν , Καιαφασ, αρχιερευσ ω ν του ενιαυτου εκεινου, ειπεν αυ τοισ, Υμεισ ουκ οιδατε ουδεν , ου δε διαλογιζεσθε οτι συ μφερει ημιν ινα εισ ανθρωποσ αποθανη υπερ του λαου, και μη ολον το εθνοσ αποληται . Τουτο δε αφ εαυτου ουκ ειπεν, αλλ α αρχιερευσ ω ν του ενιαυτου εκεινου , προεφητευσεν οτι εμελλεν ο Ιησουσ αποθνησκ ειν υπερ του εθνουσ, και ουχ υπερ του εθνουσ μονον, αλλ ινα και τα τεκνα του θεου τα διεσκορπισμενα συναγαγη εισ εν.

(But a certain one of them, Caiaphas, High Priest being of that year, said to them, Ye know nothing, nor consider that it is profitable for us that one man should die for the people, and not whole the nation should perish. But this from himself he said not, but High Priest being of that year, prophesied that was about Jesus to die for the nation; and not for the nation only, but that also the children of God who have been scattered abroad he might gather into one.)[269]

The Gospel writer wants the reader to understand that the words of Caiaphas were not simply a part of a general discussion within the Council of the Sanhedrin. They constitute a pronouncement which reinterprets the role of the High Priest as an agent of atonement for the nation

[269]Gk. and lit. trans. fr. Berry, op. cit.

of Israel. In essence, Caiaphas acknowledges that Jesus is
the atonement sacrifice, not only for Israel, but for all of
the scattered children of God. The Greek phrase "that also
the children of God who have been scattered abroad he
might gather into one" is strikingly similar to the language
of the Eucharist in the Didache:

"Just as this broken bread was scattered over the hills and
having been gathered together became one, so let thy
church be gathered together from the ends of the earth into
thy kingdom..."[270]

  The rite of atonement is now replaced by the
Eucharist. The Gospel writer has used a part of the first-
century church's liturgy to reinterpret the significance of
the atonement as declared by the High Priest,[271] that is: as
"the memorable year of the death of Jesus."[272]

**"So from that day on they planned to put him to
death."** (Jn. 11:53)

απ εκεινησ ουν τησ ημερασ εβουλευσαντο ινα
απο κ τεινω σιν αυτον.

---

[270]Hitchcock and Brown, ed. & trans., Teaching of the Twelve
Apostles, op. cit., Chapter IX, p. 17.

[271]Schrenck, "αρχιερευσ," op. cit., p. 269. "The duties of the
High Priest are primarily cultic. His unique and supreme prerogative,
which distinguishes him from all other men, is that once a year he can go
into the Holy of Holies to offer sacrifice on the great Day of Atonement.
Rabbinic tradition speaks of heavenly voices granted to the officiating High
Priest in the innermost sanctuary. Perhaps there is a reference to this in
Jn. 11: 51, where the αρχιερευσ is a prophet."

[272]Ibid., p. 270.

(From that therefore day they took counsel together that they might kill him.)[273]

"That day" appears at first to be the day in which the decision was made to execute Jesus. The theology of the Fourth Gospel suggests, however, that more is meant here. This is the day of creation, the day of rebirth, the day of resurrection. It is intended to convey the truth that though Jesus is already victorious over death, those who have been resurrected to judgement continuously, in futility, plan to put him to death (See Jn. 1: 5, 10-15).

"Jesus therefore no longer walked about openly among the Jews, but went from there to a town called Ephraim in the region near the wilderness; and he remained there with the disciples." (Jn. 11: 54)

Ιησουσ ουν ουκ ετι παρρησια περιεπατει εν τοισ Ιουδαιοισ, αλλα απηλθεν εκειθεν εισ την χωραν εγγυσ τησ ερημου, εισ Εφραιμ λεγομεν ην πολιν, κακει διετριβεν μετα τω ν μαθητων αυ του.

(Jesus therefore no longer publicly walked among the Jews, but went away thence into the country near the desert, to Ephraim called a city, and there he stayed with his disciples.)[274]

---

[273]Gk. and lit. trans. fr. Berry, op. cit.

[274]Gk. and lit. trans. fr. Berry, op. cit., p. 281.

The term translated "to remain"[275] in the NRSV is often translated "to abide," which more adequately conveys the theological intent of its use in John.[276] The witness of John the Baptist in Jn. 1: 32, that the Spirit descends from heaven upon Jesus and "remains" in him, acknowledges that life in Jesus is not limited by the boundaries of human flesh.

The Gospel records a lengthy monologue by Jesus, explaining how it is that God abides in Jesus, who in turn abides in each one of his disciples (Jn. 14). The life that "abides" in these disciples is the same life that "remains" in the world, even after body of Jesus has been sacrificed.

In the transition between the story of the raising of Lazarus and the anointing story, there is a sense of the continual presence of Jesus who "abides" or "remains" with his disciples, those who believe in him,[277] in contrast to the clear message that Jesus is now alienated from "the Jews," who do not believe. He "no longer walked openly

---

[275]See F. Hauck, "μενο," Theological Dictionary of the New Testament, op. cit., vol. IV, p. 575, n.3. "μενειν occurs 112 times in the NT, 66 times in the Johannine writings (40 in the Gospel, 23 in 1Jn, 3 in 2Jn.) Note: not all ancient manuscripts use μενο in this passage. Some use διετριβεν, which means "tarried."

[276]Ibid., pp. 575-576. "μενειν is particularly common in the Johannine writings. The statement that Jesus Himself abides in Jn. 12: 34 is undoubtedly designed to assert apologetically the eternal character of the dignity of Jesus in face of Jewish protests which deny his messiahship on the basis of His transitory earthly existence. The abiding of the Spirit of Christ in Jn. 1: 32 lifts Him above the prophets, who are honored only with temporary inspiration. It also lifts His filling with the Spirit, and the later filling of Christians, above the passing ecstatic states of pagans. The endowment of the Spirit is a continuing state in the Christian religion."

[277]See Jn. 1: 32-33, 38; 7: 9; 8: 31; 9: 41; 10: 40; 12: 24, 46; 15: 4-10, 16; 19: 31; 21: 22-23.

among the Jews" is the sad conclusion of the story all the world knows as "the raising of Lazarus."[278]

The old priesthood has alienated itself from God. Those who would continue to serve God have been called out of their old "place." Those who have responded to the call have had their priestly robes removed and are now numbered among the disciples of Jesus. The stage is set for the ordination of a new priesthood, which is what follows.

---

[278]For a further consideration of 11: 54, See above on 11: 19.

Chapter 13
The Ordination Trilogy: Act 2
The Ordination of Mary of Bethany

The Table Setting

"Now the Passover of the Jews was near, and many went up from the country to Jerusalem before the Passover to purify themselves." (Jn. 11: 55)

Ην δε εγγυσ το πασχα των Ιουδαιων, και ανεβησαν πολλοι εισ Ιεροσολυμα εκ τησ χωρασ προ πασχα, ινα αγνισωσιν εαυτουσ.

(Now was near the passover of the Jews, and went up many to Jerusalem out of the country before the passover, that they might purify themselves.)[279]

Ironically, the Jews who have turned away from Life,[280] are preparing to celebrate the Passover, the festival that recalls the gracious gift of life given by God to people who lived by faith when guided by Moses. The Passover of the Jews was near. For the disciples, Jesus is the Passover of God, the "resurrection of life" (Jn. 5: 29; 11: 25). Nevertheless, the setting for the Jewish Passover observance now becomes important in the Gospel. The eschatological banquet with the "lamb of God" as both host

---

[279]Gk. and lit. trans. fr. Berry, op. cit.

[280]That Jesus is the source of life and eternal life, See Jn. 1: 4; 3: 15-16, 36; 4: 14, 36; 5: 21, 24, 28-29; 6: 25-71; 8: 12; 10: 10, 28; 11: 25; 12: 25, 50; 14: 6; 17: 2-3; 20: 31. That rejecting Jesus means rejecting life, See Jn. 3: 36; 5: 39f; 6: 53.

and main course, first suggested in John's witness in Jn. 1: 29, is now at hand.[281]

The deacons among the disciples have set the table and prepared the meal, following instructions given to them by Jesus first at the wedding at Cana in Jn. 2: 1-11. There Jesus replaces the water of purification (Nu. 19: 1-9) with wine. John the Baptist later clarifies (Jn. 3: 29) that this is a covenant banquet with Israel and that Jesus is the Divine Host.[282] Further instructions have been provided at the feeding of the multitude,[283] where words of interpretation for the bread and wine of the Eucharist are provided (Jn. 6: 35, 51, 55-56). Words of institution are also recorded in Jn. 7: 37f., and the language in Jn. 15 is an extensive interpretation of the Eucharist.

Purification

Little more than what has already been noted is known about the Jewish rites of purification. Jn. 2: 6; 3:

---

[281]See Johannes Behm, "κλαω ," Theological Dictionary of the New Testament, op. cit., vol. III, pp. 741-742 on The Lord's Supper in John.

[282]See Is. 61, esp. 61: 5; Joachim Jeremias points out that "Nowhere in the O.T. is the Messiah presented as a bridegroom." He does acknowledge, however, that "from the time of Hosea the O.T. is acquainted with the metaphor of the marriage of Yahweh and Israel, which it uses to depict the covenant relation of God to His people." For John, Jesus *is* God, therefore the metaphor is appropriate. See J. Jeremias, "νυμφη, νυμφιοσ ," Theological Dictionary of the New Testament, op. cit., vol. IV, pp. 1099-1106.

[283]Note the material connection between the setting for the meal in 6: 4 "Now the Passover, the festival of the Jews, was near." and the setting in 11: 55. Philip (6: 5-7), Andrew (6: 8-9), and "his disciples" (6: 12) are clearly deacons in at this meal.

25 imply that these rites involved a spiritual cleansing with
water in a way that was apparently similar to the baptismal
rites performed by John the Baptist. Nu. 31: 21-24
explains the importance of purification by water. Nu. 19:
1-13 details the process of sacrificing a red heifer, the ashes
from which were mixed with water for use in purification
rites. Neh. 12: 44f. suggests that singing was a part of
these rites and that the singers and gatekeepers of the
Temple[284] were specifically involved in them. Nu. 31: 19-
20 directs that the rites take place outside of the camp and
that they require seven days, focusing on the third and the
seventh days, to cleanse those who have been defiled. Jn.
2: 6 indicates that a large amount of this water was kept on
hand for these rites.

**"They were looking for Jesus and were asking one
another as they stood in the Temple, 'What do you
think? Surely he will not come to the festival, will he?
Now the Chief Priests and the Pharisees had given
orders that anyone who knew where Jesus was should
let them know, so that they might arrest him." (Jn. 11:
56-57)**

εζητουν ουν τον Ιησουν, και ελεγον μετ αλληλω
νε τω ιερω εστηκοτεσ, Τι δοκει υμιν, οτι ου
μη ελθη εις την εορτην; Δεδωκεισαν δε και οι
αρχιερεισ και οι Φαρισαιοι εντολην, ινα εαν τισ
γνω που εστιν μηνυση, σπωσ πιασωσιν αυτον.

(They were seeking therefore Jesus, and were saying among
one another in the Temple standing, What does it seem to

---

[284]See also Neh. 13: 22.

you, that in no wise he will come to the feast? Now had given both the Chief Priests and the Pharisees a command, that if anyone should know where he is he should show [it], that they might take him.)[285]

As indicated before, these verses, quoted from Jn. 7: 11f., point out the ironic fact that many people in Israel knew who Jesus was and where he was (where Jesus abides), but the Chief Priests and the Pharisees did not know, and that is an indictment against them (Jn. 1: 10-11). The construction of Jn. 11: 56 infers, ironically, that the religious leaders, standing in the Temple during the time of preparation, were *therefore* seeking Jesus. The Christology already provided in the Gospel suggests that if they had been preparing to receive the Eucharist, they would, indeed, have been "purified."   They seek purification, but leave orders (a command) that Jesus should be arrested (taken).

The Time and Place

"Six days before the Passover Jesus came to Bethany, the home of Lazarus, whom he had raised from the dead." (Jn. 12: 1)

Ο ουν Ιησουσ προ εζ ημερων του πασχα ηλθεν εισ Βηθανιαν , οπου ην Λαζαροσ ο τεθνηκωσ, ον ηγειρεν εκ νεκρων.

---

[285]Gk. and lit. trans. fr. Berry, op. cit., p. 281.

(Jesus therefore before six days the passover came to
Bethany, where was Lazarus who had died.)[286]

        The importance of this setting has been already
considered, as has the significance of Bethany, the identity
of Lazarus and the meaning of the story of the raising of
Lazarus.

The Meal

**"There they gave a dinner for him. Martha served, and
Lazarus was one of those at the table with him."** (Jn.
12: 2)

εποιησαν ουν αυτω δειπνον εκει, και η Μαρθα
διηκονει ο δε Λαζαροσ εισ ην τω ν
συνανακειμενων αυτω .

(They made therefore him a supper there, and Martha
served, but Lazarus one was of those reclining with him.)[287]

        The note that Lazarus was at the table with Jesus
indicates that he is no longer a celebrant, but is now a
participant in the ritual meal. The Chief Priests who have
left the Temple, following Mary, and have accepted the
resurrection of life from Jesus are now among his disciples,
but they are not, at least at this point, given priestly roles.
On the other hand, the fact that they are sitting at the table
with Jesus indicates that they enjoy equal status as disciples,
persons included by Jesus as part of his own "flock."

---

[286]Gk. and lit. trans. fr. Berry, op. cit.
[287]Gk. and lit. trans. fr. Berry, op. cit., p. 282.

The Ritual

"Mary took a pound of costly perfume made of pure nard, anointed Jesus' feet, and wiped them with her hair. The house was filled with the fragrance of the perfume." (Jn. 12: 3)

Η ουν Μαρια λαβουσα λιτραν μυρου ναρδου πιστικησ πολυτιμου, ηλειψεν τουσ ποδασ του Ιησου, και εζεμαζεν ταισ θριζιν αυτησ τουσ ποδασ αυτου η δε οικια επληρωθη εκ τησ οσμησ του μυρου.

(Mary therefore having taken a pound of ointment of nard pure of great price, anointed the feet of Jesus, and wiped with her hair his feet; and the house was filled with the odor of the ointment.)[288]

Since the roles of Martha and Lazarus have been specified, and since the setting is so clearly identified with Lazarus, Martha, and Mary, then the celebrant at this meal is Mary. The Gospel writer seems to have assumed that those with eyes to see will know that this is the Eucharist, though the ritual for the Eucharist is not described.

The ritual that is described is so bizarre that it virtually requires the reader who seeks to understand it to look for signs, the most obvious of which is the "costly perfume (ointment) made of pure nard," (spikenard) the fragrance of which filled the house.[289]

---

[288]Ibid.

[289]See Gerhard Delling, "οσμα,' Theological Dictionary of the New Testament, op. cit., vol. V, pp. 493f.

The Ointment

The term used to describe the amount of perfume used λιτραν *"litran"* designates a Roman pound, that is 12 ounces. This term is used again in Jn. 19: 39 to indicate the amount of myrrh and aloes brought by Nicodemus and Joseph of Arimathea to embalm the body of Jesus for burial after it was removed from the cross. (100 *litran* -- 75 lbs. was used!)

The amount of perfumed ointment is important for two reasons. First, it contradicts the interpretation by nearly all of the scholars that this bizarre ritual is presented as a pre-figuring of the embalming of Christ's body for burial. Brown suggests that this explanation is inadequate, since there is no precedence for embalming a body before it is dead and since the amount of myrrh and aloes required for such a purpose far exceeds the amount that Mary uses. In addition, Jn. 19: 39 suggests that the perfumed ointment brought specifically for use in preparing the body of Jesus for burial was a mixture of myrrh and aloes, an aromatic sap. No aloes are mentioned in Jn. 12: 3. Instead, the signs that reveal the ointment's importance are that it is "pure" and that its fragrance "fills the house."

The term translated "pure" πιστικοσ (*pistikos*) is used only twice in the Bible, both times to describe the oil of spikenard used to anoint Jesus.[290] It belongs to the same word group as πιστισ (*pistis* -- "faith") and πιστευιεν (*pisteuein* -- believe, esp. believe in or into). *Pistikos*

---

[290]William F. Arndt and F. Wilbur Gingrich, A Greek-English Lexicon of the New Testament, op. cit., p. 668, "only as modifying *nardos* (nard) w. *polutelas* or *polutimos* (costly, very expensive) Mk. 14: 3; Jn. 12: 3."

literally means "faithful."[291] The fact that it is paired with πολυτιμου (polutimou - costly, expensive) provides a double entendre inferring for those with eyes to see a sign of the high cost and value of faith. The monetary value of the ointment (300 denarii -- Jn. 12: 5) is roughly equivalent to a full year's wages for common labor.[292]

The amount and value of this faithful and expensive oil of spikenard is important for a second reason; it allows us to compare its cost to Mary with the cost of a Nazirite vow, the most expensive of all of the sacrifices (worth all of the others combined). The ointment's value is slightly more than the cost of a Nazirite vow for an adult male of Jesus' age (250 denarii). It is twice the cost of a Nazirite vow for a female of similar age (150 denarii). If, as I have suggested, Mary gained access to the Jerusalem Temple on the night in which he was betrayed because she was due to complete her Nazirite vow then, the monetary cost of her faithfulness to Jesus was extremely high.[294] The value of her sacrifice is understandably "pleasing unto the Lord." It is no wonder that Judas, though he did not know the full extent of it, took note of her generous gesture.

---

[291]See an extensive article written by Rudolf Bultmann and Artur Weiser, "pisteuo," Theological Dictionary of the New Testament, op. cit., vol. VI, pp. 174-228, esp. pp. 222f. Perhaps because of Bultmann's work, the importance of the Fourth Gospel's use of pisteuo is well known. What is less well known is that "pistikos" ties the anointing oil used by Mary to all that pisteuo and its various forms mean in the gospel.

[292]Imagine the extraordinary cost of the 100 lbs. provided by Nicodemus and Joseph of Arimathea!

[294]Especially if we take into consideration the possibility that Mosaic Law required that a red heifer would have had to be sacrificed for her purification rites to begin. See Nu. 19: 1 through 20: 13, esp. 19: 1-9.

That the aroma of this sacrifice filled the house points directly to the proscription in Ex. 30: 1-10 that requires that an altar exclusively for burning incense shall be maintained by the High Priest inside of the sanctuary. The High Priest placed incense on the coals of this altar twice each day, so that the aroma would fill the house of the Lord. Houtman[295] explains that this was to "form an atmospheric curtain which (would) protect the place of YHWH's revelation against possible bad exhalations and fumes, which are so pungent that they manage to penetrate in the Holy Places." Mary's ointment is the new Temple's incense.

Mary's Personal Sacrifice and Glory

The correlation between Mary's sacrifice for Jesus and the Nazirite ritual, however, is not limited to the monetary value of the sacrifice. There is a direct *semeiotic* parallel in the ritual as described in Jn. 12: 3. The Nazirite must place her (or his) hair under the sacrifice and make an offering of it along with the sacrifice. When Mary dries the oil of spikenard from the feet of Jesus, she is placing her hair under the sacrifice.

That it is his feet that Mary anoints should by now be no mystery. Jesus is not only the replacement for all Jewish sacrifices, he is the new Temple, a replacement for Jacob's ladder. His feet are the altar at which Mary worships. Her faith is at once in his incarnation as the divine *logos* and in his identity as the resurrection of life. His presence, both during this soon-to-be finished walk

---

[295]See Houtman, op. cit., pp. 463-464. See also Ex. 25: 22; 30: 6; Lv. 16: 2; Nu. 7: 89.

upon the earth, and as her resurrected Lord, is symbolized by his feet. She and those who follow her example, are his footstool. His feet are now anointed, just as Moses anointed the altar in the Tabernacle and Jacob anointed the stone which for him represented "the house of God." This is truly an anointing story, and the fact that Mary does not anoint the head of Jesus is to be understood as an intentional sign, offered by Mary of Bethany, to all of the disciples present at this important meal. She understands ("sees") the *semeiotic* role that Jesus is playing, and she believes in him. She commits her life to him in a vow as sacred as any vow a Nazirite could ever make.

In the process of making this extraordinary liturgical gesture, Mary's head is anointed. Comparable to the High Priest, she is now "Holy unto the Lord" (Nu. 6: 7-8). She has consecrated herself according to God's instructions given to Moses (Ex. 19: 10-25).

"The Lord said to Moses, 'Go to the people and consecrate them today and tomorrow. Have them wash their clothes and prepare for the third day, because on the third day the Lord will come down upon Mount Sinai in the sight of all the people. You shall set limits for the people all around, saying, 'Be careful not to go up the mountain or touch the edge of it. Any who touch the mountain shall be put to death. No hand shall touch them, but they shall be stoned or shot (with arrows); whether animal or human being, they shall not live. When the trumpet sounds a long blast, they may go up on the mountain.' So Moses went down from the mountain to the people. He consecrated the people, and they washed their clothes. And he said to the people, 'Prepare for the third day; do not go near a woman.' On the morning of the third day there was thunder and lightning, as well as a thick cloud on the mountain, and a blast of a trumpet so loud that all the people who were in the camp trembled. Moses brought the people out of the camp to meet God. They took their stand at the foot of the mountain. . . . Then the Lord said to Moses, 'Go down and warn the people not to break through to the Lord, to look; otherwise many of them will perish. Even the priests who approach the Lord must consecrate themselves or the Lord will break out against them.'"

Mary not only saw the Christ in Jesus, she understood her rightful place before him; she respected the boundaries required by his holiness. She had brought the priests out of the Temple to take their stand as consecrated priests at the feet Jesus from which the Word of God came. She was preparing them for the third day on which they would see Christ face to face. She was preparing them for the most awesome event ever to occur in human or cosmic history: the death and resurrection of Jesus.

The house was filled with the fragrance of the perfume. It is Mary's faithfulness that fills the house. She is the Beloved Disciple not because she is Jesus' favorite, but because she sees so clearly and believes so completely.

The Challenge

"But Judas Iscariot, one of his disciples (the one who was about to betray him), said, 'Why was this perfume not sold for three hundred denarii and the money given to the poor?' (He said this not because he cared about the poor, but because he was a thief; he kept the common purse and used to steal what was put into it.)" (Jn. 12: 4-6)

Λεγει ουν εισ εκ των μαθητων αυτου, Ιουδασ, Ζιμωνοσ Ισκαριωτησ, ο μελλων αυτον παραδιδομαι, Διατι τουτο το μυρον ουκ επραθη τριακοσιων δηναριων , και εδοθη πτωχοισ ; Ειπεν δε τουτο , ουχ οτι περι των πτωχων εμελεν αυτω , αλλ οτι κλεπτησ ην , και το γλωσσοκομον ειχεν, και τα Βαλλομενα εβασταζεν.

(Says therefore one of his disciples, Judas, Simon's [son] Iscariot, who was about him to deliver up, Why this ointment not was sold for three hundred denarii, and given to [the] poor? he said but this, not that for the poor he was caring, but because a thief he was, and the bag had, and what was put into [it] carried.)[294]

The most glaring sign in this verse is the identification of Judas Iscariot, one of his disciples, as a thief. Jesus has already explained the role of the thief in this Gospel. Just before the trilogy begins, Jesus describes his own role as that of the Good Shepherd, the gate to the sheepfold (Jn. 10: 1-18, esp. 1, 8, 10). "The thief comes only to steal and kill and destroy (Jn. 10: 10a)." The Temple priests enter the Temple for the sake of sacrificing the sheep. In the parlance of this Gospel, these Temple priests are the thieves. Jesus intends to lead the sheep out of the Temple, to offer them life, not death. Judas, one of his own disciples, is identified with the Temple priests. He is a thief.

---

[294]Gk. and lit. trans. fr. Berry, op. cit.

The Words of Ordination

"Jesus said, 'Leave her alone. She bought it[287] so that she might keep it for the day of my burial." (Jn. 12: 7)

ειπεν ουν ο Ιησουσ, Αφεσ αυ την εισ την ημεραν του ενταφιασμου μου τετηρηκεν αυ το.

(Said therefore Jesus, Let alone her: for the day of my burial has she kept it.)[288]

     "Leave her alone," αφεσ (*aphes*) can be interpreted three ways: "to leave, to let alone or to forgive." The original Greek means "to send off, to hurl, to release," suggesting an emphatic separation. This is consistent with the word's use in the LXX.[289]

---

[287]The NRSV notes that the Greek version of this text lacks " She bought it . . ."

[288]Gk. and lit. trans. fr. Berry, op. cit., p. 282.

[289]Rudolf Bultmann, *"aphiami,"* Theological Dictionary of the New Testament, op. cit., vol. I, pp. 509-512. *"Aphienai,* 'to send off,' is richly attested in Gk. from any early period, and is used in every nuance, both lit. and fig. from 'to hurl' (e.g., missiles) to 'to release,' 'to let go' or 'let be.' . . . In the LXX *aphienai* is used for a whole series of Hebrew words, a. for those which denote either 'release,' 'surrender,' etc., or 'leave,' 'leave in peace,' etc." (Examples given: Gn. 20: 6; Ex. 12: 23; Nu. 22: 13 are negative formulations in which God does not "allow" or "let" something to happen, i.e.: God does not "let" the angel of death enter the Hebrew homes marked by the blood of the Passover lamb.) . . . "NT usage exhibits most of the possibilities. *aphienai* means "to let go" or *"to leave"* (See Jn. 4: 3, 28; 14: 18, 27; 16: 28) . . . It can also mean 'to leave in peace,' *'to let alone,'* (Jn. 11: 48) . . . There are also the instances in which *aphienai* means 'to remit' or 'to forgive,' whether in the profane sense in Mt. 18: 27, 32, or more often in the religious (Jn. 20: 23)." Note that Bultmann does not refer to Jn. 12: 7 as

The translators of the NRSV have attempted to clarify the Greek construction of this verse by inserting the sentence, "she bought it" between Jesus' emphatic defense of Mary and his explanation of her actions. The NKJV translates it "Let her alone; she has kept this for the day of My burial." The NIV has "'Leave her alone,' Jesus replied. 'It was intended that she should save this perfume for the day of my burial.'" The NASV stays closest to the Greek: "Let her alone, in order that she may keep it for the day of my burial."

Barrett suggests that the obscure construction of this sentence requires a positive, in fact an imperative translation, "Let her keep it" or "Let her alone; let her keep it."[287]

"Let her alone" sounds a lot, even in Greek, like "separate her, set her apart." In Greek, the term most properly used for that meaning would not have been αφιημι (*aphiami*), but αφοριζω (*aphorizo*), which means

---

an illustration of any of these definitions.

[287]Barrett, C.K., The Gospel According to St. John: An Introduction with Commentary and Notes on the Greek Text, The Westminster Press, Philadelphia, (1955), (2nd ed. 1978), p. 414. "In Hellenistic Greek αφεσ, αφετε had become almost auxiliaries introducing a first-person subjunctive in the sense of an imperative. Possibly a similar usage should be accepted here, and if so we should translate 'Let her keep it. . .' Alternatively we may render (a) (with substantially the same sense) 'Let her alone in order that she may keep it . . .' (b) (taking the ινα as imperatival) 'Let her alone; let her keep it . . .'; (c) 'Let her alone; (this was) that she might keep it . . .'; (d) hesitantly Dodd suggests the possibility that we should construe τηρηση as if it were τετηρηκυιαη 'Allow her to have kept it.' None of these can be dismissed on purely grammatical grounds, and the construction remains uncertain and obscure."

"to separate," "to sever,"[288] and is clearly a term that implies a distinction between the ordained (separated for holiness) and the profane (separated for uncleanness). If this latter term had been used instead of the former one, the nature of this unique ritual would have been more readily apparent: it declares that an ordination is occurring. The similarity between these two words is too striking to make the chosen use accidental, especially given the other signs already pointing to ordination as the meaning of this event.

Barrett does not restrict his observations to the difficulties in the Greek construction of the sentence, leading to his conclusion that the imperative is indicated; he focuses as well on the meaning of the term τηρειν (*tarein* -- translated as "to keep"). He asks,

---

[288]Karl L. Schmidt, "αφοριζω ," Theological Dictionary of the New Testament, op. cit., vol. V, p. 454. "In the LXX αφοριζω does not correspond to a single, definite Hebrew term . . . in Gn. 2: 10; 10: 5 it means cleavage, spacial separation; . . . in Lv. 20: 25 (twice), 26; Dt. 4: 41; Jos 16: 9; Is. 56: 3 means "division," "separation." . . . Otherwise predominantly cultic terms are the originals . . . which are all used for the bringing of sacrifices and the dedication of fields and land to religious and cultic purposes, and which all involve separation from everyday life from the LXX standpoint. . . . The dividing out of the unclean or unholy is an esp. important matter in the legal status concerning purity and holiness, Lv. 13:4. . . . In Nu. 12: 14f Miriam was cast out (αφωρισθη) of the camp seven days because of her revolt. . . .If in the NT separation is by God for a specific and express purpose, there are OT models for this too. The separation of holy men or things taking place εν αντι κυριου or τω κυριω , See the refs. to the so-called heave offering (votive offering) in Ex. 29: 24, 26; Lv. 10: 15; 14: 12; Nu. 18: 24; Ez. 45: 13; 48: 9. The Levites are an offering (αποδομα) of this kind: Aaron is to separate them (αφοριει) from the other Israelites. In the so-called Holiness Code we find the admonition: 'And ye shall be holy unto me, for I the Lord am holy,' with the statement: 'And I have severed you (o αφορισασ υμασ) from other people, that ye should be mine.'" Lv. 20: 26.

"In what sense can the woman 'keep' the ointment which she has already used? (The variant τετηρηκεν is a manifest attempt to alleviate the difficulty.) To suggest that only a small part of the ointment had been used and that the rest might be preserved is not only to miss the spirit of the narrative but also to ignore v.3c. It is equally inconsistent with the narrative to suppose that John thought of a miraculously unfailing supply of ointment. The simplest suggestion is that here τηρειν means not 'to keep,' but 'to keep in mind,' 'to remember.' We should then translate '. . . let her remember it (the ointment, or the act of anointing) on the day of my burial."[289]

Barrett focuses upon the ointment as that which is to be "kept" or "remembered." Harald Riesenfeld asserts that it is the tradition of the death of Jesus that is to be remembered. He points out that the basic meaning of this term, outside of the New Testament, is "to keep in view," "to take note," "to watch over."

In the New Testament τηρεω occurs 60 times and "the preference for τηρεω is esp. striking in the Johannine writings. It occurs 18 times in John, φυλασσω 3, and 7 in 1 Jn., φυλασσω only once."[290]

---

[289]Barrett, op. cit., p. 414.

[290]Harald Riesenfeld, "τηρεω," Theological Dictionary of the New Testament, op. cit., vol. VIII, p. 140f. "**Literal meaning**: (a) "to guard," e.g. a prison . . . (b)"to keep" until a given point in time, e.g. wine at the wedding feast, Jn. 2:10; . . . (c) "to maintain," not found expressly in the NT but echoed in some expressions . . . (d)"to protect" with ref. to the preserving or keeping of someone intact. **Transferred meaning**: (a) the object of τηρεω in the sense "to preserve," "to protect," "to guard" is the disciple, or in the Church situation, the Christian, who as he passes through the world is exposed to temptation and

Thus, Jesus' words, addressed apparently to Judas in defense of Mary's liturgical gesture, emerge with a special meaning. They serve as words of institution for a specific ordination of Mary. Jesus is commanding Judas, and the other disciples who are present, including those

---

the danger of falling (Jn. 17: 11, 12, 15) . . . (b) With an impersonal object τηρεω denotes the actual maintaining of the essential functions or realities of Christian life, e.g., "to keep faith" . . . (c) A meaning which is shown by its frequency to be characteristic of the NT is that of "to take note of," "to observe," "to fulfill," "to keep," especially with reference to doctrine or commandments or precepts . . . The keeping of feasts should also be mentioned in this connection τηρειν το σαββατον, (keep the Sabbath) Jn. 9:16 . . . That traditional catechetical material in the primitive Palestinian community was regarded as stemming from Jesus' teaching of the disciples and taken to be normative for the walk of Christians in the form of εντολαι (commandments) may be seen also from διδασκοντεσ αυ του σ τηρειν παντα οσα ενετειλ αμην υμιν (teaching them to keep all that I have commanded you), Mt. 28: 20 . . . This use of τηρεω is especially common in the Johannine writings. . . . **The saying of Jesus to Mary on the occasion of the anointing in Bethany (Jn. 12: 7) means 'let her alone, she has observed (i.e., done) this with a view to my death.'"** pp. 140-145. See also Daube, The N.T. and Rabbinic Judaism, op. cit., pp. 317-320; also Georg Bertram, "φυλασσω ," Theological Dictionary of the New Testament, op. cit., vol. IX, pp. 236-241, for consideration of the various Hebrew words (n. 4, 5, 6 p. 237) which are sometimes translated by φυλασσω and sometimes by τηρεω . φυλασσω is the verb form of φυλαζ , "watchman" "and denotes the activity or office of a watchman whose job it is 'to protect' those who are asleep from harm during the night." "In Jn. 12: 47, 'hearing' and 'observing' are Christologically oriented: He does not practice the words that he has heard, for him they will become a judgement. To observe the words of Christ corresponds to the Johannine demand to do the truth, Jn. 3:21; 1 Jn. 1:6. . . . In Jn. 17: 12 it is He Himself who 'keeps' those whom the Father has given Him so long as He dwells among them. . . The prayer for preservation refers to the community of the risen Lord. Jn. 12: 25 adopts the Synoptic dictum that promises the gaining of life to the disciple who sacrifices it." See also Nu. 6: 24 Nazirite's priestly benediction.

who once may have been Temple priests, to set Mary apart, to let her keep the tradition of his death. She is being ordained to a highly significant ministry: the teaching of the Jesus tradition, his commandments, teachings, ritual practices, and the meaning of his death.

Mary is to "watch over" this tradition and the disciples who will learn to "see" and "believe" in Christ through it. She is the authorized Teacher of Disciples, a theologian with Christ's authority to teach and interpret the Christian tradition. In ecclesiastical terms, she is a bishop, an "overseer." In traditional Hebrew terms, she is now a Rabbi. This ordination, however, is not for Mary alone. The disciples are ordained along with her.

The Ordination of the Disciples

"You always have the poor with you, but you do not always have me." (Jn. 12: 8)

τουσ πτωχουσ γαρ παντοτε εχετε μεθ εαυτω ν, εμε δε ου παντοτε εχετε.

(The poor for always ye have with you, but me not always ye have.)[291]

Barrett says that this verse could rightly be omitted altogether "since here it has no direct connection with the context." No doubt, given the interpretation offered thus far, this verse, at first glance, appears to have nothing to do with what has gone before it. An alert disciple, at this point in studying John's Gospel, will recognize such an

---

[291]Gk. and lit. trans. fr. Berry, op. cit.

obvious irrelevance as a distinctly Johannine literary tool. Its surface meaning looks so innocuous as to cause the casual reader to skip over it lightly. Indeed, if anything, the surface meaning of this short text appears to reveal a pouting Jesus, offended at Judas' critique of Mary's gesture, suggesting to Judas that he (Jesus) is a more important recipient of this precious perfume than are the poor. Such an impression of Jesus is radically inconsistent with the character of Jesus as presented in the rest of the Gospel.[292]

The Open Hand

It is generally recognized that the first thought in this text, "You always have the poor with you . . ." is a partial quotation from Dt. 15: 11, a passage well known to alms-givers, yet it is not in the first part of this particular passage where the import of the message is found, but in the second. "Since there will never cease to be some in need on the earth, I therefore command you, 'Open your hand to the poor and needy in your land.'"

Once again, the Gospel of John leads the seeker of truth to the Pentateuch, where what the casual reader sees as an all-too-human defensiveness in Jesus, is revealed as a divine being issuing a commandment: open your hand. Mary has held the feet of Jesus in her hands. In the tradition of the Temple priests, she can now offer the sacrifice of Jesus as an elevation offering before the Lord. She has been ordained to celebrate the Eucharist in remembrance of Christ's death. To follow the *semeiotic* pattern established by Moses and Aaron, the priests' portion

---

[292]See Jn. 1: 10-14, 16-18; 5: 30; 6: 15; 10: 11-18.

of the sacrifice is now to be placed in the worshipper's outstretched and open hand, then lifted up before God. Jesus is instructing Judas (and by inference, the other disciples with him) to open his hand, to symbolically receive the sacrifice that Mary has consecrated, perhaps to lift the priests' portion up before God along with Mary. The image of Aaron and his sons lifting the sacrifice before God in the Temple is now replaced with the image of countless disciples lifting the elements of the Eucharist before God. Jesus' command extends this priestly authority and role to his disciples.

Judas' complaint has been couched in terms that infer that sharing the perfume with the poor would have been a more generous way to use it. Jesus' response suggests that the most generous way to respond to the needs of the poor is for Judas to open his hand, to celebrate the sacrifice by giving it to those who worship, rather than by taking from the worshippers as the Chief Priests had been doing. This both confronts Judas with the impression that Jesus knows that he is a thief (Jn. 12: 6) and offers to him a sign of grace.

Though the Gospel of John does not identify as thieves those with whom Jesus was crucified, it seems likely that this part of the synoptic tradition was as well known as it appears the rest of the orthodox Jesus story was known by the writer or writers, because in this Gospel, Jesus offers grace to the Chief Priests and Pharisees, who *are* identified as thieves (Jn. 10). Some accept this grace, and others do not (Jn. 5: 25-29; 11: 45-46).

Jesus opens himself to Judas, offering his life as a sacrifice. It may be inferred from Jn. 10: 28-29 that this same offer is made to every disciple, for, while the hour for Jesus to be delivered into the hands of those who will crucify him is coming, Jesus vows that the thieves will "never snatch them (my sheep/ disciples) out of my hand . . . no one can snatch (what my Father has given me) out of the Father's hand." The disciples will be the new right hand of God: God's priests.

Authority to Celebrate

The second part of Jesus' response to Judas, "You will not always have me," is dismissed by some scholars because it originated in the Synoptic Gospels.[293] Such a dismissal blinds the scholar/reader to an important sign. The indicators that this phrase is a sign are: (1) The language is inconsistent with the theology of the Gospel. (2) It is linked with a LXX passage (Dt. 15: 11), which hints at a hidden meaning. (3) Part of the passage is repeated, a hint that it is not to be ignored. (4) It has a material connection with another passage in the Gospel which suggests that it may have a meaning related to that passage.

(1) The impression given by this utterance is that Jesus is jealous of the attention that Judas is suggesting should be offered to the poor. It appears that Jesus is suggesting that his need for the ointment Mary has just used to massage his feet is more important than the needs of the

---

[293]Hermann Hanse, " εχω ," Theological Dictionary of the New Testament, op. cit., vol. II, p. 824, n. 47, "See M. Dibelius, 'Glaube u. Mystik bei Paulus,' (N. Jbch. Wis. u. Jugendbildung, 7 (1931), 683ff., 696. Mt. 26: 11 = Mk. 14: 7 = Jn. 12: 8, Mk. 2: 19, reject the idea that the disciples have Jesus constantly: 'Me ye have not always.' But the reference here is to concrete, spatial presence (μεθ εαυτου). One cannot anoint the exalted Lord, but one may have Him with one in a different way (Mt. 28: 20). We need not be disturbed by this saying of Synoptic Gospel origin within the Johannine writings."

poor. This is consistent with the identity of the Good Shepherd who lays down his life for his sheep, who directs his disciples to "love one another as I have loved you."

(2) The phrase, "the poor you will always have with you . . ." comes from Deuteronomy 15: 11. It says, "Since there will never cease to be some in need on the earth, I therefore command you, 'Open your hand to the poor and the needy in your land.'" The hidden *semeion* is the open hand, and the ethic from the Mosaic Law is consistent with the Gospel's record of Jesus' commandment to love others.

(3) The word that is repeated twice in Jn. 12: 8 and translated "always," is παντοτε (*pantote*). It is used a total of six times in the Gospel, always in the context of the Eucharist (Jn. 6: 34; 7: 6; 8: 29; 11: 42; 12: 8 -- twice).

(4) "My time has not yet come, but your time is always here" (Jn. 7: 6). In refusing to go with his brothers to the Festival of Booths, Jesus declares that his hour has not yet come, but that he will always abide with them. Later (Jn. 7: 32-39) Jesus explains to the Pharisees that their time to believe and receive the Eucharist is short.

The oracular message carried by Jn. 12: 8 is not that the disciples will not always have Jesus, but that those who do not believe will not always have Jesus. It is their own refusal to receive the living bread and the living drink, elements of the Eucharist, that prevents them from "having" Jesus. Those who will receive the sacrament, in contrast, will continue to "have" Jesus, that is, to abide in Jesus and "have" Jesus abide in or remain with them. This is a tragic moment, because Jesus is telling Judas that this sacramental meal will be his last, foretelling that Judas will choose to abide in darkness, with those who do not see the Christ in Jesus and will never believe in him.

Judas, who by inference refuses to open his hand to receive the priest's portion offered by Jesus, has chosen to hold that which is already in his hand (the money bag), rather than receive what is far more valuable: authority to celebrate the Eucharist as a disciple of Jesus. Judas is confronted with a choice: accept the things of this world (as offered by the priests who abide in darkness) or accept the things of the spirit (as offered by the light).

Laying on of Hands

The sign of the hand is hidden in this verse, but it is significant, and its importance applies not only to Judas and the disciples who are offered ordination with him, but to Jesus, for Whom this ordination coincides with the hour of his sacrifice.[294]

The timing of the imposition of this important symbolic gesture is vitally important in this Gospel. Jesus refuses to reveal his identity as the true sacrifice on several occasions. The first, in Jn. 2: 4, is when he tells his mother, who seems to have prompted him to perform the miracle of the wedding feast, "Woman, what concern is that to you and to me? My hour has not yet come." Later, when Jesus appears at the Festival of the Booths,

---

[294]Remember that Daube tells us that "*Samakh*" (leaning on of hands) was a ritual with two purposes: (1) to prepare an animal as a sacrifice, and (2) to designate a disciple as one authorized to teach (i.e.: expound) upon the Torah. The former represents the transference of the guilt and holiness between worshipper and sacrificial animal; the latter represents the imposition of the priest's holiness upon the one being ordained.

"Then they tried to arrest him, but *no one laid hands on him*, because his hour had not yet come." (Jn. 7: 30)

"Εζητουν ουν αυ τον πιασαι και ουδεισ επεβαλεν επ αυ τον την χειρ α, οτι ουπω εληλυθει η ωρα αυ του ."

(They were seeking therefore him to take, but no one laid upon him [his] hand, because not yet had come his hour).[295]

Then the time (the hour) comes when it *is time* for others to lay hands upon him and bind him in preparation for his sacrifice (See Gn. 22: 9).

"So the soldiers, their officer, and the Jewish police arrested Jesus and bound him" (Jn. 18: 12).

"Η ουν σπειρα και ο χιλιαρχοσ και οι υπηρεται τω ν Ιουδαιων συνελαβον τον Ιησουν, και εδησαν αυ τον ."

(The therefore band and the chief captain and the officers of the Jews took hold of Jesus, and bound him.)[296]

Samakh (laying on of hands) was used to impose judgement, esp. judgement leading to execution[297] as well as ordination. Lv. 24: 14 proscribes this procedure for one found guilty of blasphemy. Jn. 18: 22, where an officer of

---

[295] Gk. and lit. trans. fr. George Ricker Berry, op. cit, p. 264. See 8: 20.

[296] Gk. and lit. trans. fr. Berry, op. cit.

[297] See Susannah 34; Daube, op. cit., p. 227.

the High Priest strikes Jesus in the face, and Jn. 19: 2, where Pilate's soldiers place a crown of thorns on Jesus' head, use this *semeion* in this way. Yet, when Moses laid hands on Aaron and his sons, the purpose was clearly so that they would be authorized to perform the sacrificial rituals. This was necessary for them to be able to function as priests. Daube tells us that by the first-century the purpose of laying on of hands was to pass along authority from a master teacher (Rabbi) to a disciple, so that the disciple could expound upon the scriptures, that is to teach.

"The Rabbi, who conferred authority, 'leaned' -- *samakh* -- his hands on the candidate's head . . . The master communicated his personality, his status, to the disciple, who thus became a Rabbi with *reshuth*, 'authority,' himself. Henceforth he shared that wisdom and power which, as was believed, ultimately descended from Moses."[298]

Ordination in the first-century implied more that the disciple was to be authorized to teach than that the disciple was authorized to practice religious rites, and that the authority for this teaching was transferred from the master to the disciple.

"You will not always have me," may be inferred to mean that Judas would be well advised to accept the ordination of Mary that he has just witnessed, because Judas would not always be able to learn from Jesus. The opportunity to participate in the ritual he has just witnessed will not occur again. It is, in fact, leading to his (Judas') own ordination, and if he fails to recognize the moment for what it is, it will quickly pass.

---

[298]See Daube, op. cit., pp. 207-208, 224-245, esp. 226-227.

Chapter 14
The Ordination Trilogy: Act 3
Completing the Ordination of Jesus' Disciples

The Setting

"Now before the festival of the Passover, Jesus knew that his hour had come to depart from this world and go to the Father. Having loved his own who were in the world, he loved them to the end." (Jn. 13: 1)

"προ δε τησ εορτησ του πασχα; ειδωσ ο' Ιησουσ οτι εληλυθεν αυτου η ωρα ινα μεταβη εκ του κοσμου του προ σ τον πατερα, αγαπησας τουσ ιδιουσ του σ εν τω κοσμω εισ τελοσ ηγαπησεν αυτουσ."

(Now before the feast of the Passover, knowing Jesus that has come his hour that he should depart out of this world to the Father, having loved his own which [were] in the world to [the] end he loved them.)[299]

The setting for the ordination of Mary appears to be the same setting for this, the fourth and final episode in the ordination trilogy: the ordination of the disciples. Jn. 11: 2 connects the raising of Lazarus story with Jn. 12: 3, which is set in Bethany six days before the Passover. This passage sets the action simply as "before the festival of the Passover." It is generally accepted that the Passover mentioned in Jn. 11: 55 and 12: 1 is the same Passover as

---

[299]Gk. and lit. trans. fr. Berry, op. cit., pp. 285-286.

this one. I am suggesting that the meal that took place in that context (the Eucharist) is the same meal. In other words, all of the events of the trilogy occurred at the same time that Jesus instituted the Eucharist. Thus, examining Mary and Martha for ordination after Mary brings temple priests to the fold of Jesus' disciples, Mary's anointing of Jesus' feet, and the washing of the disciples' feet by Jesus, all occurred at the same event.

In the same sentence (i.e.: as part of the setting), the narrator provides what Culpepper calls "an inside view"[300] of the mind of Jesus. In this case, that view appears to reflect a temporal awareness that spans a past, a present, and a future consciousness.[301] "Before . . . Jesus knew" reflects an awareness located in the past; "Having loved his own who were in the world" reflects an awareness that extends from the past into the present; "he loved them to the end" indicates an active presence that, given the high Christology of the Gospel and the assertion that Jesus is the resurrection and the life, suggests a consciousness of an indefinite future. In other words, the setting for this third act of the trilogy infers a conscious tie between past, present, and future.

---

[300]R. Alan Culpepper, <u>Anatomy of the Fourth Gospel</u>, Fortress Press, Philadelphia, (1983), p. 21f.

[301]See Culpepper, op. cit., p.27f, esp. 30 "In this broad sense, the Johannine narrator, who presumably expresses the perspective of the author, tells the story from a point of view which in its retrospection is informed by memory, interpretation of scripture, the coalescing of traditions with the post-Easter experience of the early church, consciousness of the presence of the Spirit, a reading of the glory of the risen Christ back into the days of his ministry, and an acute sensitivity to the history and struggles of the Johannine community."

This tie is both in the Eucharist and in the relationship between the Divine Mind (*logos*) and those who are called to intercede between God and humanity ("his own who were in the world" i.e.: priests), who celebrate the Eucharist. Significantly, this class of priests is not limited to liturgical or juristic or didactic officials (like Chief Priests, Pharisees, and Rabbis) or even to a group identified with a single culture, ethnic group, or nation (like Levites), but included all who could see Christ and believe, i.e.: every disciple of Jesus.

These are the "sheep" to which Jesus refers in chapter 10 as "his own," those whom Jesus, as the Good Shepherd, leads into the Temple through the gate, and who leads them safely out again by calling their names. By this point in the narrative, it has become clear that included in this group are some who were formerly Temple priests, and at least one of these was a Pharisee (Nicodemus). Mary and Martha of Bethany, who may have been gatekeepers in the Temple, were called out of that Temple and are included in this group.

"The end" could arguably be translated as the obvious "end" of the earthly life of Jesus, i.e.: his death on the cross. The finality of that understanding, however, inferring that the love of Jesus was extended to his own only until his death, is contrary to the Christology of the Gospel. In the Prologue (esp. Jn. 1: 11f.), it is acknowledged that all of his own did not accept him (i.e.: All whose identities were joined to his by the Mosaic covenant did not accept him), but to those who did, he gave power to become children of God. Jesus explains this carefully in Jn. 10: 7-18, making it clear that for the sake of his sheep he has "power to lay (his life) down and . . . to take it up again."

This resurrection of life is extended to those who hear (Jn. 5: 25-29). In other words, "the end" is an indefinite future, dependent upon the yet-to-be-decided response to Christ's call of future "sheep."

"The Greek expression used to describe Jesus' love "ϵιϭ τϵλοϭ" (*eis telos*) can be translated two different ways, as a comparison between the NRSV and the NIV shows. It can be translated as a temporal expression ("to the end" NRSV) or as referring to the quality of Jesus' love ("to the full extent" NIV). The Fourth Evangelist probably intended both meanings to be heard here, because it was in loving his own "to the end" that the "full extent" of Jesus' love is revealed."[302]

Eis telos could refer to "the end" of the life of the "sheep" (disciples/priests) or "to the full extent" of the relationship between the sheep and the shepherd, again referring to the willingness of the Good Shepherd to lay down his life for the sake of the (eternal) life of "his own." Interpreted this way, the meaning is that Jesus loved "his own" *into eternity*. That is, his love is timeless, and his love, represented in the Eucharist, is the means by which they enter into eternity.

---

[302]Gail R. O'Day, "The Gospel of John: Introduction, Commentary and Reflections," The New Interpreter's Bible: A Commentary in Twelve Volumes, vol. IX, Abingdon, Nashville, (1995), p. 721.

The Devil's Hand

"The devil had already put it into the heart of Judas son of Simon Iscariot to betray him.   And during supper . . ." (Jn. 13: 2)

"και δειπνου γενομενου , του διαβολου ηδη βεβληκοτοσ εισ την καρδιαν Ιουδα Σιμωνοσ Ισκαριωτου , ινα αυτον Παραδω ,"

(And supper taking place, the devil already having put into the heart of Judas, Simon's [son] Iscariot, that him he should deliver up,) [303]

    The setting is at a supper, and the devil has already "put into the heart" of Judas Iscariot a scheme to "deliver him (Jesus) up" (betray him). We have already established that the setting is not only "a supper," but *"the supper"* (the Lord's Supper). It remains to consider what might be meant by the devil's already completed action and scheme.
    βεβληκοτοσ is a form of βαλλω , which means "(a) the powerful movement of 'throwing' or 'propelling,' . . . or (b) 'to bring to a place,' 'to lay down,' 'to pour in.'"[304] It is used in the Fourth Gospel in the former sense in Jn. 15: 6 with the adverb εζω *(exo)* when Jesus says, "Whoever does not abide in me is *thrown* away like a branch and withers; such branches are gathered, *thrown*

[303]Gk. and lit. trans. fr. Berry, op. cit., p. 286.

[304]Friedrich Hauck, Theological Dictionary of the New Testament, op. cit., vol. I, p. 526f.

into the fire, and burned."[305] In addition to the present text, the word is used in the second sense in Jn. 20: 25 in the words of Thomas, who says, "Unless I see the mark of the nails in his (Jesus') hands, and *put* my finger in the mark of the nails and my hand in his side, I will not believe." The impression left by these citations is that what the devil has "*put* into the heart" of Judas Iscariot was not placed there gently, but forcefully. The devil has "laid hands" (Jn. 7: 30, 44; 10: 39) upon Judas in the same way that the Chief Priests and Pharisees had tried but failed to do, with Jesus.

The scheme, that Judas should αυτον παραδω (*auton parado*) "betray him" also implies that Judas is to play a part in laying hands on Jesus, since παραδω is a form of παραδιδωμι (*paradidomi*) which means "to hand over."[306] John's gospel irony is revealed in the fact that while the High Priest, the Chief Priests and their representatives were seeking to lay their hands upon Jesus to crucify him, Jesus was soon to lay hands upon the disciples to ordain them to the new priesthood in the new Temple, authorizing them to recall the tradition established

---

[305]The alternative form of this verb, εκ βαλλω (*ekballo*) "to throw out," "to expel," "to repel," (See Gn. 3: 24; Ex. 6: 1; Lv. 21: 7) is used in the Fourth Gospel to describe the efforts of the Jews to drive out those who confessed their faith in Christ (Jn. 9: 34f.). "In contrast, Jesus excludes from His fellowship none of those whom the Father causes to come to Him. (Jn. 6: 37); . . . επιβαλλω (*epiballo*) depicts the violent movement of "casting on or casting over" . . . (or) "hostile seizure" (in the NT) . . . the Fourth Gospel shows that the Jews cannot use force against Jesus until His hour comes (Jn. 7: 30, 44)." Hauck, op. cit., p. 528-529.

[306]See Jn. 18: 36. Jesus says to Pilate, "My kingdom is not of this world. If my kingdom were from this world, my followers would be fighting to keep me from being *handed over* to the Jews." See also Jn. 6: 64, 71; 12: 4; 13: 11; 18: 2, 5; 19: 11.

by his sacrificial death and glorious resurrection. While the temple authorities were seeking to eliminate Jesus, Jesus was eliminating their authority and roles.

The repetitive *semeion* "hand" provides a clue to the disciple seeking truth that this passage contains an oracle about the laying on of hands. By the devil's hand, the heart of Judas has been turned, and Judas in turn plans to "hand over" Jesus to the authorities sent by the Sanhedrin, so that they can "lay their hands on him" to crucify him. That the hand is an oracle meaning ordination is what follows.

Into Jesus' Hands

"Jesus, knowing that the Father had given all things into his hands, and that he had come from God and was going to God, . . ." (Jn. 13: 3)

ειδωσ ο' Ιησου σ οτι παντα δεδωκεν αυτω ο πατηρ εισ τασ χειρασ, και οτι απο θεου εξηλθεν και προσ τον θεον υπαγει,

(knowing Jesus that all things has given him the Father into hands, and that from God he came out and to God goes)[307]

Jn. 3: 31-36 is an affirmation of faith apparently given by the narrator, the implied author of the text. It is consistent with the high Christology of the Prologue. Jn. 3: 35 says, simply, "The Father loves the Son and has placed all things in his hands." This theme is carried further in Jn. 10: 27-30 when Jesus, in response to the unbelief of the Jews, says,

---

[307]Barry, op. cit., p. 286.

"My sheep hear my voice. I know them, and they follow me. I give them eternal life, and they will never perish. No one will snatch them out of my hand. What my Father has given me is greater than all else, and no one can snatch it out of the Father's hand. The Father and I are one."

The response of the Jews (Jn. 10: 31) was to take up stones to stone Jesus, then to try to arrest him again (Jn. 10: 39), "but he escaped from their hands."
We have seen that the hand is a *semeion* representing the role of the priest as an intermediary between God and humanity. That God has given all things into the hands of Jesus suggests that Jesus is authorized to lay hands upon those who are called to the priesthood, in order to grant them God's authority to function as priests, following the pattern established by Moses when he ordained Aaron and his sons.[308] In this way each disciple becomes a new "right hand" of God.
Again an inside view of the consciousness of Jesus as One who "had come from God and was going to God" is provided by the narrator, suggesting that the reader should know that Jesus knew that his authority was God's authority, and that what he was about to do would have a cosmic significance. As the Prologue indicates (Jn. 1: 18), the revelation of God by Jesus is the center-point of all history. Jesus is God-made-visible to human beings who seek to see God. The hour approaches in which Jesus will cease to be visible in the flesh that these disciples have come to know. If the Word is to continue to be "seen" and heard, then those who are called to serve as God's intermediaries will need to reveal him.

---

[308]See chapter 1 above; Lev. 8; Ex. 29.

The Eucharist is the medium for this, replacing all of the festivals and sacrifices previously used in Israel. The truth of God's continuing presence in the world with "his own" is reaffirmed in the Eucharist, which replays the cosmic event of Christ's incarnation every time it is served. With the relationship between God and humanity for all time at stake, Jesus prepares to bestow his authority upon his disciples.

Girded With a Towel

"got up from the table, took off his outer robe, and tied a towel around himself. Then he poured water into a basin and began to wash the disciples' feet and to wipe them with the towel that was tied around him" (Jn. 13: 4-5).

γειρεται εκ του δειπνου και τιθησιν τα ιματια, και λαβωνλεντιον διεζωσεν εαυτον ειτα Βαλλει υδωρ εισ τον νιπτηρα, και ηρξατο νιπτειν του σ ποδασ τω ν μαθητων, και εκμασσειν τω λεντιω ω ην διεζωσμενοσ.

(he rises from the supper and lays aside [his] garments and having taken a towel he girded himself: afterwards he pours water into the washing-basin, and began to wash the feet of the disciples, and to wipe [them] with the towel with which he was girded,)[309]

---

[309]Barry, op. cit., p. 286.

The double entendre is used again in verse 4 as the
statement is made that Jesus rises from the supper. The
NRSV translates this to mean that Jesus "got up from the
table," but that is only half of its original meaning. It is
also an oracle, for indeed, the resurrection of Jesus Christ
is directly proclaimed in the Lord's Supper; he "rises from
the supper."

In a similar way, the next phrase must be more
carefully translated in order to hear its double meaning.
The Greek term στολη (*stola)* is correctly translated "outer
garment." It represents the outer robe, worn over the tunic
and undergarments. This garment marks the specific status
of the wearer, especially in the case of the priestly robe.
The term used in this passage, τα ιματια (*ta imatia)* is
used more frequently in the New Testament as a generic
term for clothing in general.[310] If στολη had been used,
then we might well discern that Jesus was discarding a
priestly or rabbinical identity in preparation for washing the
disciples' feet, but that is not what the original text
conveys. Our literal translation portrays Jesus "lay(ing)
aside [his] garments." In this context, the reader is not
only to hear that Jesus removed his robe, but that he
stripped down to his undergarments, taking on the
appearance of a slave. The semeiotic meaning behind this
gesture goes even further. Jesus removed his earthly
identity, the body that clothes his being, his flesh. He laid
down his life for his own.

---

[310]Ulrich Wilckens, "στολη," Theological Dictionary of the New
Testament, op. cit., vol. VII, p. 690. Wilckens does acknowledge that
"In the NT στολη denotes only the "upper garment." It stands in contrast
to the usual ιματιον where special clothing is to be stressed, though the
usage is fluid."

The image that this verse portrays, Jesus with a towel wrapped around his waist, is clearly meant to convey the identity of a slave.[311]   John the Baptist, in 1: 27, identifies himself as "not worthy to untie the thong of his sandal." This implies that John the Baptist thinks of himself as less than a slave in relation to Jesus, since a slave is *expected* to untie and remove the master's sandals and then to wash his feet. As I have pointed out, this little phrase identifies John the Baptist as a disciple, since this one service, by rabbinical tradition, was *not expected or allowed of disciples*. For Jesus to take upon himself this identity is to humble himself below the station from which the disciples themselves relate to Jesus. It is a radical gesture on a par with Mary's anointing of his feet, an unthinkable, extraordinary liturgical event, designed to leave a lasting impression upon all disciples forever.

The term διεζωσεν (*diezosen*) translated as "tied" is more directly translated "girded." On the surface, it would appear that Jesus is carefully following Mosaic instructions for the Passover meal. Ex. 12: 11 provides instructions for the way to eat the Passover meal. "This is how you shall eat it: your loins girded, your sandals on your feet, and your staff in your hand; and you shall eat it hurriedly. It is the Passover of the LORD." Even within its Old Testament context, this verse paints the ironic picture of shepherds eating and walking while tending their sheep. There is no indication as to whether or not the disciples put their sandals back on after Jesus washed their feet, but Jn. 18: 1 indicates that they all went to a garden

---

[311] See Karl Heinrich Rengstorf, "δουλοσ," <u>Theological Dictionary of the New Testament</u>, op. cit., vol. II, pp. 261-280, esp. pp. 277f.

in the Kidron valley *after* the meal. Presumably, they put
their shoes on and carried their staffs for that journey.

As we have noted, the High Priest's girdle (ephod)
contained the oracle used to discern God's will and
direction. While there is much mystery surrounding this
oracle and the ephod which contained it, it seems clear that
the High Priest held the oracle tightly against his body; he
was girded with the ability to discern God's will.

The body of Jesus is, in itself, an oracle -- both in
the flesh and in the Eucharist, through which the will of
God may be discerned. It must be seen through the eyes of
faith, recognized as bearing more meaning than is apparent
on the surface.   The incarnation indicates a level of
humility far below the station of the Word of God, yet that
is the station to which Jesus invites his disciples. His
message is clearly intent upon preventing these new disciple
priests from adopting the kind of attitudes that the High
Priest, the Chief Priests and the Pharisees of the Herodian
Temple had adopted: arrogance, spiritual blindness and
reliance upon political power and influence, rather than
upon faith in God and sensitivity to the spiritual needs of
God's people. In addition, if the function of an oracle is to
guide those who seek God to a deeper understanding of
what it is that they see, then Jesus is most assuredly an
oracle *par excellence*.

The key to this passage, of course, is what Jesus
does. What exactly does he do and why does he do it?
What does it all mean? If one comes to this passage from
the perspective offered by the current study, i.e.: that Jesus
observes the *semeiotic* patterns in the Mosaic law regarding
the ordination of priests, then his actions are easier to
interpret and their meaning more simply understood.

The Greek term νιπτειν (*niptein*) refers to the partial washing (i.e.: of hands and feet) of living persons.[312] Priests were supposed to wash both their hands and their feet before entering the sanctuary or ministering on the altar. God tells Moses,

"You shall make a bronze basin with a bronze stand for washing. You shall put it between the tent of the meeting and the altar, and you shall put water in it; with the water Aaron and his sons shall wash their hands and their feet. When they go into the tent of the meeting, or when they come near the altar to minister, to make an offering by fire to the Lord, they shall wash their hands and their feet, so that they may not die: it shall be a perpetual ordinance for them, for him and for his descendants throughout their generations" (Ex. 30: 17-21).

However, on one occasion, the priests did not wash themselves, but were washed by the one who represented the authority of God. Moses washed Aaron and his sons *as a first step in their ordination to the priesthood* (Lv. 8: 6;=Ex. 29: 4).[313]

---

[312]F. Hauck, "νιπτω ," Theological Dictionary of the New Testament, op. cit., vol. IV, p. 946-947.

[313]See The Septuagint Version, op. cit., p. 135, vss. 6-9. "And Moses brought nigh Aaron and his sons, and washed them with water, and put on him the coat, and girded him with the girdle, and clothed him with the tunic, and put upon it the oracle, and put upon the oracle the Manifestation of the Truth. And he put the miter on his head, and put upon the miter in front the golden plate, the most holy thing, as the Lord commanded Moses."

Not only does Jesus wash the feet of the disciples, but he dries them *with the towel with which he was girded.* The towel represents Christ's own priesthood. He is girded by his own ministry of self-sacrifice and humility. Into this ministry the disciples are ordained.

Consider for a moment the significance of Jesus laying his hands upon the feet of the disciples, rather than upon their heads. Mary of Bethany has worshipped at the feet of Jesus, because she recognizes that the incarnate Christ is the foot of Jacob's ladder. The priests are to continue the ministry of Jesus after his death. They, too, are to be the "feet" of Jacob's ladder. Their holy head is Jesus, and the head does not require washing. Their hands, already washed as part of the liturgy of the Passover meal,[314] are already clean. It is their feet which must be washed in order for them to serve as priests at the new altar in the new Temple, consecrating the new sacrifice: Jesus.

This washing of their feet is what Jesus does in terms defined by Mosaic Law, "so that they may not die." While Jesus expects to become the sacrificial lamb, he is taking this *semeiotic* step to assure that his disciples are not executed with him and that they are symbolically prepared to take on his ministry.

---

[314]See Chaim Raphael, trans, <u>Passover Haggadah</u>, Behrman House, New York, (1972), p. 52. The host washes his hands at the beginning of the meal, after the first cup of wine. All who are celebrating the Passover wash their hands after the second cup of wine, with this blessing: "Blessed be God, who made each *mitzvah* (commandment) bring us holiness and laid on us the washing of hands before food."

Peter's Reaction

**"He came to Simon Peter, who said to him, 'Lord, are
you going to wash my feet?' Jesus answered, 'You do
not know now what I am doing, but later you will
understand.' Peter said to him, 'You will never wash
my feet.' Jesus answered, 'Unless I wash you, you have
no share with me.'"** (Jn. 13: 6-8)

"ερχεται ουν προσ Σιμωνα Πετρον και λεγει
αυτω εκ ειν ο σ, Κυριε, συ μου νιπτεισ τουσ
ποδασ; Απεκριθη Ιησουσ και ειπεν αυτω , "Ο
εγω ποιω συ ουκ οιδασ αρτι, γνωση δε μετα
ταυτα. Λεγει αυ τω Πετροσ, Ουμη νιφησ τουσ
ποδασ μου εισ τον αιωνα. Απεκριθη αυ τω ο
'Ιησου σ, 'Ε αν με νιφω σε, ουκ εχεισ μεροσ
μετ εμου..

(*He comes, therefore to Simon Peter, and says to him he,
Lord, thou of me dost wash the feet? Answered Jesus and
said to him, What I do thou not knowest now, but thou shalt
know hereafter. Says to him Peter, in no wise mayest thou
wash my feet forever. Answered him Jesus, Unless I wash
thee, thou has not part with me.*)[315]

Jesus' response to Peter's objection to the foot
washing is consistent with our understanding that Jesus was
consecrating Peter and the other disciples as priests. The
term translated "share" in the NRSV and "part" in Barry's
literal translation, is μεροσ (*meros*).

---

[315]Gk. and lit. trans, Barry, op. cit., p. 286.

"In the New Testament we find the two basic senses of μεροσ seen through the writings of antiquity, namely, 'part' and 'share.' 1. 'Part.' part of the body. . . . 2. 'share.' One can have a share in a person (Jesus, Jn. 13: 8), a group of persons, . . . a thing . . ., or an event."[316]

In Jn. 19: 23 *meros* is used in reference to the "parts" into which the soldiers who crucified Jesus divided his clothes. Again these soldiers perform the priests' *semeiotic* function: separating the sacrifice into "parts." There is another, similar sounding, Greek word with almost exactly the same meaning. That word is μελοσ (*melos*) and it is used in the LXX to denote the "parts" or "bodily members" into which an animal is cut up when it is sacrificed,[317] when it is "separated" (αφοριζω - *aphorizo*) before God.[318]

When Jesus says to Peter, "Unless I wash you, you have no share (*meros*) with me," he is telling Peter that his refusal will prevent his sharing in the priest's portion of the sacrifice. It means that Peter will not be allowed to celebrate the Lord's Supper. If Peter will not submit to the foot washing, then he cannot be ordained. Jesus' touch, imprinting his humble identity upon each disciple as he washes their feet, *is* their ordination ritual.

---

[316]J. Schneider, "μεροσ," Theological Dictionary of the New Testament, op. cit., vol. IV, pp. 594-598.

[317]J. Horst, μελοσ, Theological Dictionary of the New Testament, op. cit., vol. IV, pp. 555f., esp. 557f.; See Ex. 29: 17; Lv. 1: 6, 12; 8: 19f.; 9: 13.

[318]See Ex. 29: 24, 26; Lev. 10: 15; See esp. Nu. 18: 20 "Then the LORD said to Aaron: You shall have no allotment in their (Israel's) land, nor shall you have any share (μεριο - *meris*) among them; *I am your share* and your possession among the Israelites." (NRSV)

"Simon Peter said to him, 'Lord, not my feet only but also my hands and my head!" (Jn. 13: 9).

"Λεγει αυ τω Σιμων Πετροσ, Κυριε, μη του σ ποδασ μου μονον , αλα και τασ χειρασ και την κεφαλην .

(*Says to him Simon Peter, Lord, not my feet only, but also the hands and the head.*)[319]

Peter now understands that Jesus is performing an ordination ritual; however, he assumes that *his* ordination should be distinct from the others, since he believes that he is to be the High Priest. If the foot washing is to be linked with the sacrifice of Jesus, then the blood of that sacrifice must be applied to the right earlobe (the head), the right thumb (the hand), and the right big toe (the foot) of the High Priest in order to consecrate him.[320]   Peter seems to understand that the water Jesus is using represents his sacrificial death. However, the water is not the significant symbol; rather water is being used as part of the rite that grants authority to celebrate the Eucharist. The significant symbol is the feet of each disciple, including Peter's, which are now identified with, washed by, and touched by Jesus. These are the feet of those who will ascend to the altar to consecrate the sacrifice, to stand before God.

---

[319]Gk. and lit. trans., Barry, op. cit., p. 286.
[320]See Lev. 8: 22-24; Ex. 29: 19-20.

Jesus' Explanation

"Jesus said to him, 'One who has bathed does not need to wash, except for the feet, but is entirely clean. And you are clean, though not all of you." (Jn. 13: 10)

Λεγει αυτω ο 'Ισους, "Ο λελουμενοσ ου χρειαν εχει η τουσ ποδασ νιψασθαι, αλλ εστιν καθαροσ ολοσ και υμεισ καθαροισ εστε, αλλ ουχι παντεσ.

(Says to him Jesus, He that has been laved not need has [other] than the feet to wash, but is clean wholly and ye clean are, but not all.)[321]

Jesus corrects Peter's understanding by drawing a distinction between λουειν -- *(louein)* "to bathe" and νιπτειν *(niptein)* "to wash."   "One who has bathed," says Jesus, "does not need to wash." It seems unlikely that Jesus actually spoke Greek to Peter or the other disciples,[322] but this appears to be a semantic distinction, because the meanings for the two words are very close. This is not the first instance where the author (or authors) of the text have chosen to convey meaning through paired words with similar definitions.   This text suggests that careful consideration of the fine points of meaning in the language is required, not only by the writer(s), but by Jesus himself!

---

[321]Gk. and lit. trans., Barry, op. cit., p. 286.

[322]See Jn. 12: 20f. The signal to Jesus that His hour has come is the arrival of some Greeks who come seeking Jesus. The text does not indicate that Jesus spoke with them directly. Of course, the fact that the Fourth Gospel was originally written in koine Greek suggests that the intended readers could read Greek.

Λουειν refers to the bathing required of those who must be purified or liturgically "clean." In the Old Testament "the priest in particular had to bathe before consecration and official actions."[323] Jesus is referring to the fact that those who are about to perform priestly functions must bathe their entire body before they put on their vestments. They are thus ritually and literally clean as they approach the altar. There is no need to wash their head or their bodies *in addition* to the bathing that they have already given themselves.

However, in the performance of priestly duties, it *is necessary* for the priest to wash (νιπτειν) his hands and feet *each time* the priest ascends or descends from the altar (Ex. 30: 17-21). As indicated earlier, washing the hands was an intrinsic part of the Passover Haggadah, and can be presumed to have already occurred, so all that remained for the disciples to be ritually clean in order to perform the priestly functions relating to the new sacrifice on the new altar, is for their feet to be washed.

"For he knew who was to betray him; for this reason he said, 'Not all of you are clean.'" (Jn. 13: 11)

"υδει γαρ τον παραδιδοντα αυ τον δια τουτο ειπεν, Ουχι παντεσ καθαροι εστε."

(For he knew him who was delivering up him: on account of this he said, Not all clean ye are.)

---

[323] A. Oepke, "λουω ," Theological Dictionary of the New Testament, op. cit., vol. IV, p. 300f; See Ex. 29: 4; 40: 12; Lv. 8: 6; 16: 4; Nu. 19: 7f.

The NRSV implies that Jesus' comment, "You are clean, though not all of you," is directed not only at Peter, but to all of the disciples who are (εστε) present (i.e.: all of you). Indeed, if this message had been addressed to a single person, it seems obvious that it would refer, not to Peter, but to Judas. Jn. 13: 21-30 indicates that Jesus knew ahead of time that Judas would betray him. That Judas will betray Jesus is what seems obvious on the surface of this passage, though it could well be argued that Peter also betrayed Jesus by denying him three times as Jesus predicted he would (Jn. 13: 36; 18: 15-18, 25-27).

The surface level interpretation of "You are clean, though not all of you," (Jn. 13: 10) appears to be, "All of you are clean except one among you," since Jn. 13: 11 implies that some *one* would betray him. There is another possibility, however. It may mean, "You are all completely clean, except for one part of each of you (i.e.: your feet)." This is born out by the actions of Jesus, who is in the process of washing each disciple's feet as he says it.[324] The actions of at least one disciple defiles all of them, requiring that all of them have their feet cleansed.

Jesus knows that one (or two) from among the disciples will betray him, therefore he takes initiative to preserve the sanctification of all disciples, so they may function as priests.   This is consistent with the understanding of Jesus as the theophany of the Word.[325]

---

[324]The NRSV translators note, "other ancient authorities lack 'except for the feet' in verse 10. This interpretation of verse 11 is consistent with the inclusion of that phrase in the text.

[325]Konrad Weiss, "που σ ," Theological Dictionary of the New Testament, op. cit., vol. VI, pp. 624-631, esp. 630f. "Understood as the One who according to His divine character forgives sins, Jesus in the totality of His person is already far above sinful man. As in theophanies

This foot washing represents the ritual cleansing from sin (forgiveness of every one for the sinful actions of any one) of those who are to serve at the altar.

"After he had washed their feet, had put on his robe, and had returned to the table, he said to them, 'Do you know what I have done to you? You call me Teacher and Lord - and you are right, for that is what I am. So if I, your Lord and Teacher, have washed your feet, you also ought to wash one another's feet. For I have set you an example, that you also should do as I have done to you. Very truly, I tell you, servants are not greater than their master, nor are messengers greater than the one who sent them." (Jn. 13: 12-16)

"Οτε ουν ενιψεν τουσ ποδασ αυτων, και ελαβεν τα ιματια αυτου, αν απεσων παλιν, ειπεν αυτοισ, Τινωσκετε τι πεποιηκα υμιν; υμεισ φωνειτε με ο διδασκαλοσ και ο κυριοσ, και καωλσ λεγετε, ειμι γαρ. ει ουν εγω ενιψα υμων τουσ ποδασ, ο κυριοσ και ο διδασκαλοσ, και υμεισ οφειλετε

(p. 627, 17ff), only His feet still stretch into the sinful world, and therefore it is to His feet that honor and worship must be paid and a sacrificial offering made. . . . this helps us to understand the act of foot washing . . . It is a paradox that the Lord of glory should stoop to the feet of men. The point of the story, however, is precisely in the paradox. Its goal is not to establish a fixed rite of washing of which this is the etiological foundation, nor is it to provide a safeguard against erroneous rites. The act offers an interpretation of the saving work of Jesus. He humbles Himself to the menial task of foot-washing, i.e.: He lays aside His divine glory and by so doing accomplishes salvation for the man on whose behalf He performs this service." (i.e.: all disciples and through them all people.--My note.)

αλλ ηλ ω ν νιπτειν τουσ πο δασ. υπυδειγμα γαρ
εδωκα υμιν, ινα καθωσ εγω εποιησα υμιν, και
υμεισ ποιητε. αμην αμην λεγω υμιν, ουκ εστιν
δουλοσ μειζων του κυριου αυτου, ουδε αποστολοσ
μειζων του πεμφαντοσ αυτον ."

(When therefore he had washed their feet, and taken his
garments, having reclined again, he said to them, Do ye
know what I have done to you? Ye call me the Teacher
and the Lord, and well ye say, I am [so] for. If therefore
I washed your feet, the Lord and the Teacher, also ye ought
of one another to wash the feet; for an example I gave
you, that as I did to you, also ye should do. Verily verily
I say to you, Is not a bondman greater than his lord, nor a
messenger greater than he who sent him.)[326]

Jesus has completed his liturgical act, humbling
himself as though he were a slave. This is at once an act of
humility, similar to, but more extreme, than the one Mary
performed when she anointed his feet, and an intimate act
of self-revelation. He is revealing the nature of his
incarnation, the extent to which God has gone in order to
abide with "his own." He takes upon himself, once again,
his garments, that is his identity by which he is more
customarily recognized, and returns to his role as the
Teacher and Lord of his disciples, engaging them in a
lesson, so that they will understand that his act is to serve
as an example for their actions. They are to model their
relationships with those to whom he sends them after his
relationship with them. They are to humble themselves as
though they are servants, revealing the Christ who abides

---

[326]Gk. and lit. trans. fr. Barry, op. cit., pp. 286-287.

within them as one who seeks a personal and intimate relationship with them, and they are to prepare other disciples to serve God's people in the same way.

It could be argued that Jesus is establishing a ritual for the ordination of disciples, though that does not appear to have been the practice of the early church, nor has it become a tradition in the church since the first-century. Given Jesus' instructions, this is surprising.

Of particular interest are the illustrations Jesus provides, apparently as a rationale to convince the disciples that they should follow his example. A slave δουλοσ *(doulos)* is not greater than his lord κυριοσ *(kurios)*; a messenger αποστολοσ *(apostolos)* is not greater than the one who sends the messenger πεμφασ *(pemphas)*.

"Washing feet was one of the duties of slaves, and indeed of non-Jewish rather than Jewish slaves. (Wives have the same duty, as also sons and daughters towards their father.) In performing this service, Jesus puts himself in the position of a δουλοσ who must unthinkingly fulfill his office. By thus rendering to the disciples a service which even they did not owe to him, though the duties of the disciple to his teacher were very much the same as those of a slave to his master, he displayed to them the degree of condescension and self-sacrifice which his office entailed. In view of his majesty, only the symbolic position of the slave was adequate to open their eyes and to keep them from illusions in respect to his office."[327]

---

[327]Karl Heinrich Rengstorf, "δουλοσ," Theological Dictionary of the New Testament, op. cit., vol. II, p. 277, n. 113; See Strauss-Billerbeck., II, p. 557; I, p. 706; T. Qid, 1, 11).

. This liturgical gesture by Jesus affirms the liturgy performed for him by Mary of Bethany in Jn. 12: 3. It is an act of solidarity with her, having taken upon himself the humble servant role which she assumed as a woman and as his disciple. Jesus now asserts that his identity as a humble servant is the identity into which every disciple is to be ordained. It is to be passed perpetually by these disciples to all other disciples.

The term αποστολοσ (*apostolos*) is a Greek term referring to a Jewish institution in which an emissary represents the authority of a definite group or community.[328]

"It is as an authorized representative of the local community that the leader prays for the assembled congregation in the individual synagogue, and any lapse is a bad sign for those whom he has to represent before God. Again, the High Priest acts as a fully accredited representative of the priesthood, which for its part is charged by the Sanhedrin to see that he correctly carries out the prescribed actions, and then on the Day of Atonement he represents the national community as a whole."[329]

"As representatives of the scribes, and in their name again of all Israel, we have to mention supremely the rabbis who were sent out to the whole *diaspora* by the central

---

[328]Karl Heinrich Rengstorf, "αποστολοσ," Theological Dictionary of the New Testament, op. cit., vol. I, p. 416. See also pp. 398-406 on the synonyms "αποστελλω " and "πεμπω ". Both mean the same as "αποστελλειν": to send forth.

[329]Ibid. The Gk. "αποστολοσ" is sub. for the Heb. term used in this article. See Ber., 5, 5; Yoma 1, 5.

authorities; for them the designation (αποστολοσ) became an official title in the true sense. Their commission was many-sided enough, but it was always made possible by the authority which stood behind them in the person of those who sent them. Moreover the (αποστολοσ), who were usually ordained rabbis, were specially set apart for their task by the laying on of hands in the name of the community which sent them. Their mission thus acquired a religious as well as an official character. Perhaps this final element is also specifically expressed in the fact that (αποστολοσ) were not sent out alone but usually two or more together."[330]

"The laying on of hands, with which, e.g., the representative High Priest on the Day of Atonement was designated for his supreme office, but which was above all customary in ordination, seems to have been later abandoned by the Jews in view of its adoption by Christians. Its earlier link with the institution of (αποστολοσ) emphasizes the importance of the latter."[331]

". . . The Rabbis often used the term (αποστολοσ) of one who was commissioned and authorized by God. Two groups might be mentioned in this connection, first, the impersonal one of the priesthood in the priest as such, and second, a small number of outstanding personalities, especially Moses, Elijah, Elisha, and Ezekiel. In offering sacrifices the priest was the commissioned minister of God and not of the Jewish community. Behind this statement

---

[330]Ibid., p. 417.

[331]Ibid., pp. 417-418; See Yoma., 1, 1; T.Sanh.., 1, 1; Strauss-Billerbeck, II, 653f.

stands the whole (αποστολοσ) idea that the one authoritatively commissioned is as the one who commissions him. If the priest were the (αποστολοσ) of the community, the latter might also offer sacrifice. But if so, the priest would be superfluous. Hence the priest can be only the (αποστολοσ) of God."[332]

"Moses, Elijah, Elisha, and Ezekiel are called (αποστολοσ) of God because there took place through them things normally reserved for God. Moses causes water to flow out of a rock; Elijah brings rain and raises a dead man; Elisha 'opens the mother's womb' and also raises a dead man; and Ezekiel receives the 'key to the tombs at the reawakening of the dead' (Ez. 37: 1ff)."[333]

"There is full identity between αποστολοσ and (the Hebrew term) at Jn. 13: 16. Here αποστολοσ is simply the rendering of the legal term in its purely legal sense of one who is lawfully charged to represent the person and cause of another. This meaning is confirmed by the juxtaposition of the two pairs δουλοσ *(slave)*/κυριοσ *(lord)* and αποστολοσ *(authorized messenger -- sent one)*/ πεμψασ *(authority or sending one)*. The δουλοσ *(servant)* stands fully under the jurisdiction of his master and derives from him all that he is. But this is also a mark of the (αποστολοσ)."[334]

---

[332]Ibid., p. 419; See Rab. Huna b. Jehoshua, c. 350 A.D.; b. Kid., 23b.

[333]Ibid., p. 419; See b. B.M. 86b; Midr. Ps. 78: 5; See b. Taan. 2a; b. Sanh., 113a.

[334]Ibid., p. 421. (Definitions set off by italics in parenthesis are my own.)

Jesus has taken upon himself the identity of the δουλοσ (*slave*) and is now asserting that his disciples, who call him Master and Lord, are not greater than he. As those whom he sends by God's authority, they are not greater than God. They are now authorized to function as priests. Though couched in language that appears to be a teacher's lesson, these words are in fact the words of institution for the ordination of the disciples of Jesus.

Two additional illustrations could have been provided by Jesus, but were not: a disciple is not greater than the Teacher, and a priest is not greater than the Lord. Though these illustrations would have flowed naturally from the titles that Jesus acknowledges are used by the disciples to identify him, they do not convey the hidden message that the paired terms slave/lord and messenger/sender do. Implied in those terms (esp. αποστολοσ) is the authority of humble disciple/messengers (apostles) to carry out the mission of Jesus by remembering his sacrifice whenever they serve the Eucharist.

The Blessing

"If you know these things, you are blessed if you do them" (Jn. 13: 17).

"ει ταυτα οιδατε, μακαριοι εστε εαν ποιητε αυ τα."

(*If these things ye know, blessed are ye if ye do them.*)[335]

---

[335]Gk. and lit. trans., Barry, op. cit., p. 287.

This short sentence provides a hint as to the importance of what has just preceded it. It is almost as though Jesus has said, "If you have eyes to see, then believe." The operative words are: know "οιδατε (*oidate*)" and do "ποιητε (*poiate*), a play on words. They are words that have already been defined in the Gospel.[336]

Jn. 9 deals extensively with the contrast between a man born blind who "knows" and the Pharisees who do not "know," culminating in the frustrated response of the man born blind to the questioning by the Pharisees after his blindness is healed by Jesus. "I have told you already, and you would not listen. Why do you want to hear it again? Do you also want to become his disciples?" (Jn. 9: 27). The disciples look to see, listen to hear, seek to know. The Pharisees are characterized as blind to the light, deaf to the truth and "not knowing." They do not know where Jesus abides or who he is. They do not want to know.[337]

---

[336]There are 115 references to the various forms of "γινωσκω " (know, knowing, known and knows) in John. The word "know" is found in every chapter of the gospel. See Rudolf Bultmann, "γινωσκω ," Theological Dictionary of the New Testament, op. cit., vol. I, pp. 689-719, esp. pp. 711 - 713.

[337]See Jn. 1: 26; 2: 9; 3: 8-10; (to a Samaritan woman) 4: 22; 5: 12f; 6: 42; (Jesus says that the Jews do not know God) 7: 28; 8: 14, 55; 9: 12, 21, 29, 30; 10: 5; (Caiaphas admits that none of them know) 11: 49; (Jesus explains why some do not know) 12: 35; (It is important to Jesus that his disciples know) 13: 7, 12, 17; (Jesus tells the disciples, who admit they do not know) 14: 4f; (Jesus calls those who know him, his friends) 15: 15; (The disciples admit again that they do not know, and Jesus tells them) 16: 18f; (Jesus prays that the disciples will know God) 17: 3; (When the High Priest questions Jesus, he tells him to ask those who have heard his teachings, and therefore know) 18: 21; Pilate understands the power of knowing and not knowing (19: 4, 10); (Mary Magdalene and the disciples do not know about the resurrection) 20: 2, 9, 13, 14; 21: 4; (Jesus knows everything) 21: 15, 16, 17; (The B.D.'s

Disciples are blessed by doing what they know. What these disciples know now is the meaning of the Eucharist and the nature of their own ministries. The traditional Passover beatitude quoted in Jn. 12: 13 comes from Psalm 118: 26. Though Jesus makes reference to it by quoting only a brief portion of it, the full benediction conveys a sense of closure to the ordination. "Blessed is the one who comes in the name of the Lord. We bless you from the house of the Lord." These are the words of priests. The ordination ritual is complete.

---

witness is known by the writers of the Gospel) 21: 24.

Chapter 15
Who Wrote the Gospel of John?

The Name Is Not the Author's

Scholars are generally agreed that the Gospel According to John was not written by a disciple named John (John Mark or John the son of Zebedee). By consensus the date of its publication is no earlier than 90 AD and is generally set at about 120 AD. The fact it has been named "The Gospel According to John" may have more to do with the custom in that era of referring to un-titled works by the name of the first person identified in it. Since most documents were written in the form of letters, this was usually an indication of authorship. Letters began with a salutation similar to the ones used by the Apostle, Paul: "From Paul, a servant of Jesus Christ . . . to the church in . . ." One would expect the Gospel of John to begin, "From John, a disciple of Jesus Christ, to his other disciples," but that is not the way the Gospel begins. In fact, there is no direct indication as to who the author is or for whom the gospel was originally intended.

Just as surely as scholars agree that John Mark is not the author of the Gospel of John, they are clear that John the Baptist is not the author of the Gospel. As we have seen, John the Baptist does have an important role in the Gospel, one that is appropriately identified at the beginning of the narrative. He provides the model for all disciples, setting the criteria of seeing Christ in Jesus and witnessing to their belief in him. While that role is of crucial importance in the Gospel, (It could be called The Gospel According to the *Perspective* of John the Baptist), his importance does not extend to that of "author."

A Number of Different Hands and Voices

Throughout this study, references have been made to "the author or authors" of the Gospel. James Charlesworth, following the lead of Raymond E. Brown, has articulated the current consensus among scholars regarding the probability that a number of different roles must be defined in answer to the question, "Who wrote the Gospel According to John?"[338]

The Beloved Disciple may be identified, as Brown suggests, as "the source" of the Gospel. From this study it seems fair to suggest that the Beloved Disciple may well have been the female leader of a community of disciples who were engaged in the process of educating disciples using the existing Gospels (especially Luke)[339] and the scriptures of the Septuagint. The Beloved Disciple may well have provided narrative commentaries of the sort that would have emerged from the midrash method of instruction. These commentaries, filled with language borrowed from the Septuagint and elaborating on words and characters identified in the orthodox versions of the Jesus story, may be the gospel's "source."

---

[338]Charlesworth, op. cit., pp. 25f.

[339]See Randel McCraw Helms, Who Wrote the Gospels?, Millennium Press, Altadena, California, (1996). Helms contends that the Gospel of Luke was written by a woman, citing the numerous references to women in important roles, including the only other reference to Mary and Martha (Luke 10: 38-42) and Jesus' response to a woman who cries out "Happy is the womb that carried you and the breasts that suckled you!" "He rejoined, 'No, happy are those who hear the word of God and keep it' (Luke 11: 27-28)." - p. 74. Luke is also the source of the name of Lazarus as a symbolic figure in one of Jesus' parables (Luke 16: 19-31).

An Intimate Knowledge

That still doesn't answer the question, however, as to "who wrote the Gospel According to John?" As we have said, the identity behind the gospel, the person from whom the tradition came, the one who shaped the theological perspective in the Fourth Gospel is the Beloved Disciple, Mary of Bethany. The "inside views" of Jesus in the Gospel reflect an intimate relationship, a sensitivity to Jesus the man as well as an acute awareness of Jesus the Christ, the Holy One. The extensive use of oracles and the intricate way in which they are woven together with the orthodox Jesus story suggests a deep and well-informed theological mind. The person who fits that identity is the Beloved Disciple, whom this study has identified as Mary of Bethany.

An Old Testament Professor

Clearly, however, there are other roles. Brown and Culpepper suggest that the gospel may have been the product of an entire community or even a school. Without a doubt someone with an extraordinarily deep understanding of the Pentateuch and Nehemiah as well as other parts of the Old Testament, had an influence over what was written, perhaps even how the tradition was shaped. While Mary of Bethany may have been the leader, even the principal theologian of the community of scholars and student disciples, Nicodemus seems the most likely candidate for the role of "Old Testament Professor."

The Scribe

As to the identity of the writer, the scribe who literally placed words on parchment, at least two different persons must be identified: the scribe who recorded the words, and the person who "caused the words to be written" (Jn. 21: 24). I suspect that the identity of the former (the writer) may be the same as that of the author of the second epistle of John, "the elder to the elect lady and her children, whom I love in the truth, and not only I but also all who know the truth, because of the truth that abides in us and will be with us forever" (1 Jn. 1: 1-2). The elect lady is not *the church* as tradition suggests, but the Beloved Disciple, Mary of Bethany. The author of these epistles identifies himself as "the elder to the elect lady . . ." This study has shown that Thomas was identified as an elder in the community. It is not difficult to imagine Thomas, the Elder, working closely with the Beloved Disciple, Mary of Bethany, as her scribe. He writes conveying her words, her thoughts, her theology. He is the person in whose possession the actual manuscript from which the Gospel According to John was originally to be found. He is the one who is suspected by many scholars to have added what we know as the 21st chapter to the Gospel, following the death of the Beloved Disciple.

The Publisher

As to the identity of the person who "caused the words to be written," there is but one clue in the Gospel as to this person's identity, and it seems impossible to believe. This one person had the authority to direct, "Let it be written," as if a new law were being recorded (as, indeed, it was). He literally caused a sign to be written, attesting to the

identity of Jesus as the King of the Jews (Jn. 19: 19-22).
I mean, of course, Pontius Pilate. Remember that the
model for discipleship established by John the Baptist is that
a seeker sees the Christ in Jesus and testifies to that truth.
Look carefully at what may have been the very first written
affirmation of faith in Jn. 19: 19-20. In the Hebrew
tradition there is only one King of Israel: Yahweh, God.
When Pilate identifies Jesus as "King of the Jews," he is
ironically declaring that it is the Hebrew God that is being
crucified. In Jn. 19: 15, Pilate asks these authorities,
"Shall I crucify your King?" The Chief Priests answer,
"We have no king but the emperor." That was a politically
correct response for those hoping to use Pilate's authority
to crucify one they considered to be a blasphemer (Jn. 19:
12). It was a devastating assertion of their loss of
relationship with the *logos*, Yahweh, King of Israel.

Note that this sign that Pilate caused to be written
was inscribed in Hebrew, Latin and Greek. While Pilate
did not consider himself to be a Jew (Jn. 18: 35), he
apparently intended that people from every culture would
be able to read his affirmation of faith. Could it be that he
caused the whole story of Jesus to be written by supporting
what we now call the Johannine community? When Jesus
informed Pilate that "my kingdom is not of this world" (Jn.
19: 36-38), could it be that Pilate saw the need for a
witness addressed to the world, composed in the universal
language of Greek? As unthinkable as it sounds at first,
Pilate could have been the gospel's publisher.

One More Theory

Who wrote the Gospel According to John? The complete answer to that question may never be known, but here is one more theory to add to the collection. The Gospel According to John was originally composed by Thomas from a collection of sermons or commentaries on the life of Jesus that were originally provided by the leader of his community, Mary of Bethany. This Gospel became the text book for the training of new disciples of Jesus in that community, and was subject to being "polished" by the scholars of considerable talent who "remained" in the community. As such, it may have been a work in progress, subject to the adjustments offered by a number of scribes, when a crisis occurred that caused the community to break up. That crisis occured sometime after the destruction of the second temple in Jerusalem (70 A.D.) and after the Beloved Disciple died. Many of the leaders of the Christian community who emerged after the turn of the first century may well have been influenced, directly or indirectly, by people who had, at one time, been a part of what we call the Johannine community.

Chapter 16
The Rest of the Story

The End of a Very Old Story

The Fourth Gospel is not written just to tell the story of the ordination of Mary of Bethany and the other disciples. The story is about Jesus, and the death and resurrection of Jesus provides the dramatic conclusion to the narrative. The setting is a blend of both historical and cosmic time and place.

In 13: 17-18, the transition to the conclusion of the plot, Jesus says,

"I am not speaking to all of you; I know whom I have chosen. But it is to fulfill the scripture (Gn. 3: 15), "The one who ate my bread (or ate bread with me) has lifted his heel against me."

It is the ordained disciple, Judas, who represents enmity with Christ. From the perspective of the Fourth Gospel, this enmity is not only with Christ, but with the tradition of Christ. Mary of Bethany is the keeper of that tradition. The feet of Jesus are the focus of her faith. She is a servant, but Judas, whose enmity with Mary is apparent in Jn. 12: 4-6, strikes at Jesus' head ("lifted his heel against me") symbolically in the betrayal in Jn. 18.

The story is interrupted at this point by a series of monologues (Jn. 13: 21 - 17: 26) which bring the seeking disciple (the implied reader of the Gospel) into the heart, mind, and soul of Jesus. The seeker makes the rest of the journey, not as one who follows Jesus, but as one who experiences what Jesus experiences as his or her own.

The Setting: In the Garden of Eden

The setting is carefully described in Jn. 18: 1. "After Jesus had spoken these words, he went out with his disciples across the Kidron valley[340] to a place where there was a garden, which he and his disciples entered." This serves both as a *geographic map*, indicating the route taken by Jesus and the disciples as they left Jerusalem and journeyed to the garden, and as a *sign* that bears a message for those with eyes to see.

The Kedron valley was a deep gorge which made travel between Jerusalem and the King's Garden possible without being seen. Nehemiah made an inspection of the broken walls of Jerusalem (and of the Temple), the sign of Jerusalem's shame for having turned from the covenant with God.

"Then I went on to the Fountain Gate and to the King's Pool;[341] but there was no place for the animal I was riding to continue. So I went up by way of the valley by night and inspected the wall. Then I turned back and entered by the Valley Gate, and so returned. The officials did not know where I had gone or what I was doing; I had not yet told the Jews, the priests, the nobles, the officials, and the rest that were to do the work" (Neh. 2: 14-16).

---

[340]In the LXX, literally, ". . . beyond the winter stream of Kedron . . ."

[341]Also called the Pool of Shelah or Pool of Siloah. See G.A. Barrois, "Shelah, Pool Of," The Interpreter's Dictionary of the Bible, Vol 4, Abingdon Press, Nashville-New York, (1962), pp. 319-320. See also Barrois, "Kidron, Brook," The Interpreter's Dictionary of the Bible, Vol. 3, op. cit., pp. 10-11.

The sign indicates that the whereabouts of Jesus, because of the secret route he had taken, were still unknown to "the Jews, the priests, the nobles, the officials, and the rest that were to do the work" of the final hour of Jesus.

As has already been established, the hour of Jesus begins on the Day of Preparation, historically the day before Passover. If Passover was to be celebrated on the Sabbath,[342] then the six-day period of ritual purification would conclude on Friday, which would begin after sundown on what we would call Thursday evening. This is important, because the events that the Fourth Gospel reports as occurring that night could not have occurred on the Sabbath, which was to be a day "of complete rest, a holy convocation; you shall do no work: it is a Sabbath to the Lord . . ." (Lv. 23: 3). Jesus had replaced the Sabbath, but the general population and certainly the Chief Priests had not.

On that night (the beginning of the Day of Preparation) having spoken the words included in the monologues, Jesus goes to a garden. The garden represents the Garden of Eden, because what transpires there completes a story that began, as just mentioned above, and according to the story of creation in Genesis, in the garden. It is there that the enemy of Jesus and of the tradition of Jesus strikes against the holy head of Jesus.

---

[342] See Lv. 23: 1-8. Vs. 5 reads "In the first month, on the fourteenth day of the month, at twilight, (Heb. *between the two evenings*) there shall be a passover offering to the Lord . . ." Assuming that the first day of the first month would always be the first day of the week (beginning after twilight on the previous Sabbath), the fourteenth day of the first month (*Nissan*) would be the Sabbath.

Judas Priest

"Now Judas, who betrayed him, also knew the place, because Jesus often met there with his disciples. So Judas brought a detachment of soldiers together with police from the Chief Priests and the Pharisees, and they came there with lanterns and torches and weapons." (Jn. 18: 2-3)

Judas was a disciple. He knew where Jesus was and where Jesus would be, because he knew where it was that Jesus met his disciples. The Teacher in the Johannine school quizzes her students, "Where does Christ abide?" The students reply, "Christ abides in me." "When Judas betrays Christ, who does he betray?" "He betrays himself." He is a priest who sees the light, yet he stands with those who abide in darkness, the dead priests, the servants of the serpent.

As we have seen, whenever the writer of the Fourth Gospel uses the word "stands" in reference to a disciple or priest, it refers to their priestly role as one who "stands before God (i.e.: at the altar, making a sacrifice.)" For Judas to stand with the Temple priests and their hired hands (Jn. 10: 10a, 11-13) means that he stands before God prepared to offer Jesus as a sacrifice. This point is reinforced by what happens next.

Whom Do You Seek?

Jesus asks the same question of Judas and those who accompany him as he asked the first two disciples (Jn. 1: 39) "Whom do you seek?" They respond in a manner that sounds just like the response of a faithful disciple, "We seek Jesus of Nazareth." To which Jesus says, simply and powerfully and subtly, "I am." When Jesus identifies himself in the same words that God uses to identify himself to Moses at the burning bush, the priests of the darkness step back and fall to the ground, essentially genuflecting to acknowledge the holiness of Jesus.

Jesus repeats the question. "Whom do you seek?" The hired hands respond again, "We seek Jesus of Nazareth (or Jesus the Nazorean)." Jesus again says, "I am." By this repetition there is to be no doubt in the mind of the disciple who is reading this Gospel that Jesus is the Holy One of God and those who arrest him, who lay hands upon him, know it and believe it.

This strike against the head of Jesus is reported again in the Gospel. In Jn. 18: 22 one of the Temple guards strikes Jesus on the face, ostensibly in defense of the High Priest's dignity and holy authority, which the guard believes Jesus has defiled. In this context, Jesus makes it clear that the true blow is the response he gets: violence against him instead of a profession of faith or an acknowledgement of Truth. The doubt of a disciple (Jn. 20: 29) tears at his insides, but violence to his holy head is an abomination, an offense to God.

Summary

The sign that concludes the story of Adam and Eve in the Garden of Eden is given as the Gospel of John begins its dramatic conclusion. In addition, the story of Miriam, the archetype of all female priests, has now been finished, asserting the will of Jesus that women be brought back into the camp where they are called to serve as priests.

All of this and much, much more, is contained in the context of a Jesus story that was written to appear as a re-telling of the Jesus story that was already accepted in the orthodox Christian church. The writer or writers of this Gospel have simply trusted that those who really want to see the truth will eventually recognize the connection between the ancient oracles of the Mosaic tradition and the secret story line in the Gospel of the Johannine community, a Gospel that would become known as the Gospel According to John.

For nearly two millennia this truth has remained hidden, waiting for the day when the world would be ready to see its light. As the time for the third millennium approaches, the voice of the Great Shepherd calls out to those who have ears to hear and eyes to see. That voice calls us each to become disciples. To those who refuse to know that our Lord has always called women as well as men into ministry, we say with Jesus, *"Let her keep it!"*

Plan of The Second Temple [343]

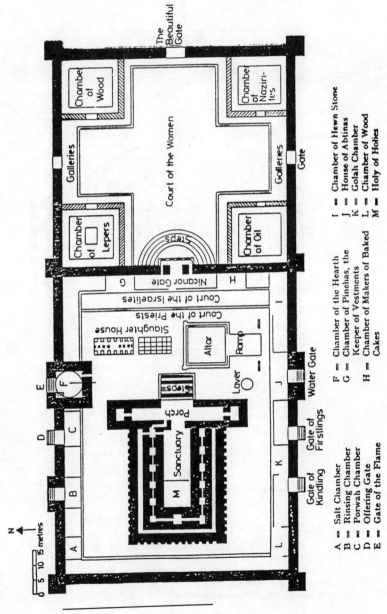

A = Salt Chamber
B = Rinsing Chamber
C = Porwah Chamber
D = Offering Gate
E = Gate of the Flame

F = Chamber of the Hearth
G = Chamber of Pinchas, the Keeper of Vestments
H = Chamber of Makers of Baked Cakes

I = Chamber of Hewn Stone
J = House of Abtinas
K = Golah Chamber
L = Chamber of Wood
M = Holy of Holies

[343]Joan Comay, <u>The Temple of Jerusalem</u>, Holt, Rinehart and Winston, New York, (1975), p. 166.

The "Eye" of Reader-Response,[344]

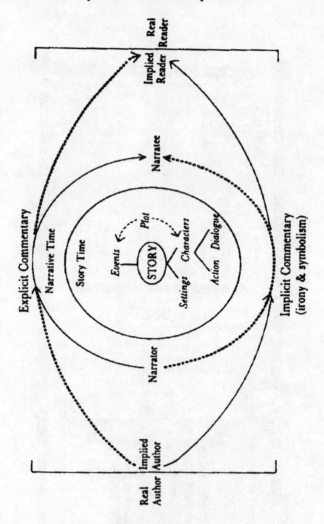

[344]Culpepper, <u>Anatomy of the Fourth Gospel</u>, op. cit., p. 6.
Culpepper credits Seymour Chatman, <u>Story and Discourse</u>, p. 267, who
in turn "owes a great deal to the communicational model of Roman
Jakobson." He acknowledges that some of his own modifications appear
on this model, which I have named.

APPENDIX C

Concordance
Of Mosaic and Johannine Signs

Anointing Oil: scented oil used to mark that which is holy
Recipe for temple use only: Ex. 30: 22-38; 25: 6
Ordination: Ex. 29: 7; Lev. 8: 10-12
Sacrifices:
-Grain: Lev. 2: 1-10, 15; 6: 14-15; 7: 13
-Animals: Ex. 29: 40-41; Lv. 2: 16
Consecration of holy objects: Gn. 28: 18; 35: 14
To anoint the feet of Jesus: Jn. 12: 3

Believe: action of faith; discipleship
Moses' hand: Ex. 4: 1-17, esp. 6-8 (see Hand)
God to Moses in a cloud: Ex. 19: 9
John the Baptist: Jn. 1: 7
Nicodemus: Jn. 3: 1-21
Samaritan woman brings believers: 4: 21, 42, 48
Jesus identifies witnesses: Jn. 5: 38-47; 10: 25-38
God's purpose in Jesus: Jn. 6: 29-65
Unbelievers:
-Jesus' brothers Jn. 7: 5
-Pharisees Jn. 11: 48
-People Jn. 12: 36-40
Consequences of believing: Jn. 8: 23-24, 45-47
Man born blind unbelief: Jn. 9: all
Jesus' promise to believers: Jn. 11: 26-27, 40-42
Fulfillment of God's prophesy (Gn. 3:15): Jn. 13:19
Rewards for belief: Jn. 14: all; 16: 29-33; 17: 20-21
Trusworthy testimony, believe it: Jn. 19: 35
Thomas to touch wounds: Jn. 20: 24-31

Bethany: sign of near gate to the temple; house of Ananiah
      House of Ananiah near temple gates: Neh. 3: 23
      Town outside Jerusalem: Neh. 11: 32
      Town of Lazarus, Mary, Martha: Jn. 11: 1; 12: 1
      Near Jerusalem: Jn. 11: 18

Bethany beyond Jordan: sign of far temple gate
      Cities of refuge: Nu. 35: 9-12; Dt. 19: 1-13
      John the Baptist baptises there: Jn. 1: 28

Blood: sacred sign of life, belonging exclusively to God
      Blood is life: Gn. 9: 4; Dt. 12: 23-27
      Without offering: Lv. 17 all; Dt. 12: 16; 15: 23
      Water to blood by Moses: Ex. 4: 09; 7: 17-19
      Moses is bridegroom of blood: Ex. 4: 24-26
      Passover: Ex. 12: 1-13, 22-23
      Blood of the covenant: Ex. 24: 1-8
      Ordination: Ex. 29: 12-21; Lv. 8: all; 9: all
      Atonement: Ex. 30: 10; Lv. 16: all
      Offerings
      -Burnt: Lv. 1: all
      -Well-being: Lv. 3: all
      -Sin: Lv. 4: all; 5: 9; 6: 24-30
      -Guilt offerings: Lv. 7: all;
      Sign of guilt: Lv. 20: all; Dt. 21: 7-9; 22: 8
      Song of Moses: Dt. 32: 14, 42-43
      Born not of blood: Jn. 1: 13
      Blood of Son of Man: Jn. 6: 53-56
      Jesus' body pierced: Jn. 19: 34-37

Body: All not head or legs on animal or person; entrails
      Purify body in water: Lv. 14: 8; 15: 13, 16, 19f
      Atone for body in water: Lv. 16: 24, 28

Ordination: Ex. 29: 13, 17, 22; Lv. 8: 21; 9: 14
Jesus' body as the temple: Jn. 2: 21
Jesus heals, compared to circumcision: Jn. 7: 21-24
Soldiers pierce side (body) of Jesus: Jn. 19: 33-34
Remove and bury Jesus' body: Jn. 19: 38-42
Two angels where body, feet had been: Jn. 20: 12

Bosom: Breast or chest; sign of close, intimate relationship
Moses' hand in: Ex. 4: 6-8
Moses to carry God's people?: Nu. 11: 12
"Wife you embrace": Dt. 13: 6; 28: 54
Jesus in God's: Jn. 1: 18
Beloved Disciple in Jesus': 13: 23, 25; 21: 20

Caduceus: Serpent(s) on pole; symbol of healing
God instructs Moses: Nu. 21: 4-9
Jesus to be lifted up: Jn. 3: 14-15

Charcoal Fire: holy coals: sign of true worship
Unholy fire on the altar: Lv. 10: 1-3
Peter seeks warmth: Jn. 18: 18
Jesus feeds the disciples: Jn. 21: 9

Creation: The divine act in birth, re-birth
God creates: Gn. 1; 2; 5: 1-2; Dt. 4: 32; 32: 6
Jesus tells Nicodemus to be reborn: Jn. 3: 1-8
Jesus heals a man born blind: Jn. 9: all, esp. vs. 6
Jesus calls to Lazarus Come forth! : Jn. 11: 43

Darkness: Belief that life, light exists without God
Primordial darkness, before creation: Gn. 1: 2
God names night and day: Gn. 1: 4, 5
Pilars of dark and light: Gn. 13: 21-22: 14: 19-20

Blazing mountain, shrouded in dark: Dt. 4: 11
Light shines in the darkness: Jn. 1: 5
Light in world; people love darkness: Jn. 3: 19-21
Follows walk not in dark: Jn. 8: 12; 12: 35-36, 46

Day: In cosmic time: the day of creation / new creation
Day of creation: Gn. 2: 4
Day of the covenant: Gn. 15: 17-21
Third day: Abraham prepares sacrifice : Gn. 22: 4
Day breaks: Gn. 32: 22-32
Disciples of John abide with Jesus: Jn. 1: 39
The third day: wedding festival in Cana: Jn. 2: 1
All who believe on the last day: Jn. 6: 39-40, 54
Last day: come to me and drink: Jn. 7: 37-38
Ancestor rejoiced to see my day: Jn. 8: 56
Work while it is day: Jn. 9: 4, see vs. 14
Walk by day, do not stumble: Jn. 11: 9-10
Martha's belief on the last day: Jn. 11: 24
Leave her alone, that she might keep it: Jn. 12: 7
Last day my word will serve as judge: Jn. 12: 48
On the last day you will know: Jn. 14: 20
Ask of the Father in my name: Jn. 16: 23, 26
Day of preparation: Jn. 19: 14, 31, 42
The resurrection of Jesus on the first day: Jn. 20: 1
Jesus appears on the evening of the first: Jn. 20: 19
Day break: Jn. 21: 4

Defilement: soiling one's holiness, ritually unclean
Going near a dead body: Lv. 21: all; Nu. 19: 11-13
Corpse on a tree not permitted to remain: Dt. 21: 22
Leprous persons put out of the camp: Nu. 5: 1-4
Test for wife accused of adultery: Nu. 5: 11-33
Ritual for re-starting Nazirite vow: Nu. 6: 9-12

Purification after a sudden death: Nu. 19: 14-20
Pilate's headquarters unclean: Jn. 18: 28
Jesus is buried on day of preparation: Jn. 19: 42

Disciple: one who sees Christ and witnesses.
Isaiah binds testimony of his disciples: Is. 8: 16-18
See chapter 6 for a listing of disciples in John
See chapter 10 on the Beloved Disciple

Dust: the stuff of creation; sign of human sinfulness
God creates Adam from dust: Gn. 2: 7
God curses ground: Gn. 3: 14, 19
Jesus washes the disciples' feet: Jn. 13: 1-11

Elevation Offering: sacrifice placed in palms, lifted up
Ordination: Ex. 29: 24-25; Lv. 7: 28-30
Jesus to be lifted up: Jn. 12: 32; see also Caduceus

Feet: Sign of contact with dust of the earth
Moses told to remove shoes: Ex. 3: 5
Passover: eat standing with sandles on: Ex. 12: 11
Moses anoints the base (foot) of the altar: Lv. 8: 11
Ordination: blood on big toe: Ex. 29: 20
Priests wash hands, feet: Ex. 30: 17-21; 40: 31
Legs of sacrifice washed: Ex. 29: 17; Lv. 8: 21
Mary kneels at the feet of Jesus: Jn. 11: 32
Mary anoints the feet of Jesus: Jn. 11: 2; 12: 3
Jesus washes the disciples' feet: Jn. 13: 1-11
Jesus' grave cloths, believes: Jn. 20: 1-8
Angels where Jesus' head, feet had been: Jn. 20: 12

Footstool: sign for the altar in God's House
        David's vow to worship at footstool: Ps. 132: 1-7
        Heaven is throne, earth is footstool: Is. 66: 1
        God does not remember his footstool: Lam. 2: 1
        See Feet, esp. re: Mary at feet of Jesus' feet

Gate: Entry to the temple; sign of access to God.
        Jacob's ladder dream - gate of heaven: Gn. 28: 17
        Temple gates: Neh. 2, 3, 8, and 12
        See Bethany

Girdle/Ephod: Tight fitting apron; sign of close to God
        High Priest to wear: Ex. 28: 6-14;
        Jesus girded himself: Jn. 13: 4, 5

Hair: Sign of God's glory in one dedicated to God
        Priests not to dishevel their hair: Lv. 10: 6
        Purification from leprosy - shave hair: Lv. 14: 8-9
        Men shall not trim hair or beards: Lv. 19: 27
        High Priest may not dishevel hair: Lv. 21: 10
        Unbraiding hair: Nu. 5: 18
        Nazirite shall not shave hair: Nu. 6: 5
        Nazirite shaves hair to complete vow: Nu. 6: 18
        Mary of Bethany wipes Jesus' feet: Jn. 11: 2; 12: 3

Hand: Sign of power, authority, control; God's power
        Adam's potential power acknowledged: Gn. 3: 22
        Curse from Cain's hand: Gn.. 4: 11
        Abraham's hand is stopped: Gn. 22: 10, 12
        Moses' hand: Ex. 4: 1-5
        Keep Passover sign on hand: Ex. 13: 9
        Moses' song - strong right hand of God: Ex. 15: 6
        Miriam's song -tambourine in her hand: Ex. 15: 20

Sacred boundaries - no hand shall touch: Ex. 19: 13
Lay hand on burnt offering: Lv. 1: 4; 3: 8
Ordination: Gn. 48: 17; Dt. 34: 9; See Dt. 31: 23
Ordination: blood right thumb: Lv. 8: 23
Priest pours anointing oil into his: Lv. 14: 15, 26
Blood on leper's right thumb: Lv. 14: 14, 25
Anointing oil on leper's right thumb: Lv. 14: 18, 28
No priest with injured hand: Lv. 21: 19
Love the Lord, bind sign on your hand: Dt. 6: 4-9
Remember the mighty hand of God: Dt. 7: 19
Open your hand: Dt. 15: 7-11
All things in the Son's hands: Jn. 3: 35
No one shall snatch sheep out of my: Jn. 10: 28, 29
Guard strikes Jesus on the face: Jn. 18: 22
Thomas must place his into Jesus: Jn. 20: 25-27

Head: Body part that represents the holiness
God's curse - serpent's head bruised: Gn. 3: 15
Jacob's dream: Gn. 28: 11, 18
Lay hands on heads (blessing): Gn. 48: 14-18
Ordination turban: Ex. 29: 6
Ordination - anoint head with oil: Ex. 29: 7
Ordination - hands on heads: Ex. 29: 10, 15, 19
Ordination, sacrifice - head not washed: Ex. 29: 17
Nazirite consecration on head: Nu. 6: 7, 9, 11, 18
Captive woman's head shaved: Dt. 21: 11, 12
Peter asks Jesus to wash his head: Jn. 13: 9
Crown of thorns on Jesus' head: Jn. 19: 2
Jesus bows his head and dies: Jn. 19: 30
Grave cloth on Jesus' head: Jn. 20: 7
Angels where Jesus' head, feet were: Jn. 20: 12

High Priest's Signet turban emblem
Holy to God: Ex. 28: 36-28, 39: 30; Lv. 8: 9

Holiness: Set apart for God, sanctity
Of nation of priests (Israel): Ex. 19: 6, Dt. 14: 2
Of Priests: Lv. 21: all; (see defilement)
Of Sabbath Day: Ex. 20: 8
Curtain separates holy place: Ex. 26: 33
Touches altar, sacrifice is: Ex. 29: 37; Lv. 6: 27
Altar of incense is holy to the Lord: Ex. 30: 10
Altar of burnt offering is most holy: Ex. 40: 10
Grain offering: a most holy part: Lv. 2: 3; 6: 17
Priests must be holy: Lv. 10: 3
Priests separate holy and common: Lv. 10: 10
Priests holy because God is holy: Lv. 11: 44-45
High Priest washes body in holy place: Lv. 16: 24
For violating: Lv. 20: all; Nu. 4: 15; Lv. 21: all
Use of holy offerings: Lv. 22: all; 27: all
Festivals are holy convocations: Lv. 23: all
Blasphemy and its punishment: Lv. 24: 10-23
Nazirite is holy to the Lord: Nu. 6: 8
Remember and be holy: Nu. 15: 40
Waters of Miribah show God's holiness: Nu. 20: 13
John the Baptist- baptise with holy spirit: Jn. 1: 33
Peter declares Jesus Holy One of God: Jn. 6: 69
Fear loss of holy place, nation: Jn. 11: 48
Jesus - Leave her alone: Jn. 12: 7
Advocate will become Teacher: Jn. 14: 26
Jesus prays to protect the disciples: Jn. 17: 11
Jesus breaths on the disciples: Jn. 20: 22

Hour: Kairos moment (divinely appointed meaning)
See Chapter 8 for a listing of 24 Hours in John

House: Sign for abode, dwelling, family; God's house
   Jacob - This is the house of God: Gn. 28: 10-22
   Joseph overseer in Pharoah's house: Gn. 39: 5
   When you sit in your house: Dt. 6: 7
   Not make father's a house of trade: Jn. 2: 16, 17
   Jesus - place for a slave, a son: Jn. 8: 35
   Mary sat in the house, praying: Jn. 11: 31
   The house was filled with its aroma: Jn. 12: 3
   In my father's house are many rooms: Jn. 14: 2
   A week later in the house: Jn. 20: 26

Incense: Fragrant oil and / or fiber to mark all that is holy
   Altar of incense: Ex. 30: 1-10
   Recipe for anointing oil and incense: Ex. 30: 22-38
   Incense cloud must cover mercy seat: Lv. 16: 12-13

Jacob's Ladder: Dream vision
   Jacob's ladder dream: Gn. 28: 10-22

Jews: Sign for leaders of the temple in Jerusalem
   Temple officials - had not been told: Neh. 2: 16
   Send priests, Levites to question John: Jn. 1: 19
   Passover of the Jews: Jn. 2: 13; 6: 4; 11: 55
   Ask Jesus for a sign: Jn. 2: 18-22
   Nicodemus, leader of: Jn. 3: 1
   Have no dealings with Samaritans: Jn. 4: 9
   Salvation from the Jews: Jn. 4: 22
   Festival of the Jews where Jesus heals: Jn. 5: all
   Confused: Jn. 6:41, 52; 7:15, 35; 8:22, 48, 52, 57;
    10: 24
   Seek Jesus: Jn. 7: 1, 11; 10: 31-33; 11: 8; 18: 12,
    14; 19: 7
   Fear of: Jn. 7: 13; 9: 22; 11: 54; 19: 38; 20: 19

Who believed: Jn. 8: 31; 10: 21; 11: 45; 12: 11
Who did not believe: Jn. 9: 18; 10: 19-20; 11: 46
Who were close to Mary and Martha: Jn. 11: 19
Who followed Mary to Jesus: Jn. 11: 31, 33, 36
Who come to see Jesus and Lazarus: Jn. 12: 9
Jesus - As I said to the Jews: Jn. 13: 33, 18: 20
Jews not permitted to execute: Jn. 18: 31
King of the Jews: Jn. 18: 33, 39; 19: 3, 14, 19-22
Followers would fight to keep Jesus: Jn. 18: 36
Tell Jews: no case against Jesus: Jn. 18: 38; 19: 12
Body of Jesus left on cross: Jn. 19: 31
Burial custom of the Jews: Jn. 19: 40

Leprosy: A skin disease that makes a person unclean
Rituals regarding: Lv. 13: all; 14: all
White as snow:
-(Moses) Ex. 4: 6
-(Miriam) Nu. 12: 10

Light: The first emanation of God; sign of divine presence
Let there be light: Gn. 1: 3-5; 15-18
9th Plague - darkness: Ex. 10: 23
Pilar of fire: Ex. 13: 21
Light kept burning: Lv. 24: 2
Eleazar oversees oil for light, etc.: Nu. 4: 16
Life was light of all people: Jn. 1: 4
Witness to the light: Jn. 1: 7-8; 5: 31-35
Light in world: Jn. 3: 19-21; 11: 9-10; 12: 35-36
I am the light of the world: Jn. 8: 12; 9: 5; 12: 46

Linen Grave Cloths: signs of priesthood.
  Linen tunics for Aaron and his sons: Ex. 28: 40-43
    Ex. 39: 27; Lv. 16: 4, 32
  Jesus grave cloths of Lazarus removed: Jn. 11: 44
  Jesus is buried in linen cloths: Jn. 19: 40
  Jesus' separated grave cloths: Jn. 20: 6-8

Oracle: Word, image, event bears deeper spiritual meaning
  Oracle defined: Nu. 24: 3-4, 22: 31
  Eyes will be opened: Gn. 3: 5-7
  What your eyes see: Dt. 4:9-20; 10:21; 11:1-7, 18;
  eyes to see, ears to hear: Dt. 29: 4
  Jesus heals blind man: Jn. 9: all; 10: 21; 11: 37
  Lord blinds eyes, hardens heart: Jn. 12: 40; Is. 6:10

Ordination / Consecration: Set apart for service to God.
  7 Days to ordain: Lv. 8: 33
  Ritual of Ordination: Ex. 29: all; Lv. 8: all
  Consecration of a Nazirite: Nu. 6: all
  Jesus ordains his disciples: See chapters 11-14

Purification: to reclaim holiness after having been defiled
  See Defilement, Hand, Feet
  After Childbirth: Lv. 12: all
  Of Lepers: Lv. 14: all
  After Bodily Discharges: Lv. 15: all
  Ceremony of the Red Heifer: Nu. 19: all
  See chapter 13, section on purification in John

Priest's Portion: breast, thigh of sacrifice, offering bread
  Due to priests, Levites: Lv. 7: 30-37; Nu. 18: 8-32
  Jesus to Peter- Unless I wash you: Jn. 13: 8

Sheep/Goats: represent people of God as sacrifices
       Without blemish: Lv. 22: 17-20
       Ordination and Ritual Sacrifice: see Chapter 2
       Nazirite: See Chapter 3
       Good Shepherd gives life, not death: Jn. 10: all
       Peter re-ordained to feed, tend sheep: Jn. 21: 15-19

Sign: See Oracle

Stone: Sign of the holy place where God is
       Stone marks house of God: Gn. 28:10-22
       Roll stone from well: Gn. 29: 1-14
       Altar to be built of unhewn stones: Ex. 21: 25
       Commandments on tablets of stone: Ex. 24: 12
       Water comes from the rock at Horeb: Ex. 17: 1-7
       Jesus turns water in stone jars into wine: Jn. 2: 6
       Lazarus' grave - cave with a stone on it: Jn. 11: 38
       Jesus - Remove the stone: Jn. 11: 39
       Stone had been removed from the tomb: Jn. 20: 1

315

Appendix D

Bibliography

Abba, R., "Priests, Levites," *Interpreter's Dictionary of the Bible,*
ed. Butterick, Abingdon, Nashville, vol. 3, (1962)

Aichele, George, et. al., *The Postmodern Bible*, Yale Univ.
Press, New Haven and London, (1995)

Arndt, William F. and F. Wilbur Gingrich, *A Greek-English
Lexicon of the New Testament and Other Early Christian
Literature,* trans. adapt. of Walter Bauer, *Griecheisch -
Deutsches Wortenbuch zu den Schriften des Neuen
Testaments und der ubrigen urchristlichen Literatur,*
Univ. of Chicago Press, Chicago, (1957, 12th print. 1969)

Balz, Horst, "υπνοσ," *Theological Dictionary of the New
Testament*, ed. Friedrich, trans.ed. Bromiley, Eerdman's,
Grand Rapids, vol. VIII, (1972)

Barrett, C.K., *The Gospel According to St. John*, Westminster,
Philadelphia, (1978)

Barrois, G. A.,
"Kidron, Brook," *Interpreter's Dictionary of the Bible*, ed.
Butterick, Abingdon, Nashville, vol. 3, (1962)

"Moriah," "Shelah, Pool," *Interpreter's Dictionary of the
Bible*, ed. Butterick, Abingdon, Nashville, vol. 4, (1962)

Beck, H.F, "Consecrate, Consecration," *Interpreter's Dictionary of
the Bible*, ed. Butterick, Abingdon, Nashville, vol. 1, (1962)

Behm, Johannes, "κλαω," *Theological Dictionary of the New
Testament*, ed. Kittel, trans. ed. Bromiley, Eerdman's,
Grand Rapids, vol. III, (1965)

Berry, George Ricker, *The Interlinear Literal Translation of the*
        Greek New Testament, Zondervan, Grand Rapids, (1958,
        19th printing, 1977)

Bertram, Georg, "φυλασσω, φυλακη," *Theological Dictionary*
        of the New Testament, ed. Friedrich, trans. ed. Bromiley,
        Eerdman's, Grand Rapids, vol. IX, (1974)

Betz, Otto, "φωνεω," *Theological Dictionary of the New*
        Testament, ed. Friedrich, Eerdman's, Grand Rapids, vol. IX,
        (1974)

Beyer, Hermann W., "επισκεπτομαι, επισκοπεω, επισκοπα,
        επισκοπασ, αλλοπριεπισκοπασ," *Theological*
        Dictionary of the New Testament, ed. Kittel, Eerdman's,
        Grand Rapids, vol. II, (1964)

Blackwood, Andrew W., Jr., *Commentary on Jeremiah*, Word,
        Waco, (1977)

Blair, E.P.
        "Mary," *Interpreter's Dictionary of the Bible*, Abingdon,
        Nashville-New York, vol. 3, (1962)

        "Thomas," *Interpreter's Dictionary of the Bible*,
        Abingdon, Nashville - New York, vol. 4, (1962)

        "Didymus," *Interpreter's Dictionary of the Bible*,
        Abingdon, Nashville-New York, vol. 1, (1962)

Bornkamm, Gunther, "πρεσβυσ, πρεσβυτεροσ, πρεσβυτησ,
        συμπρεσβυτεροσ, πρεσβυτεριον, πρεσβευω,"
        Theological Dictionary of the New Testament, ed.
        Friedrich, Eerdman's, Grand Rapids, vol. VI, (1971)

Brenton, Sir Lancelot C.L., *The Septuagint with Apocrypha: Greek*
        and English, Orig. Pub. Samuel Bagster and Sons, Ltd.,
        London, (1851), (fifth print . in U.S.A. 1995)

Brown, Raymond E., S.S., The Community of the Beloved Disciple,
        Paulist, New York, (1979)

Buchsel, Friedrich,
> "ιστορεω (ιστορια)," *Theological Dictionary of the New Testament*, ed. Friedrich, trans. ed. Bromiley, Eerdman's, Grand Rapids, vol. III, (1965)

> "ειμι," *Theological Dictionary of the New Testament*, ed. Kittel, Eerdman's, Grand Rapids vol. II, (1964)

> "λυο," "κρισισ," "κρινο," *Theological Dictionary of the New Testament*, ed. Kittel, Eerdman's, Grand Rapids, vol. III, (1965)

Bultmann, Rudolf and Artur Weiser, "πιστευω," *Theological Dictionary of the New Testament*, ed. Friedrich, trans. ed. Bromiley, Eerdman's, Grand Rapids, vol. VI, (1968)

Bultmann, Rudolf,
> "ςαω," *Theological Dictionary of the New Testament*, ed. Kittel, trans. ed. Bromiley, Eerdman's, Grand Rapids, vol. III, (1967)

> "γινωσκω," "αφιαμι," *Theological Dictionary of the New Testament*, trans. ed. Bromiley, Eerdman's, Grand Rapids, vol. I, (1964)

Charlesworth, James H., *The Beloved Disciple: Whose Witness Validates the Gospel of John ?*, Trinity, Valley Forge, (1995)

Comay, Joan, *The Temple of Jerusalem*, Holt, Reinhart and Winston, New York, (1975)

Cullman, Oscar,
> *Early Christian Worship*, Wyndall, (1953, reprint 1987)
> *The Johannine Circle*, Westminster, Philadelphia, (1976)

Culpepper, R. Allen,
    Anatomy of the Fourth Gospel: A Study in Literary Design,
    Fortress, Philadelphia, (1983)

    *The Johannine School: An Evaluation of the Johannine
    School Hypothesis Based on An Investigation of the
    Nature of Ancient Schools*, Scholars Press, Missoula,
    (1975)

Daube, David, *"The New Testament and Rabbinic Judaism,"*
    Univ. of London, the Athlone Press, (1956)

Davies, G. Henton, "Ephod (Object)," *Interpreter's Dictionary of
    the Bible*, Abingdon, Nashville, vol. 2, (1962)

DeJong, M., "Jesus: Stranger from Heaven and Son of God,"
    SBLSBS, Scholars Press, Missoula, vol. II, 1977

Delling, Gerhard,
    "απαρχη," *Theological Dictionary of the New Testament*,
    ed. Kittel, trans. ed. Bromiley, Eerdman's, Grand Rapids,
    vol. I, (1964)

    "οσμα," *Theological Dictionary of the New Testament*,
    ed. Friedrich, trans. ed. Bromiley, Eerdman's, Grand
    Rapids, vol. V, (1967)

Denton, R.C., "Hand," *Interpreter's Dictionary of the Bible*,
    ed. Butterick, Abingdon, Nashville, vol. 2, (1962)

Dodd, C.H., *The Interpretation of the Fourth Gospel*,
    Cambridge U. Press., Philadelphia, (1953)

Eco, Umberto, *The Limits of Interpretation*, Indiana U. Press,
    Bloomington and Indianapolis, (1990)

Edersheim, Alfred, *The Temple*, Kregel, Grand Rapids, (1997)

Foerster, Werner, "Lord in Later Judaism: the Choice of the Word
Κυριοσ in the LXX," "Lord in Rabbinic Judaism,"
Theological Dictionary of the New Testament, ed. Kittel,
trans. ed. Bromiley, Eerdman's, Grand Rapids,
vol. III, (1965)

Friedrich, Gerhard, "σαλπιγε," *Theological Dictionary of the New
Testament*, ed. Friedrich, trans. ed. Bromiley, Eerdman's
Pub., Grand Rapids, vol. VII, (1971)

Gealy, F.D., "Twin Brothers," *Interpreter's Dictionary of the Bible*,
ed. Butterick, Abingdon, Nashville, vol. 4, (1962)

Gray, John, "The Book of Exodus," *Interpreter's One Volume
Commentary on the Bible*, ed. Charles M. Laymon,
Abingdon, Nashville, (1971)

Grundman, Walter,
"δεςιοσ," *Theological Dictionary of the New Testament*,
ed. Kittel, trans. ed. Bromiley, Eerdman's, Grand Rapids,
vol. II, (1964)

"στηκω, ιστημι," *Theological Dictionary of the New
Testament*, ed. Friedrich, trans.ed. Bromiley, Eerdman's,
Grand Rapids, vol. VII, (1971)

"κραςω," *Theological Dictionary of the New Testament*,
ed. Kittel, trans. ed. Bromiley, Eerdman's, Grand Rapids,
vol. III, (1965)

Gutbrod, Walter,
"Ισραηλ, ισραηλιτησ, Ιουδαιοσ, Ιουδαια, Ιουδαικοσ"
Theological Dictionary of the New Testament, ed. Kittel,
trans. ed. Bromiley, Eerdman's, vol. II, (1964)

"Israel: ii in John," *Theological Dictionary of the New
Testament*, ed. Kittel, trans. ed. Bromiley, Eerdman's,
vol. III, (1965)

320   Let Her Keep It

Hans, Herman, "εχω," *Theological Dictionary of the New Testament*,
    ed. Kittel, trans. ed. Bromiley, Eerdman's, Grand Rapids,
    vol. II, (1964)

Hauck, F.,
    "Βαλλω," *Theological Dictionary of the New Testament*, ed.
    Kittel, trans. ed. Bromiley, Eerdman's, Grand Rapids, vol. I,
    (1964)

    "μενο," "νιπτω," *Theological Dictionary of the New
    Testament,* ed. Kittel, trans. ed. Bromiley, Eerdman's,
    Grand Rapids, vol. IV, (1967)

Helms, Randel McCraw, *Who Wrote the Gospels?*, Millennium
    Press, Altadena, (1996)

Hermann, Johannes, "ιλασκομαι, ιλασμοσ," *Theological
    Dictionary of the New Testament*, ed. Kittel, trans. ed.
    Bromiley, Eerdman's, Grand Rapids, vol. III, (1965)

Hess, Franz, "χπιω, χριστοσ, αντιχριστοσ, σρισμα, χριστιανοσ,"
    Theological Dictionary of the New Testament, ed. Friedrich,
    trans.ed. Bromiley, Eerdman's, Grand Rapids, vol. IX, (1974)

Hitchcock, Roswell D. and Francis Brown, ed. trans., *Teaching of the
    Twelve Disciples*, Charles Scribner's Sons, New York, XV,
    (1885)

Horst, J., "μελοσ," *Theological Dictionary of the New Testament*, ed.
    Kittel, trans. ed. Bromiley, Eerdman's, Grand Rapids, vol. IV,
    (1967)

Houtman, C., "On the Function of the Holy Incense (Exodus XXX 3-8)
    and the Sacred Anointing Oil (Exodus XXX 22-23)," *Vetus
    Testamentum*, XLII, vol. 4, (1992)

Iser, Wolfgang, *The Act of Reading: A Theory of Aesthetic Response*,
    Johns Hopkins U., Baltimore, (1978, 5th print. 1987)

Jeremias, J., "νυμφη, νυμφιοσ," *Theological Dictionary of the New Testament*, ed. Kittel, trans. ed., Bromiley, Eerdman's, Grand Rapids, vol. IV, (1967)

Kittel, Gerhard and Gerhard von Rad, "δοςα," *Theological Dictionary of the New Testament*, ed. Kittel, trans. ed. Bromiley, Eerdman's, Grand Rapids, vol. II, (1964)

Kittel, Gerhard,
"αινιγμα," *Theological Dictionary of the New Testament*, ed. Kittel, Eerdman's, Grand Rapids, vol. I, (1964)

"λογιον," *Theological Dictionary of the New Testament*, ed. Kittel, Eerdman's, Grand Rapids, vol. IV, (1967)

"λεγω," *Theological Dictionary of the New Testament*, ed. Kittel, trans. ed. Bromiley, Eerdman's, Grand Rapids, vol. IV, (1967)

Lohse, Eduard,
"χειρ," *Theological Dictionary of the New Testament*, ed. Friedrich, trans. ed. Bromiley, Eerdman's, Grand Rapids, vol. IX, (1974)

"σαββατον," "συνεδριον," *Theological Dictionary of the New Testament*, ed. Friedrich, trans. ed. Bromiley, Eerdman's, Grand Rapids, vol. VII, (1971)

"Zion -- Jerusalem in the New Testament," *Theological Dictionary of the New Testament,* ed. Friedrich, trans. ed. Bromiley, Eerdman's, Grand Rapids, vol. VII, (1971)

Mauch, T.M.   "Zattu," *Interpreter's Dictionary of the Bible*, ed. Butterick, Abingdon, Nashville, vol. 4, (1962)

Meyer, Rudolf,
"κολποσ," *Theological Dictionary of the New Testament*, ed. Kittel, trans. ed. Bromiley, Eerdman's, Grand Rapids, vol. III, (1965)

Meyer, Rudolf, (continued)
"φαρισαιοσ," *Theological Dictionary of the New Testament,*
ed. Friedrich, trans.ed. Bromiley, Eerdman's, Grand Rapids,
vol. IX, (1974)

Michaelis, Wilhelm, "οραω, ειδον, βλεπω," *Theological Dictionary*
of the New Testament, ed. Friedrich, trans. ed. Bromiley,
Eerdman's, Grand Rapids, vol. V, (1967)

Michel, O.,
"μναμα, μναμειν," "μιμνησκομαι," *Theological*
Dictionary of the New Testament, ed. Kittel, trans. ed.
Bromiley, Eerdman's, Grand Rapids, vol. IV, (1967)

"σπενδομαι," *Theological Dictionary of the New Testament,*
ed. Friedrich, trans.ed. Bromiley, Eerdman's, Grand Rapids,
vol. VII, (1971)

Milgrom, Jacob, *Leviticus 1-16: A New Translation with Introduction*
and Commentary, Doubleday, New York, vol. 3, (1991)

Muilenberg, J., "Holiness," *Interpreter's Dictionary of the Bible,*
ed. Butterick, Abingdon, Nashville, vol. 2, (1962)

Oepke, Albrecht,
"ςωνα," *Theolgoical Dictionary of the New Testament,*
ed. Friedrich, trans. ed. Bromiley, Eerdman's, Grand Rapids,
vol.V, (1967)

"αναστασισ, εςαναστασισ," "ανισταμι, εςανισταμι,"
Theological Dictionary of the New Testament, ed. Kittel,
trans. ed. Bromiley, Eerdman's, Grand Rapids, vol. II, (1964)

"λουω ," *Theological Dictionary of the New Testament,* ed.
Kittel, trans. ed. Bromiley, Eerdman's, Grand Rapids, vol.
IV, (1967)

O'Day, Gail, "The Gospel of John: Introduction, Commentary and
Reflections," *The New Interpreter's Bible: A Commentary in*
Twelve Volumes, Abingdon, Nashville, vol. IX, (1995)

O'Sullivan, Kevin, O.F.M., "Barefoot," *Encyclopedic Dictionary of the Bible,* trans. adapt. of A. Van de Born, *Bijbels Woordenboek,* 2nd rev. ed. (1954, 57) by Lois Hartman, McGraw-Hill, New York, (1963)

Pope, H.M., "Seven, Seventh, Seventy," *Interpreter's Dictionary of the Bible,* ed. Butterick, Abingdon, Nashville, vol. 4, (1962)

Quell, Gottfried, "Κυριοσ: The Old Testament Name for God: The Name for God in the LXX," *Theological Dictionary of the New Testament,* ed. Kittel, trans. ed. Bromiley, Eerdman's, Grand Rapids, vol. III, (1965)

Raphael, Chaim, trans., *Passover Haggadah,* Behrman, New York, (1972)

Reed, W.L., "Ephraim," *Interpreter's Dictionary of the Bible,* ed. Butterick, Abingdon, Nashville, vol. 2, (1962)

Reisner, Rainer, "Bethany," "Bethany Beyond the Jordan," *The Anchor Bible Dictionary,* ed.Noel Freedman, Doubleday, New York, (1992)

Rengstorf, Karl Heinrich,
"σημειον," *Theological Dictionary of the New Testament,* ed. Friedrich, trans. ed. Bromiley, Eerdmans, Grand Rapids, vol. VII, (1971)

"αποστολοσ," *Theological Dictionary of the New Testament,* ed. Kittel, trans. ed. Bromiley, Eerdmans, Grand Rapids, vol. I, (1964)

"κλαιο, κλαιθμοσ," *Theological Dictionary of the New Testament,* ed. Kittel, trans. ed. Bromiley, Eerdmans, Grand Rapids, vol. III, (1965)

"δουλοσ," *Theological Dictionary of the New Testament,* ed. Kittel, trans. ed. Bromiley, Eerdmans, Grand Rapids, vol. II, (1964)

Richardson, Alan, "Sacrament, Sacramental Theology," *A Dictionary of Christian Theology*, ed. Richardson, Westminster, Philadelphia, (1969)

Riesenfeld, Harald, "τηρεω," *Theological Dictionary of the New Testament,* ed. Friedrich, trans.ed. Bromiley, Eerdman's, Grand Rapids, vol. VIII, (1972)

Rigato, Maria Luisa, "Maria Di Betania Nella Redazione Giovanna," *Antonianum: Periodicum Trimestre*, editum cura Professorum Pontificii Athenaei, Antoniani de Urbe, Roma, (1991)

Ryaarsdam, J.C. "Nazirite," *Interpreter's Dictionary of the Bible*, ed. Butterick, Abingdon, Nashville, vol. 3, (1962)

Sasse, Hermann, "γη," *Theological Dictionary of the New Testament*, ed. Kittel, trans. ed. Bromiley, Eerdman's, Grand Rapids, vol. I, (1964)

Schlier, Heinrich, "παρρασια, παρρασιαςομαι," *Theological Dictionary of the New Testament*, ed. Friedrich, trans. ed. Bromiley, Eerdman's, Grand Rapids, vol. V, (1967)

Schmidt, Karl L., "αφοριςω," *Theological Dictionary of the New Testament*, ed. Friedrich, trans. ed. Bromiley, Eerdman's, Grand Rapids, vol. V, (1967)

Schneider, Carl, "καθαμαι, καθιςο, καθεςομαι," *Theological Dictionary of the New Testament,* ed. Kittel, trans. ed. Bromiley, Eerdman's, Grand Rapids, vol. III, (1965)

Schrage, Wolfgang, "αποσυναγογοσ," *Theological Dictionary of the New Testament*, ed. Friedrich, trans. ed. Bromiley, Eerdman's, Grand Rapids, vol. VII, (1971)

Schrenk, Gottlob, "αρχιερευσ," *Theological Dictionary of the New Testament*, ed. Kittel, Eerdman's, Grand Rapids, vol. III, (1965)

Schweitzer, Albert, *The Quest for the Historical Jesus*, Macmillan, New York, (1906 German, 1910 English, 9th print. 1964)

Schweizer, Eduard and Friedrich Baumbartel, "σαρς, σαρκικοσ, σαρκινοσ," *Theological Dictionary of the New Testament*, ed. Friedrich, trans. ed. Bromiley, Eerdmans, Grand Rapids, vol. VII, (1971)

Seesemann, Heinrich, "οιδα," *Theological Dictionary of the New Testament*, ed. Kittel, trans. ed. Bromiley, Eerdman's, Grand Rapids, vol. V, (1967)

Signer, Michael A. "How the Bible Has Been Interpreted in Jewish Tradition," *The New Interpreter's Bible*, Abingdon, Nashville, (1994)

Stahlin, Gustav, "ασθενασ," *Theological Dictionary of the New Testament*, ed. Kittel, trans. ed. Bromiley, Eerdman's, Grand Rapids, vol. I, (1964)

Stauffer, Ethelbert, "εγω ειμι," *Theological Dictionary of the New Testament*, ed. Kittel, Eerdman's, Grand Rapids, vol. II, (1964)

Throckmorton, B.H., Jr., "Figurehead," *Interpreter's Dictionary of the Bible*, ed. Butterick, Abingdon, Nashville, vol. 2, (1962)

Torgesen, Karen Jo, *When Women Were Priests*, Harper, San Francisco, (1993)

Weiss, Konrad, "αναφερω," *Theological Dictionary of the New Testament*, ed. Friedrich, trans.ed. Bromiley, Eerdman's, Grand Rapids, vol. IX, (1974)

"πουσ," *Theological Dictionary of the New Testament*, ed. Friedrich, trans. ed. Bromiley, Eerdman's, Grand Rapids, vol. VI, (1968)

Weiss, W. F., "φαρισαιοσ," *Theological Dictionary of the New Testament*, ed. Freidrich, trans.ed. Bromiley, Eerdman's, Grand Rapids, vol. IX, (1974)

Wilckens, Ulrich, "στολη," *Theological Dictionary of the New Testament*, ed. Friedrich, trans.ed. Bromiley, Eerdman's, Grand Rapids, vol. VII, (1971)

APPENDIX E

INDEX